Top of the Heap

A Yankees Collection

Also by Glenn Stout (and Richard A. Johnson)

Yankees Century: One Hundred Years of New York
Yankees Baseball

Red Sox Century: One Hundred Years of Red Sox Baseball

Ted Williams: A Portrait in Words and Pictures

DiMaggio: An Illustrated Life

Jackie Robinson: Between the Baselines

Edited by Glenn Stout

The Best American Sports Writing 1991–present
(series editor for annual volumes)

The Best American Sports Writing of the Century
(with David Halberstam)

Chasing Tiger: The Tiger Woods Reader

Impossible Dreams: A Red Sox Collection

Top of the Heap

A Yankees Collection

Glenn Stout, Editor

Houghton Mifflin Company
Boston · New York 2003

Library of Congress Cataloging-in-Publication Data

Top of the heap : a Yankees collection / Glenn Stout, editor.
p. cm.
Includes index.
ISBN 0-618-30399-5
1. New York Yankees (Baseball team)—History. 2. Baseball
players—United States—Biography. I. Title: Yankees collection.
II. Stout, Glenn.
GV875.N4 T66 2003
796.357'64'097471—dc21 2002191270

Printed in the United States of America

Book design by Robert Overholtzer

QUM 10 9 8 7 6 5 4 3 2 1

To all the men and women
who have written about the Yankees,
and to all the readers who make
that task worthwhile

ACKNOWLEDGMENTS

Collections such as this are always group efforts. My thanks first go to the writers responsible for the fine work collected in this volume, which easily could have been much, much larger. My gratitude also goes to all my friends who have supported me throughout various projects and to those who alerted me to material that I may never have found otherwise. They include Richard A. Johnson, Howard Bryant, John Dorsey, Al Lizotte, Mike Hourihan, Max Frazee, and Tony Morante. Jack Curry, Adrian Wojnarowski, Ira Berkow, and Mike Vaccaro were all kind enough to suggest items for inclusion. The collections of the Sports Museum of New England, the Boston Public Library, the Lamont Library of Harvard University, the Library of the National Baseball Hall of Fame, the New York Public Library, and the Brooklyn Public Library were invaluable, for they are responsible for the preservation of the words in this book. My editor, Susan Canavan, continues to let me do the books I choose to do, and Jaquelin Pelzer, Gracie Doyle, Larry Cooper, and Cindy Buck of Houghton Mifflin always make my work easier. But Siobhan and Saorla are really at the top of the heap.

CONTENTS

PART VII: NEW YORK, NEW YORK

INTRODUCTION

Top of the Heap is not just a metaphor of excellence, but a literal description.

I don't collect baseball cards or uniforms or autographs or other memorabilia, and quite frankly I don't understand those who do. But I do collect the sentences and paragraphs that provide the language of this game; the words vibrate between my ears in a way nothing else does. Ever since I was a kid I've stashed away the newspapers and magazines that spoke to me, and I have the nightmare of a basement, contact lenses, an understanding spouse, and the occasional bad back to prove it.

Although I didn't realize it then, my tendency to collect words was the beginning of the process that led me to become a writer. For most of the last twenty years I have spent my time writing and editing more than fifty books and hundreds of articles, a career that includes the stewardship of the *Best American Sports Writing* series as well as books on the Red Sox, the Yankees, Joe DiMaggio, Ted Williams, Jackie Robinson, and a series of juvenile sports biographies. I've written about every major sport and many minor ones and about personalities both prominent and obscure, poring over indexes and microfilm and spending a fortune on copies and way too many hours online. For someone like me, the Internet, with all its indexes and databases, is the equivalent of an open line of credit for the inveterate gambler.

Somewhere along the line my collecting was done with an eye toward posterity. I just can't throw away a written word that I like, one that I think I might one day have reason to return to, even if just for my own pleasure.

The Yankees, at first by accident and more recently by plan, have often been the subject of this passion. Several years ago I realized that this book already existed, that it lay buried somewhere in those piles of paper. To create *Top of the Heap* I culled through that collection, supplemented by suggestions and submissions from some trusted colleagues to make sure I hadn't missed anything essential. While other anthologies of this type have tended to exhaust the same familiar material again and again or to favor book excerpts over work from other sources, I wanted this volume to be not only better but different. So with only a few exceptions, I have chosen not to reprint work too well known, instead giving prominence to writing from newspapers, magazines, and other sources.

Of course, this volume includes such heavy hitters as Red Smith, Ring Lardner, and Jimmy Cannon, as well as other recognizable names, but my open-minded approach also led me to some unexpected places. I remembered laughing till I cried when I heard Phil Rizzuto's inimitable 1994 induction speech at the Hall of Fame, so I dug up a transcript and laughed and cried again while reading it. Yankee manager Joe McCarthy's "Ten Commandments of Baseball" deserve revisiting for both their simplicity and their enduring wisdom; McCarthy, as much as any other man, recognized and nurtured a "Yankee tradition," and one can find the genesis of that tradition in his brief edicts. Howard Bryant of the *Bergen Record* shared with me his orphaned account of game seven of the 2001 World Series, his running story in which Alfonso Soriano was the Series MVP and world championship banner number twenty-seven was poised to be raised. Of course, in the bottom of the ninth those facts became fiction, at which point Bryant and every other beat writer had to stop, turn, and write the opposite story.

The bulk of the writing in this collection is the work of a wonderful roster of writers—some famous and some forgotten—who have covered the Yankees over the past one hundred years. In a way, this book represents a source book for the history of the Yankees— the best game stories, columns, and features. All were selected without too much regard to the author or source, sometimes for their artistry and sometimes for their historicity, but always for their ability to transmit something essential about this team, to create a sense of what the Yankees are and why so many fans have been drawn to them.

And of all the many reasons that have been offered for why the New York Yankees are the most popular and successful franchise in pro sports, from the size of their market to the size of their pocketbook, from the House That Ruth Built to the Bambino himself, none adequately explains the most significant part of that phenomenon: Why do the Yankees resonate so loudly and clearly, not just in America, but throughout the baseball-aware world?

After compiling this book, I think I know. It's the writing.

Ruth was magnificent, as were Gehrig, DiMaggio, Mantle, and Maris, and Reggie and Mattingly and Jeter, but until recent years, unless one lived near New York, fans had few and rare opportunities to actually see the Yankees, to experience the team that for so long has had the word "dynasty" embroidered on its chest.

But one has never needed to live in or around New York to follow the Yankees, for the Yankees and their deeds were spread far and wide by writers whose talents at least equaled and often eclipsed those of their subject. For just as the Yankees assumed their place atop the American League standings year after year, many of the writers covering the team have held a similar place in the pantheon of American sports writing. John Kieran, Grantland Rice, Red Smith, and Dick Young are as distinguished as Ruth, Gehrig, DiMaggio, and Mantle. Their skilled writing and reporting about the team, often syndicated nationwide, exalted the Yankees beyond their record. It was the writer who made Babe Ruth *Babe Ruth,* the writer who recognized the curious genius of Stengel and the grace of DiMaggio. It is the writer who sees within a single swing or game something singular and draws us back to it, again and again.

Despite what one might believe, I think the Yankees' success has actually made it more difficult to write something lasting and memorable about the club. With victory so commonplace, one would expect the work of the writers covering the team to have become predictable. Yet the writers continue to put out work that is both lasting and memorable, creating their own kind of dynasty. Writing about the Yankees' achievements has inspired a kind of verbal Darwinism among writers. In an earlier age, Ring Lardner and Damon Runyon and John Kieran and W. O. McGeehan all stood toe to toe in the press box and tried to outwrite each other, just as Bill Heinz, Red Smith, and Jimmy Cannon did a few years later, and Dick Young, Leonard Shecter, and their contemporaries, and Ira

Berkow, Mike Lupica, and the writers who cover the team today. More than sixty years after DiMaggio first took the field, writers continue to try to pen his definitive portrayal. Sixty years from now they will still be trying to do the same for Derek Jeter.

Top of the Heap is the result of that competition. And page by page, byline by byline, we, the readers, are the ones who win.

GLENN STOUT
December 2002

PART I

THE VIEW FROM THE HEIGHTS

In the beginning, of course, they weren't even called the Yankees, and the notion that they would someday create the greatest dynasty in the game was but a distant dream. The team that would be called the Yankees in the popular press within a year of its birth (and officially so a few years later) was created from the ashes of the old Baltimore Orioles by American league founder and president Ban Johnson. They were thrust upon New York in the spring of 1903. Never mind the fact that they lacked both an owner and a place to play. Both requirements were soon satisfied, barely, as the corrupt Tammany politicians Frank Farrell and William Devery managed a somewhat unfriendly takeover of the team. The club then carved out a ballpark from the rocky outcrops of Washington Heights.

With stars like Wee Willie Keeler on board, the ballclub challenged for the American League pennant in their second season, battling Boston into the final day. But on that day ace pitcher Jack Chesbro uncorked a fatal wild pitch that delivered the pennant to their rivals, a blow as devastating to that team as the ball that rolled between Bill Buckner's legs would be to the Red Sox in 1986. Chesbro never got over it, and neither did the early Yankees, who spiraled into a decade of mostly unmemorable mediocrity. The defeat was the apex of the first era in Yankees history. But it would be the last time that loss has ever been considered a defining character-istic of the team.

The New York sports press didn't quite know what to do with the Yankees at first. They were all National League men, partial to the more established Giants and Dodgers. The Yankees were outsiders, immigrants. They were often disparagingly referred to in print as "the Invaders." And baseball coverage, as yet, was not an integral part of the daily newspaper in New York. Deadlines were too narrow for comprehensive coverage in many of the afternoon and evening pa-pers, while the morning papers considered the results of the previ-ous day "yesterday's news." The Yankees would have to earn their way onto the sports pages by winning.

ANONYMOUS

AM. GROUNDS ON WASHINGTON HEIGHTS

Ban Johnson Makes Good His Promise to
Have a Baseball Aggregation in New York City.
Joseph Gordon Head of New Organization.
New Park at Broadway, 165th and 168th
Streets — Full Details of Deal

from *The New York World,* March 13, 1903

President Ban Johnson, of the American League, this time promptly on the hour, last night made his oft-deferred announcement of where the New York Club of the American League will play its games, and other particulars, and also gave the reasons for the delay. The grounds of the club are located between One Hundred and Sixty-fifth street on the south, One Hundred and Sixty-eighth street on the north, Eleventh avenue on the east and Fort Washington road on the west. The location, of course, is on Manhattan Island and fulfils the promise made by the American League. The grounds are not intersected by One Hundred and Sixty-sixth and One Hundred and Sixty-seventh streets, and are the largest in the country. On the east side they are 797 feet long, while on the west side the length is 778 feet. On the north they are 638 feet wide, while on the south they are 536 feet wide.

The One Hundred and Sixty-eighth street station of the new underground road is located at the northeast corner of the grounds. As the subway will not be completed in time for use this year, patrons of the American League Club will be compelled to use the surface roads, which pass within a block of the property, on Amsterdam avenue. The Third and Sixth avenue trolleys go direct, while all the elevated roads transfer to the One Hundred and Twenty-fifth street crosstown line, which also goes past the grounds.

Joseph Gordon Its President

Joseph Gordon will be the President of the new club. He was born in New York and has always lived here. He was interested in base-ball in the eighties during the regime of John B. Day, and was President of the Metropolitan club before New York went into the National League. When Day controlled the New York club Gordon was closely identified with the club. John B. Day will be interested in the new club.

Gordon is a member of Tammany Hall, and John B. Sexton is his political sponsor. Gordon was member of Assembly in 1888. In 1901 he was Superintendent of Buildings. He is in the coal and wood and building business. He is a member of the New York Athletic, Democratic, Tilden and Pontiac Clubs.

Gordon said last night:

"The corporation of which I am to be President is a very strong one financially, being backed by several wealthy and prominent citizens. The plans for the erection of the stands and the improvement of the grounds have been filed with the Building Department and approved, and a permit has been issued. Work will begin immediately, so that playing will begin in season. The grounds will be ready for use for the first scheduled game on April 30.

"No drawing of the stands has been made as yet. There will be four stands: the grandstand and three others. The grandstand will accommodate 6,000 persons, and the other three will accommodate 10,000. At present we will only complete the ball ground, but we have the privilege of putting in a bicycle track, football and athletic field. The property belongs to the New York Institute for the Blind and has been leased by the American League club for ten years."

Ban Johnson's Statement

Ban Johnson's account of the negotiations and obstacles overcome follows:

"It was in the latter part of August, at a meeting of the American League Club held in Cleveland, that we took our first official action toward invading New York City. By force of circumstances we were compelled to place the cart before the horse. That is to say, we were forced to sign all of our players for the New York Club before we got grounds or backing here. In order to do this the American League voted to foot all the bills until satisfactory partners had been secured in New York, and as the money was quickly forthcoming, little time was lost in securing the necessary players. It took a great deal of money to land this team, which I have every reason to believe will rank high among the leaders in the American League race.

"Early steps were then taken to secure grounds in this city. So much had been said about the advisability of locating on Manhattan Island that it was natural for us to look for grounds below the Harlem River. W. F. Caliender, a real estate man, acted as our agent here, and it was he who opened negotiations for the Lenox avenue property, extending from One Hundred and Forty-second street, east to the Harlem River. These negotiations were opened the latter part of September. From the very beginning the lawyer for the estates positively assured us that One Hundred and Forty-third street could be closed according to law. The petition was to be made by Mrs. Pinckney asking that the street be closed for business purposes. But before this was done the advantages of interesting Mr. August Belmont were shown to us. Douglas Robinson was the man who made the proposition to Mr. Belmont for the purchase of the Pinckney estate. The American League furnished satisfactory financial references, and we finally received advices that everything would go through without a hitch.

Could Not Close 143d Street

"We never knew the matter would come before the Board of Directors of the Rapid Transit Construction Company, else we would have taken a different shift. It is now generally known how the matter was sidetracked. The lawyer for the estates then tried to carry out his original arrangements with us, much time being lost thereby, and at the end of three weeks he threw up his hands, declaring that it was impossible to close One Hundred and Forty-third street.

"This whole proceeding absorbed so much time that we were naturally hard pressed, so that quick action seemed necessary. Early in the winter I was advised by Mr. Gordon that he had an option on a plot of ground on Manhattan Island. I met him early in January, and at that time he said that if we failed at Lenox avenue he would be glad to take the matter up with us.

"At the time of the peace conference at Cincinnati I was confined to my bed for a month, which prevented me from reaching Mr. Gordon, so there was another delay. When I finally arrived here I learned that it would take even more time to close Mr. Gordon's proposition, for he informed me that no lease could be executed for the property before March 4.

"The Board of Directors for the New York Institute for the Blind, which controls the property, do not meet except at certain times, and President Schermerhorn said it would be impossible to call a meeting of the board to specially consider the matter, so that we had to wait until March 4 before a committee from the directors of the institute could meet the Gordon syndicate.

Lease Signed at 3:30 Yesterday

"That committee did not report back to the institute until 3:30 o'clock this afternoon, when the whole deal was ratified and everything was placed in black and white. Had there been a slip-up on this property we had everything shaped to the minute to sign a lease for the Astor estate, at One Hundred and Sixty-first street and Jerome avenue, in which event the American League would have conducted the club. Other sites that we looked at were One Hundred and Sixty-sixth street and Amsterdam avenue, One Hundred and Twenty-ninth street and Second avenue, and four sites in the Bronx. It was the Astor estate which had to be surveyed on Tuesday, so that the public can see how closely we had to draw the lines.

"We could not fail in this undertaking, for we always had an anchor to windward, and there never was a moment when we were not confident of success. We appreciate the consideration and courtesy of the New York press and the indulgence of the public, and we would also like to say that, in spite of the obstacles thrown in our way, of which we do not care to go into particulars, we have no hard feelings against anybody, but simply want to see the game of baseball once more thrive and prosper in the metropolis.

"It has been a long, tedious affair from start to finish, but the American League has made good, as it has in every proposition it has undertaken."

W. R. RANKIN

PICTURESQUE SPOT

Site of the American League's New York Park.

from *The Sporting News*, March 23, 1903

NEW YORK, MARCH 22 – SPECIAL CORRESPONDENCE: — "Well, I took a day off last week and went to see the new ball park," said the Man from Up Cedar Creek. "What do you think of it?" asked the Head Barber. "I don't believe one could gather thoughts enough in a week to express an opinion on the subject," answered the Man from Up Cedar Creek.

"That's rocky!" exclaimed the Head Barber.

"Yes. Rocks and hollows describe it, with some trees as a side issue," replied the Man from Up Cedar Creek. "Johnson's wild, woolly, Western experience sent him into that unexplored region to look for a ball park. No native would have dared to venture into its profundity. Could Mr. Owen Wister only have gotten a peep at that site before he wrote the 'Virginian,' he would never have wasted so much time and space in describing such a tame place as the 'Hole in the Wall.' This would have been a far better subject, and, then, too, it would have been so much nearer to civilization. Oh, what a lost opportunity! Had he sailed up the Hudson he might well have said: 'Steep ranges and forests walled me in from the world on both sides without a single break, except the entrance to the summit — now being utilized as a ball park — which lays through intricate solitudes.' The noble Hudson ripples along past the site, which is covered with mournful pines and heavy underbrush, and rolls on to the Atlantic Ocean in blissful ignorance of the use the march of improvement intends making of that mountainous peak. Grey Rock rises majestically in the center of the range, and from its summit can be seen Long Island in the far East, with its farms under cultivation and here and there dotted with boroughs, villages and hamlets, while the palisades, in all their grandeur, stand forth like a huge giant beyond the Hudson in the far West. As far as the eye can see to the North there is an extensive district of thickly wooded country, and to the South is the beautiful and striving village of Manhattan. Undoubtedly it is the most picturesque and romantic spot that the white man has ever selected for a battle field between the base ball warriors of the present generation. In the near future it will undoubtedly gain great renown, and many thousands of people will be attracted there to see the place."

Ready for Opening Game

"Do you think they will have everything ready for the opening game?" asked the Head Barber.

"Sure, Mike. If they are not particular as to when it is played," replied the Man from Up Cedar Creek. "However, they had better wait until the underground coffins get to skating up that way. Then one may be able to see a ball game played and return to his home on the same day, but under the trolley system now in vogue such a thing is practically impossible or near.

"It would be a great stroke of genius if the new club should build its dressing-rooms on the banks of the Hudson so that its players could take a plunge without using the city's water, and thus avoid coughing up a season pass every time the water was turned on. That bombastic talk about cutting streets through the ball park died aborning. The guys who tried to throw out that scare knew perfectly well that they were barking at a knothole. If they made their talk with the expectation of getting season passes they showed their 'newness' at the game. Streets might easily be started from the East side of the grounds and could go merrily along until they struck the West side, when toboggan slides would have to be built to enable one to reach his destination — the Hudson river. When the natives up there get next to the push who have had some experience in running a ball club they will get wiser than they are now and hunt up some other kind of a scheme to work passes." Thus writes one who knows whereof he speaks.

The selection of a ballpark site on Washington Heights between 165th and 168th Streets represented the end of a protracted process to place an American League franchise in Manhattan. At nearly every step, American League founder and president Ban Johnson found his way blocked. The National League New York Giants were not eager for the competition, and their connections in Tammany Hall, the political machine that ran New York, did all they could to stop the new team. Each time Johnson identified a site for a new ballpark, Tammany Hall responded by turning the parcel into a park or creating a new street through the center of the property.

But Tammany miscalculated. Some factions of Tammany did want the new team, particularly if they were cut in. Johnson was steered to the site on Washington Heights, and by the time the rest of Tammany found out, it was too late. The team that would become the New York Yankees had a toehold in New York.

ALL GAMBLING A MYSTERY TO FRANK FARRELL

As a High-Toned Turfman Who Nods to Many
Kinds of People at Races He Gives Evidence.
Never Saw Roulette Played in New York.
Inside of Pool-Rooms Unknown to the Man
Who Only Bets in the Ring

from *The New York World*, March 19, 1903

The things that Frank J. Farrell, the sporting man, does not know would fill volumes. He told some of these things in the Supreme Court yesterday.

He was a cool witness. Never did he lose his self-possession. He conveyed the impression that his examination was a joke. Only once did he take serious exception to questions. That was when he was drawn out on the legitimacy of race-track betting. Then in a petulant manner he said it was legitimate, and that August Belmont and other racing men made bets at the track and regarded it as proper.

Then, turning to the newspaper men, Farrell said: "Perhaps it would be just as well not to say anything about Belmont. He might not like me to associate his name with mine."

With a face as solemn as a judge's Farrell swore he had never played roulette, that he was not a gambler, that he never ran a gambling-house, that he never had any interest in a gambling club, and that he had never seen the inside of a pool-room.

Farrell was in court in obedience to an order of Justice Scott directing his examination before the trial of a suit of Rogers L. Barstow, jr., to recover from Farrell and certain alleged associates of his $11,000 he says he lost in the Commercial Clerks' Club at a gambling game.

Joined with Farrell in the suit are James L. Kennedy, Gottfried Walbaum, Frank Burbridge and the club itself. Barstow charges that Farrell and the others named, to all intents and purposes, constitute the club. It is denied by Stear, Hoffman & Wahle, attorneys for Farrell, Kennedy, Walbaum and Burbridge, that the defendants are proprietors of the Commercial Clerks' Club or of any other gambling-house.

His Business Is Horse Racing

Henry C. Quinby, counsel for Barstow, began the bombardment by politely asking Farrell what his business was.

"Oh, I am in the horse business," said Farrell, with a twirl of his black mustache.

"Explain."

"Oh, well, I own a few race horses," scowled Farrell, looking bored.

"Are you accustomed to race horses belonging to you and to bet on their success?" asked the lawyer.

"Certainly I am," was the reply.

"Don't you consider that gambling?"

"No, certainly not. Not any more than I consider dealing in stocks down in Wall street to be gambling," and Farrell laughed outright.

"Then perhaps you do not consider playing roulette to be gambling."

"I know nothing about roulette." The air of injured innocence with which this was said was a study.

"Have you ever played with a roulette wheel?"

"No," snapped the witness.

"Have you never seen a roulette wheel?"

"Oh, yes. Come to think of it, I believe I saw one once in Saratoga and also in Hot Springs."

"Did you ever see one in the city of New York?"

"Never, to my knowledge."

Farrell was then questioned as to his acquaintance with "Jim" Kennedy. He replied that he had met Kennedy all over the country,

at racetracks and elsewhere, but had never asked him his occupa-
tion, nor had he ever had any business relations with him.

"Do you always make your bets at the racetracks?" asked the lawyer.

"Yes."

"Have you ever bet on a race in a pool-room in the city?"

Here Farrell's lawyer objected. The Court will rule hereafter on
that question.

He Interrupts Like Morgan

"I wish you would hurry up," interrupted Farrell. "I've got a date. I
want to give you all the information I can, but don't know anything
about this club." He spoke with the manner of J. P. Morgan at a railroad merger inquiry.

He said he had never heard of the Commercial Clerks' Club until
he was sued by Barstow. He only knew Walbaum from having met
him on the race-tracks, and from having occasionally made some
bets on horse races with him.

Farrell was next questioned as to being interested with Walbaum
and Burbridge in negotiations for the purchase of a house in Saratoga or in this city, but denied that he had.

"Did you ever make any arrangements for the buying of Canfield's house in this city?"

"I never did. That's a little free advertising the newspapers gave
me."

"But you know Mr. Canfield?"

"Yes."

"Have you ever heard of a partnership or combination between
gamblers?"

"No. That's absurd. It's just a dream."

Does as Mr. Belmont Does

"What do you call your connection with Walbaum on the racetracks
if there is no gambling?"

"That's legitimate. Mr. Belmont and all other racing men do
that."

"Have you ever referred to the activity of the local administration
concerning gambling with Walbaum?"

"No."

"Or commented upon it?"

"No."

"Have you ever been interested in a pool-room in this city?"

"No, sir."

"Ever secure any profits from a pool-room in this city?"

"No, sir."

"Are you acquainted with William B. Devery, former Chief of Police?"

"Yes, sir."

"Have you ever been interested in a gambling house on West Thirty-third street?"

"No."

"Were you ever arrested for —"

"Never in my life, except once for violating the excise law, when I was a bartender."

Farrell was then asked if he had ever met Walbaum at the Thirty-third street house and whether he was in the house when it was raided.

"No," replied Farrell. "I guess you are getting away up in the sky."

Farrell having denied being interested at any time in his life in a faro game he was questioned again as to Kennedy. He then volunteered the information that there were two "Jim" Kennedys. One had a smooth face, and one had a black mustache. One frequented the racetracks and one was to be seen at athletic exhibitions. This concluded his examination.

At the turn of the century, Frank Farrell was one of the most notorious and colorful figures in New York City. With the help of Tammany Hall, he rose from a position as a bartender to become a partner in New York's largest gambling syndicate. Operating a string of gambling parlors and poolrooms, by 1900 Farrell's syndicate was raking in over $3 million per year.

Everyone knew how Farrell earned his living, but everyone also knew that Farrell was so far above the law that he considered the courts little more than a distraction. New Yorkers took obvious delight in this account of Farrell's testimony after a disgruntled gambler charged him with cheating. What they didn't yet know was that Frank Farrell, along with his partner William Devery, the corrupt former police chief of New York, was a co-owner of the new American League franchise.

NEW TEAM WINS FIRST GAME — BEATS WASHINGTON 6 TO 2

Field and Men Win Favor.

from *The New York Telegram*, May 1, 1903

Shakespeare, when he wrote "the cat will mew and the dog will have his day," was ignorant of the Deveryite Baseball Club. The adage, however, certainly applies to the way in which that club had its day yesterday. It was the opening of the club's season on the home grounds and the local team won from Washington by a score of 6 to 2.

It indeed was a glorious occasion, not only from the point of view of the great numbers of office boys and old rooters, but from that of the backers of the local team. If any one should say that the national game is not once more popular he would probably be considered a poor judge of the drift of baseball affairs. The small boys have been in the grasp of the baseball craze for some weeks, and the grasp is becoming stronger every time the local baseball players make a hit. The popularity of baseball is easily proved by these same lads. Last year few of them had more than one aunt or uncle who conveniently got sick and needed them at home when there was a professional baseball game scheduled to be played here. Now most of these boys have many aunts and uncles whose physical condition is perplexing because one day they are well and the next they are near death's door. When these considerate relatives are very sick the boys are bent on seeing a game.

There were no pumps among the moral decorations on the grounds. Devery, by his presence in the grandstand, made amends for this oversight. Politicians were there in force, and one of the most conspicuous was "Big Tom" Foley of the Fourth Ward. Many looked with disgust at the sandwich and lemonade men. The sandwich man reminded them of the free lunch counter which was far away and the lemonade brigade brought visions to them of schooners of beer. There were enough diamonds in the shirt fronts of the politicians to start a fair sized jewelry store. There are three kinds of diamonds, it is said, which most politicians know much about — the diamond that glitters, the ace of diamonds and the baseball diamond.

It was a perfect day for the sport. The sun was strong, and a gentle breeze blew across the stand just strong enough to make it comfortable. The field is not yet completed, there being a deep hollow space on the Broadway side in back of first base, where the pond is yet to be filled in. This hollow space is about a sixteenth of the field, and when it is filled in the grounds will be the largest and handsomest baseball grounds in the world. When a ball was hit in this space, which is several feet deeper than the other part of the field, it counted for two bases. The grandstands were without roofs, but it seemed remarkable how the grounds could have been put in such a good condition for the opening in less than a month and a half. The diamond has been sodded and was a great relief to the glare of the sunbaked dirt of the outfield. The whole field will be sodded as soon as possible. Outside the grounds the "fakirs" gathered in force, and as each spectator entered the grounds he received a small American flag.

It was about 3:35 p.m. when Bayn with his 69th Regiment band escorted the players onto the diamond. It was found necessary for the men to dress at a hotel near by, as the club's dressing rooms have not yet been built. When the men came marching on the field to the tune of a patriotic song the spectators rose as if one, and stood until the band stopped playing. The decorations of flags and bunting on the stands and bleachers added to the impressive sight. As on all opening days spectators brought horns and whistles, and in the bleachers cowbells were numerous. When the game was called there were fully fifteen thousand people present, a remarkable number, considering that the rapid transit road will not be completed this season, and that the spectators had to come on surface lines.

President Ban Johnson of the American League had the honor of throwing the first ball. The home team proved themselves to be a swift lot of players, while the field work of the Washington team was also good. The most notable player to be missed on the local side was Fultz, who, it was announced, would not play. McFarland took his place, and held it in a creditable way.

The Deveryites began their first inning by making one run. Davis was first to the bat, but his hard hit went to Robinson, and he was put out at first. Keeler sent a hit to left, and got to second on Ryan's fumble. McFarland's hit was caught by Robinson. Williams came next and sent out a two bagger, tallying Keeler. Ganzel was the third man to be caught out. In the second inning the local team added another run to its lead. Conroy, first to the bat, made a hit for two bases. Courtney made a neat sacrifice to Townsend. O'Connor's hit past third allowed Conroy to score. Chesbro and Davis were the next two to be put out.

It was not until the fifth inning was reached that more runs were made. In this inning the Deveryites scored two more runs. Davis got to first on a nice hit. Keeler got to base on balls, while Davis stole second: McFarland bunted, but Davis was forced out at third by Drill's quick throw. Williams hit to right field for two bases and scored Keeler. McFarland tallied on Ganzel's long fly, caught by Robinson. Conroy's high hit was caught by Robinson.

In the seventh inning the local team made two runs, while the Washington team tallied their first run. Coughlin, first for Washington to the bat, made a single, followed by a double by Demont. Drill hit to Courtney, forcing out Demont, but Coughlin tallied on the play. Townsend's grounder was got in time by Courtney to put Drill out. Robinson fouled to Ganzel. For New-York Davis and Keeler walked to first. Coughlin was put out, while the first two men stole. Williams was struck out. Ganzel was hit and got to first. This filled the bases. Conroy's hit for two bases scored Davis and Keeler and Courtney's fly was handled nicely by Delehanty. In the eighth inning the Senators got one more run when Selbach got to first on a muff by Davis and scored on Ryan's fine hit. The score:

NEW-YORK	AB	R	LB	PO	A	E
Davis 1f...............	4	1	1	0	0	2
Keeler cf...............	2	3	2	1	0	0
McFarland cf..........	3	1	0	0	0	0
Williams 2b............	4	0	2	2	3	0
Ganzel 1b...............	3	0	0	12	1	0
Conroy 3b...............	4	1	2	6	1	0
Courtney ss...........	3	0	1	2	1	1
O'Connor c.............	4	0	1	4	1	0
Chesbro p...............	4	0	0	1	5	0
Totals..................... 31		6	9	27	12	3

WASHINGTON	AB	R	LB	PO	A	E
Robinson...............	4	0	2	2	2	0
Selbach rf...............	5	1	0	0	0	0
Delehanty lf............	4	0	0	3	0	0
Ryan cf...................	4	0	2	8	1	0
Casey 1b...............	4	0	0	0	0	0
Coughlin 3b............	4	1	2	2	1	1
Demont 2b..............	4	0	1	0	3	0
Drill c......................	4	0	0	5	1	0
Townsend p............	3	0	0	1	2	0
*Holmes..................	1	0	0	0	0	0
Totals*................... 37		2	7	24	10	1

```
New York........................... 1 1 0   0 2 0   2 0 x — 6
Washington...................... 0 0 0   0 0 0   1 1 0 — 2
```

Earned runs — New-York. 2. Two base hits — Keeler 2. Williams 2. Conroy 2. Coughlin, Robinson. Sacrifice hits — McFarland, Courtney. Stolen base — O'Connor. Double play — Ryan and Drill. Left on bases — New-York, 7; Washington 9; First base on balls — Off Chesbro, 1; off Townsend, 3. First base on errors — New-York, 1; Washington, 3. Hit by pitched ball — By Townsend, 1. Struck out — By Chesbro, 1; by Townsend, 4. Time, 1:30. Umpires — Connolly and Caruthers.

*Batted for Townsend in ninth inning.

Despite their initial success, the new team was not immediately embraced by New York. The new ballpark, officially known as "American League Park" but popularly known as the Hilltop Grounds, was hard to get to from downtown and uncomfortable. New York was still a National League town. Although the New York press had yet to fully embrace baseball and most accounts concerning the new team were surprisingly brief, the Giants still received most of the attention from the city's sportswriters. In 1904, the American League club's second season, pitcher Jack Chesbro unveiled the spitball to forge a 41–12 record. But on the last day of the season, with New York needing to sweep a doubleheader with Boston to win the pennant, Chesbro threw a wild pitch in the last inning of the first game, costing him the game as the pennant went to Boston. Chesbro never recovered, and neither did the team. For most of the next decade the team failed to challenge for the pennant.

PITCHER CHESBRO TELLS FOR FIRST TIME OF HIS FAMOUS "SPIT BALL," AND SHOWS HOW IT IS THROWN

Greatest Box Artist of the National Game Is Spending the Winter at His Home at Conway, Mass. — Says Boston Will Be Strong This Year, but New York Will Win Out

from *The Boston Post,* January 22, 1905

The spit ball has come to stay, and in my opinion it will be the most effective ball that can possibly be used.

I can make the spit ball drop two inches or a foot and a half.

It is an easy ball on the arm. I pitched 54 games last season, and my arm never troubled me.

In the last 30 games of the season I pitched spit balls entirely. In those 30 games I didn't pitch over half a dozen balls that weren't spit balls.

I have not yet read any explanation of the spit ball that was any way near correct.

You have never read of Gibson or Dineen telling how to throw spit balls.

Gibson of the Collins team had better control of the spit ball than any other pitcher I saw use it last season.

The spit ball is worked entirely by the thumb. The saliva one puts on the ball does not affect its course in any way.

The saliva is put on the ball for the sole purpose of making the fingers slip off the ball first.

Excepting the spit ball every ball that goes from the pitcher leaves the fingers last. In throwing curves the fingers do the work.

By wetting the ball it leaves the fingers first, and the thumb last, and the spit ball could be rightly called a thumb ball.

It is not necessary to thoroughly wet the ball. All you need to do is to moisten it so as to remove the friction from the part of the ball the fingers cover, and which slides off the fingers.

The ball is gripped the same as if you were throwing a curve.

Stricklett was the first pitcher I ever saw use it. I don't believe the ball was used before under other names as some people have claimed.

When I saw Stricklett throw it I said to myself: "There is something, Mr. Chesbro, that you must learn." I studied Stricklett and soon discovered that the thumb did the work.

Clark Griffith didn't know last season how the ball was pitched. Few people know how Griffith throws his slow ball, and Griffith, in my opinion, has got the best slow ball in America.

I see Pop Anson claims he could hit the spit ball. Anson couldn't hit it in a thousand years, and I am ready to wager that Anson couldn't even catch it.

The spit ball is easy to control. It will not be a very hard ball for the catchers once the pitchers have mastered it.

It was only in the first part of the season that my catchers were bothered. Towards the end I signaled just how far the ball would drop and whether it would drop straight or to the outside.

The spit ball cannot be made to drop in towards a right-handed batsman. It drops straight or to the outside. Of course, to a left-handed batsman it will drop in towards him.

Sluggers of the Freeman type are apt to be bothered more by the spit ball than scientific place hitters like Keeler.

"Won't the batters run up to meet it?" [I] was asked, and [I] replied, "What if they do? They run up now to meet a curve. Any batter can hit a ball if he knows how it is coming."

It is up to the pitcher to try and see the batsmen first, that is to try and find out if the batter is going to run up and to make his ball drop accordingly.

That last game in New York is still a dreadful nightmare.

by Jack Chesbro

No longer is the spit ball a mystery. Neither is the ball a supposition as many believe. Happy Jack Chesbro, the acknowledged king of the spit ball, the pitcher who won 41 games for the New York American team last season, the one man who Boston fans feared would deprive us of the pennant, and the same pitcher, who by a fatal wild throw allowed Criger to score from third with the run that gave Boston the pennant, tells for the first time of the spit ball, its effects, his discovery of it and its part in baseball's future.

Never before has Chesbro told, at least for publication, how he throws the spit ball. Manager Clark Griffith of the New York team tried in vain last season to discover Chesbro's method. Chesbro's fellow pitchers pleaded with him to let them "in," and from Napoleon Lajoie down the American league batsmen could not connect with Chesbro's elusive delivery.

Chesbro's explanation of the spit ball will make many pitchers open their eyes in astonishment. It will make hundreds of experts wonder, and it will make the ball players themselves gape. Since the pitch first came into vogue column after column has been printed, explaining its virtues. Never, according to Chesbro, has a correct explanation of it been made, and the pitcher who won 41 games during last season, and who attributes the greater part of his success to his gift with the spit ball, should know whereof he speaks.

Spit Ball Is a Reality

It is useless to laugh at the spit ball. Years ago when the curved ball was first pitched many tried to laugh it down. The public as a rule likes to laugh at new discoveries. When the telegraph was first invented only a brave few took it seriously and the same was the case with the telephone.

The writer has seen the spit ball pitched by Chesbro, by Gibson and by Dineen. Lou Criger has gone on record regarding the spit ball; so has Lajoie, Wagner, Griffith, Collins, and all of baseball's leading players. It is, then, indeed foolish for many of the baseball fans to ridicule the spit ball.

The spit ball has come to stay. Every pitcher in the land is thinking these cold winter days of it. Chesbro next season expects even greater results. Chesbro's secret is now out and from coast to coast the pitchers will be able to begin the coming season with a definite knowledge of the ball that threatens in a way to revolutionize America's great sport.

Chesbro's explanation puts the ball in an entirely new light. It has been argued that the ball was made possible because of the saliva on it. It is only in a small way that the saliva has anything to do with the ball.

Could Be Called a Thumb Ball

Properly the ball could be called a thumb ball. Except with the spit ball every pitcher and everyone who ever threw a ball knows that a baseball leaves the fingers last. The moistening of the ball makes it leave the fingers first and the thumb last, and from the thumb alone does Chesbro make the ball drop when it reaches the plate. As Chesbro says he can make the ball drop two inches or he can make it drop 18 inches.

Chesbro was easily the best pitcher in either league last season. He pitched in 54 games and won 41. Another game he tied. Few pitchers in either league pitched over 30 games. Last season's schedule called for 154 games, so that Chesbro pitched over one-third of the games played by New York. Chesbro also won 14 straight games, this great winning streak being stopped by Norwood Gibson.

Chesbro Enjoying Himself

Up among the Berkshire hills in the little town of Conway, Chesbro is enjoying himself as few people can. The proud owner of two of the fastest horses in western Massachusetts, Chesbro gets more enjoyment out of the winter season than any ball player in the land. Conway is a small town of about 1500 people and Chesbro is the most famous man that the town can boast of. He knows everyone and is better known than any of his fellow townsmen. Five miles from Conway is the railroad station of South River, and it took but a second for the writer to ascertain where Chesbro lived.

Chesbro with his wife and mother-in-law lives in one of the largest houses in Conway. The scenery of the Berkshire hills is said to be unrivalled in the United States, and from Chesbro's house this scenery can be viewed in all its magnificence. Across the street from the Chesbro house is one of the largest hills or rather mountains in the

State. From South River one takes a trolley car to the Conway village. The motorman had pointed out Chesbro's house, but as I prepared to climb the steep hill to it Chesbro himself walked out of the postoffice, and with a warm shake of the hand welcomed the Post man to Conway.

Chesbro Is a Farmer in Cold Weather

Chesbro is a farmer during the winter, and he glories in it. A five minutes' walk found us at the Chesbro house. Three fine hunting dogs had met us half way and Mrs. Chesbro welcomed us at the door with the gladsome remark that dinner was ready. Never did the writer accept an invitation to dine with more alacrity, for to reach Conway one must leave Boston at 6:30 in the morning and it was 1:30 before the little town was reached. One week ago Chesbro had killed one of his hogs and the roast pork was indeed relished, for seven hours of travelling on steam and trolley cars on a crisp day tends to give one a wholesome appetite.

After dinner Chesbro acted as guide. His two fast trotters received the most attention. For his great pitching last season, Owner Farrell of the New York club gave Chesbro a magnificent looking trotter with a mark on the New York speedway of 2:14. On the arrival of the horse in Conway, Chesbro christened him "Spit Ball" and "Spit Ball" the horse is as well known in western Massachusetts as is the spit ball to baseball lovers. Chesbro showed me the large barn which he built himself and it is the equal of any barn ever built. It is roomy with two box stalls. Up in the loft Chesbro has a dozen or more of fancy pigeons, the gift of one of his North Adams admirers.

Chesbro's farm comprises several acres, and in addition he owns three other large farms in Conway, which he rents at handsome figures.

Chesbro Is a Berkshire Boy

Chesbro has always lived among the Berkshire hills and was born in North Adams, which is only 25 miles from Conway.

He is known far and wide, and behind "Spit Ball," muffled up in the fur coat presented to him as he went to bat in that memorable game in New York, the gift of Harry Reinhart and other North Adams friends, Chesbro can be seen almost daily, the picture of health and contentment. When not behind his fast trotter, Chesbro is usually seen with a gun and two dogs, for rabbit hunting is Chesbro's delight and he is a crack shot.

Chesbro was glad to see the Post man. His welcome only showed this too plainly, and late in the afternoon after Chesbro had told the mysteries of the spit ball the writer enjoyed a 10-mile sleigh ride behind Spit Ball. Snow is plentiful in Conway and Chesbro had his hands full in keeping Spit Ball from breaking the speed regulations of the town.

Chesbro Didn't Tell All He Knows

Chesbro didn't tell all he knows about the spit ball. It was only after a long argument that Chesbro consented to tell about the part his thumb plays in pitching. He refused to tell how it is possible for him to make the ball drop two inches or 18 inches. The other pitchers must find out the secret themselves. Chesbro had no outside help, and no one can blame him for being secretive, for last year he baffled the batsmen by the use of the spit ball and would be indeed foolish to let his rival pitchers know the "something he now has on them."

Chesbro Loves the Sport

Chesbro loves baseball. He is in the sport for the glory there is in it. "I don't care about the money," said he. "I like to pitch and I like to win. I am well off. I have enough here to keep me for the rest of my life. I would rather have the credit of winning more games than any other pitcher than in being given the biggest salary. I have wanted to retire from baseball for the past three years, but when the spring comes around the baseball feeling gets into me, and the first thing I know I am off for the South.

"Baseball surely keeps one in the best of health. I have not had a sick day in ten years. How did I break in? Like all boys, I played baseball around North Adams. When but a youngster I discovered that I could pitch a little and played with several local teams. My pitching seemed to attract some attention, and in 1894 I was offered a job in the Middletown, N.Y., Insane Asylum. Part of the job was to pitch for the Middletown team. I had a good season, and in '95 went to Springfield. In '96 I was with the Roanoke team, and in '97 went to Richmond, where I remained until July, 1899, when [I] joined the Pittsburg Pirates."

Chesbro stayed with Pittsburg until the spring of 1903, when with Tannehill and O'Connor he jumped the Pirates for the New York Americans.

That Great Game in New York

No game ever played in the history of baseball was more important than that memorable contest in New York on Oct. 12 last, between Boston and New York. A victory for Boston meant the pennant, while a victory for New York meant that Boston would have to win the second game in order to land the pennant.

Had New York won both games she would have captured the championship.

No man played a bigger part in that game than Chesbro. On Friday of the week before Chesbro beat Boston. On Saturday in Boston Chesbro was knocked out of the box. The test came on Monday, and in the early part of the game Chesbro had smashed out a three-base hit. Leading Boston by two runs, New York's cause looked good.

Then came Williams' bad throw to the plate and the score was tied. The innings wore on and Criger was on third with Parent at the bat. The biggest crowd ever seen in the park yelled for Chesbro to retire Parent, for two were out. Parent was down for two strikes and three balls, and Chesbro sized him up with deadly precision; but Chesbro realized the responsibility. In another second the whole aspect was changed, for Chesbro's ball had hit the grand stand and Criger ran home.

Chesbro Will Never Forget One Game

Chesbro will never forget that game, neither will the Boston rooters who were present, and reluctantly he told of that game, with the remark that he would never forget it.

"It is an old, old story," said Chesbro. "I have thought it over and over. I don't believe I will ever forget it. You were there when I made that wild pitch, and in all New York I don't believe there was a more sorrowful individual. I would have given my entire year's salary back could I but had the ball back. I wanted that game badly. It practically meant the pennant, for if we won the first we would have won the second. We had the game clinched at one time with a two-run lead.

"Boston was a lucky team without doubt, for in addition to my wild pitch Williams' low throw helped to give Boston her two runs that tied the game up.

"How did I make the wild pitch? How does any pitcher make one? I used a spit ball, but the spit ball had nothing to do with it. I simply put too much force into the throw. Then Dineen had been using the spit ball and had made the ball rather slippery. I am not blaming Dineen, however. I put too much force into the ball and that's all. It hit the grand stand, and it's a long story of what happened. We lost the pennant, but this year we will win it."

Chesbro Is a Modest Fellow

Chesbro was willing enough to talk baseball, but preferred to keep himself out of the discussion. In speaking of the spit ball Chesbro was obliged to bring himself in. What he said about the spit ball he meant. Chesbro, like all great players, is modest. He didn't want to tell about the ball until it was put up to him that he would be doing all young pitchers a big favor and that baseball would be the gainer.

Chesbro looks the part of a happy farmer. He is weighing 200 pounds, or 20 more than he does during the summer. In the middle of the next month he will come down to Harvard to teach the Crimson pitchers how to pitch. He may tell them something about the spit ball.

"Collins will have a great team this season," said Chesbro, as we drove to the station. "Burkett, in my mind, is a great player, although it will be a shame to see men as good as Selbach or Freeman sitting on the bench. Gibson had the spit ball down fine last year. Collins is a great general, and if New York doesn't win the flag this season, I look to see Boston capture it. Collins as a leader has few equals. His team never gives up, and I guess I faced them as often as any pitcher in the past two years, and I guess I know.

"Something I think should be done to increase the hitting. The spit ball is sure to work to the detriment of the batting game. I wouldn't mind having the foul strike abolished, provided the umpires would have the nerve to get after the men who foul balls on purpose. It is pretty tough to pitch to men who deliberately foul them off, and there are quite a few batters who can do the trick."

The visit came to an end almost too soon. It was a glorious day and behind Spit Ball the Berkshire hills never seemed more attractive. Chesbro is unselfish and he freely gave his views on the spit ball that will enable other pitchers to master it to be used against his own team.

Chesbro was the greatest pitcher in the game last year, and among the Berkshire hills, with his horses, dogs and cows, Chesbro is leading the Simple Life that will surely enable him to pitch winning ball the coming year.

by Frederic P. O'Connell

In the off-season following Chesbro's infamous wild pitch, Boston sportswriter Frederic P. O'Connell traveled to Chesbro's western Massachusetts farm for this rare profile of the star pitcher, one of the first successful practitioners of the "spit ball." It appeared at the time as if Chesbro's success would continue unabated.

But a combination of the high life and a sore arm would cut short Chesbro's career. He put on weight, and the toil of pitching 445 innings in 1903 affected his arm. Over the next five seasons he would win only 67 more games in the major leagues.

ANONYMOUS

BUILDING A WINNING CLUB IN NEW YORK

Some of the Difficulties a Magnate Encounters
in Trying to Develop a Major League Baseball
Property. As Revealed in an Interview
with Col. Jacob Ruppert, President of the
New York Yankees

from *Baseball Magazine,* June 1919

Those who wish to see the magnate in person may best find him in
the immense brewing establishment which the Ruppert genius has
built up in New York City. Through the marble corridor which leads
out from the main entrance, past uniformed guards who greet you
courteously, you gradually penetrate through one ante room to another, as though you sought audience with the late Czar of Russia,
when the Romanoffs still controlled one-sixth the land surface of
the globe. Everything is sumptuously neat though the atmosphere
suggests the yeasty fermentation that is continually going on in the
monstrous copper cauldrons. You catch a glimpse of these bur-
nished receptacles as you mount the smoothly gliding elevator to
the office, and your guide informs you (to the grief of our prohibition friends be it said) that from those same cauldrons eight thousand barrels of beer go foaming daily, with a sudsy current of good
cheer to the huge thirsty city which lies all about you.

At last the order is given; you are admitted to the presence of the
magnate himself as he sits, in solitary state, in a spacious room dec-
orated very simply with massive bronze statuary, at a huge desk lit-
tered with papers. And it was here, with the distant purring hum of
the brewery for an accompaniment, that he unfolded the dreams he

had entertained for bearing the standards of the American League to victory in the greatest of cities.

Col. Ruppert is in every sense a man of big business, quick of speech, decisive in his statements, yet courteous and discriminating in his treatment of the men who approach him in a continual stream on a thousand varied errands. "I was always interested in baseball," he said, "in fact, in my younger years I played it in an amateur way. But up to the time when I became identified with the Yankees I was a strong National League rooter. The Polo Grounds are a feature of the big city quite as much as the Statue of Liberty or Brooklyn Bridge, and the team which has appealed the strongest to the local fans are the Giants with all their long tradition of pennants won and famous diamond stars.

"It would be impossible for me to say when the idea of becoming an owner first came to me. Probably it was a gradual process. The first time the matter was brought to my attention in a concrete form, however, was when Charles Murphy was selling out his controlling interest in the Chicago Cubs. A gentleman who knew of my fondness for baseball ventured the suggestion that I purchase them. I told him that I had no desire to become an owner of a club in Chicago, or for that matter, of any club outside of New York. In fact, the Cub transaction did not interest me at all, but it did bring the idea of some day becoming an owner prominently into my mind, and no doubt, made the later acquisition of the Yankees an easier undertaking than it otherwise would have been.

"The first intimation I had that the Yankees were for sale, was through an item to that effect, in the newspapers. The idea instantly occurred to me that here was a prospect to become interested in a Major League club at home. About the same time the matter was further impressed upon me by some of my good friends, who wished to see me get into a good thing. Through the papers I learned that Capt. Huston was also mentioned as a possible purchaser, and I accordingly arranged a meeting with him. It was the first time I had ever met Capt. Huston. We found that we agreed on all important items of the transaction and allowed it to be known that we might be possible purchasers of the franchise.

"The next act in the little drama occurred in a friendly club room where I met Ban Johnson and other members of the American League. We were treated royally by these good friends. I addressed them in an informal way and outlined our attitude. I told them that it seemed to Capt. Huston and myself that there wasn't much of a club to purchase, merely a few individual players of merit and a rather disorganized team. But I stated that we would be interested in acquiring the property, provided the other members of the American League assisted us in the construction of a winning club in New York. I emphasized the fact that we asked no charity, that we were able and willing to pay a liberal cash price for all assistance rendered to us, but that we felt we must depend upon the co-operation of our fellow magnates, in building up a powerful club in the greatest city of the world, a club in which their interest would not be an entirely unselfish one since a strong team in New York meant better patronage for every other club in the circuit. My sentiments met with a most hearty approval from all present and I began to think that the lot of the Big League owner was a close parallel to the proverbial bed of roses.

"After Capt. Huston and myself had actually acquired possession of the Yankees, we were approached by several American League owners. One of them said, 'I have one of the finest young shortstops in the country. He is yours for only $5000.' Another had a star young outfielder he was willing to dispose of for the slight consideration of $5000. Still another had a promising pitcher fresh from the bush leagues who was also ours for the paltry sum of $5000. And time revealed the fact that all these young phenoms were lemons. In fact, the only concrete evidence that the American League would give us its unqualified support, finally simmered down to players Pipp and High, for both of which men we paid the full market price.

"Now it requires no wizard of finance to see that the presence of the New York Giants in the line-up, is an immense asset to the National League, and is recognized as such by the remaining club owners. But in the American League there seems to have been an entire lack of any concerted campaign to build up a club in New York which should rival the Giants on an even basis. This is, to my mind, a failure to appreciate facts at their face value, which has cost the American League a lot of prestige it might have had, and has cost every club owner in the circuit the loss of valuable revenue. In fact, this attitude of the American League is a thing I have never been able to fathom.

"Let me cite two concrete instances of this attitude. For several years I have had my eye on Pratt of St. Louis. I cannot say that he is a better player than Gedeon, but he has played better ball and we wanted him. Well, how did I get him? I paid fifteen thousand dollars in cash and gave away a number of good players for him. But what can you do? I needed this player, everyone knew I needed him. One thing was certain, I couldn't come back empty handed. I had to do something to build up the club after the loss of several valuable men to army service. And I got what I went after, though I had to pay out of all reason for him.

"This is a deal which actually went through. Let me cite another deal which I believe, should have gone through, but didn't. For some time I have had my eyes on Joe Bush and Amos Strunk of the Athletics. Last year I asked Mack if it would be possible to interest him in a deal for these players. He said to me, 'I have sold my last player.' 'All right,' I said, 'if you change your mind let me know.' 'I will,' said he.

"Time went on and finally I received word that Mack would be willing to see me and talk things over. He didn't want to be observed discussing things with me in Philadelphia, because he was afraid some newspaper man would see him and start the story of a sensational trade. Neither for the matter of that, did he want to come to New York. So he suggested that we meet and talk it over at Trenton. Nobody ever goes to Trenton unless he has important business to negotiate. But I met him at Trenton and we adjourned to a small hotel where we, no doubt, were looked upon as a couple of gunmen discussing a future hold up game. 'I can't talk to you about Bush,' began Mack, 'because I already have given a certain club an option on Bush. But I can't say that this club will go through with the option. If they fall down, I will let you know. However, for certain reasons, I have decided to let go of Strunk and Schang and if you want these men I am willing to talk business. I want $25,000 for Schang.'

"'Well, Mack,' I said, 'I'm not so particular about Schang. I don't really need a catcher so much, anyway.' 'Well,' said Mack, 'He can certainly hit. But I don't know as Schang would be the man you need most on your club.'

"'Not at that price,' I told him. 'But I would make you an offer of $10,000 for Strunk.'

"'I couldn't consider it,' said Mack. 'I couldn't even think of it. I must get $75,000 for these three men. I will sell them for that figure, but if I had to sell two of them separately, I would want more than $50,000 for them. I wouldn't agree to let them go for $50,000, but there isn't any hurry. Think it over and decide what you are willing to do.'

"'I will do that, Mack,' I said, 'only be sure to let me know before you go through with this thing with any other club, for I certainly want Strunk and Bush anyway.'

"So we adjourned. Mack went back to Philadelphia, and I took the same train for Washington. But Mack sat in one end of the car, entirely oblivious of my presence at the other end.

"Well, you all know what happened. The Red Sox got Bush and Schang and Strunk in a sensational deal.

"When I made the offer of $10,000 for Strunk I was willing to go higher and Mack has certainly done enough trading in his day, to know that I would go higher. A man seldom makes his highest bid first.

"Capt. Huston and myself have spent over $200,000 in strengthening the Yankees since we purchased the club. We paid $37,500 for Frank Baker; we paid $25,000 for Lee Magee, and we have got rid of a young fortune on other players who couldn't deliver the goods. And we have had some of the most frightful luck I ever heard of. This may be a common alibi of the loser, but it has the substantiation of fact, in our case, at least. For at one time we had no fewer than eleven men on the hospital list. Bill Donovan was the finest fellow in the world and I hated to let him go. But business won't wait. He had been handicapped by the worst of luck as I well realized, but after three years we didn't seem to be advancing very fast and I felt that it was to the best interests of the club to make a change. Prior to the time I sent for Miller Huggins to come to my office and talk things over. I had never met him but I had followed his work and been impressed with his shrewdness in directing the Cardinal Club and believed that he would get results with the Yankees. I still contend that my judgment was sound and am perfectly willing to abide by the decision of the season.

"I shall take personal credit for Miller Huggins' appointment if he succeeds as I believe he will, and I shall also take full blame for his failure if he fails. It is true that he was suggested to me by several people as a prospective manager, but so were many other men. I listened to all the advice that was given me, but I had already made up my mind before I tried to secure him to lead my club.

"I do not begrudge the money I have lost so far in trying to build up a winner for the American League in New York. This is one city where the public demands a winner. New Yorkers will pay any reasonable amount for the best, but you can't palm off inferior goods on them. I have got a lot of excitement out of this magnate business and no doubt there is much more coming to me before I am through. But it's all a part of the game and really not so unlike other business ventures, for whatever you consider as an investment has a certain element of risk and is, to a certain extent, a gamble. Baseball is a little bigger gamble than most, and the stakes are pretty high. But if I can get a winner in New York within the next year or two, I shan't begrudge a nickle I put into the club, or a lot more that I shall probably send after what has already gone, before I am through."

Thus briefly and to the point did Jacob Ruppert outline his experiences as a magnate up to date. He had no complaints to offer, no criticism of individuals. But in stating as he did, that the establishment of a strong club in New York City was a vital concern of the American League as a whole, not merely the labor of an individual magnate he struck, to our mind, at the weakest point in the policy of the American League since that organization rose from obscurity to a commanding place in professional Baseball. No one can blame Ruppert or his associates. They have spent a fortune for players. But they do not seem to have met with quite that element of helpful co-operation which the most enlightened business foresight would warrant. The American League had made very few mistakes. But hasn't it erred a trifle in its failure to estimate at its true worth, the value to the league as a whole of a powerful club in the world's new metropolis, New York City.

As much as Babe Ruth, and perhaps even more so, beer baron Jacob Ruppert saved the Yankees, for Farrell and Devery had run the franchise into the ground. Ruppert, with partner Cap Huston, rescued the team after the 1914 season, buying it for $460,000.

It was a new day for the Yankees. Under Ruppert, the Yankees put into place the semblance of a plan for success and acquired some much-

needed stability. Moreover, Ruppert would also put pressure on American League president Ban Johnson to make good on some long-standing promises to help the team acquire talent. Johnson's failure to do so would eventually lead the Yankees to take control of their own destiny. The result would be a dynasty.

JOHNSON'S BELATED ACTION THREATENS NEW BALL WAR

American League "Czar" Stirs Up Trouble by Placing Pitcher Under Ban for Old Offense After Local Club Secures Him from the Red Sox

from *The New York Tribune,* August 1, 1919

The suspension of Carl Mays by President Ban Johnson of the American League, immediately after the pitcher's services had been secured by the New York American League Club, threatens to start a new baseball war. Ban Johnson sent out the notice yesterday to the effect that Mays would be suspended indefinitely.

The notice of suspension came as a complete surprise to Colonel Jacob Ruppert and Colonel T. L. Huston, owners of the Yankees, who had made the dicker for Mays with Harry H. Frazee, owner of the Boston Red Sox, in good faith. They point out that Johnson did not order a suspension of Mays when it was known that Charlie Comiskey, of the Chicago White Sox, was offering $40,000 for the services of the underhand pitcher.

In announcing the suspension of Mays, Ban Johnson declared that six clubs in the American League had protested against the pitcher working for any club but the Red Sox. When he was requested by wire by the Yankee owners to name the six clubs, Johnson replied with an expressive silence.

Local supporters of the American League believe that the Yankees have been discriminated against time and again by their own league. Every effort of the Yankees to strengthen the team since the present owners obtained control seems to have met with opposition.

This last action by the self-styled Czar of Baseball certainly will strengthen this impression.

National Policy Differs

The policy of the National League toward the New York fans seems to be entirely the opposite. There is almost a parallel case in Davey Robertson, of the Giants. Robertson refused to report for duty to the Giants. Yet there was no objection on the part of President Heydler of the National League when Robertson was traded to the Cubs for "Shufflin' Phil" Douglas. This trade probably will help to cinch the National League pennant for the Giants.

Johnson declares that the suspension of Mays is necessary for the preservation of discipline in the American league. The "Czar" is a stickler for discipline when discipline suits his own ends.

During a game at Shibe Park, Philadelphia, Mays threw a ball at a spectator. For this offense Mays was fined $100 by Johnson. Mays refused to pay the fine himself, and deserted the Boston club. Immediately Harry Frazee started negotiations to trade Mays. The White Sox started to dicker and offered something like $40,000 in cash for the rebellious player.

All this time the "Czar" of baseball remained mute as a Great South Bay clam. The "Czar" does not crack his disciplining knout in the direction of the Old Roman of Chicago, Charles Comiskey. The Old Roman is something of a Czar himself. Some time back he was accused of attempting to buy a pennant, that is, to purchase players necessary to win a pennant. Ban Johnson did not crack his knout once in the Old Roman's direction while the negotiations were going on. The Czar is not ruler of that small strip of the baseball world which includes Chicago.

Yankee Owners Calm

It remains to be seen whether or not there will be a little side insurrection in New York. For the present the Yankee owners are speaking very softly. Colonel Tillinghast l'Hommedieu Huston is ominously calm. Colonel Jacob Ruppert has not yet expressed even 2¾ per cent of wrath.

Colonel Ruppert wired Ban Johnson last night, pointing to the fact that if the conduct of Mays had called for an indefinite suspension, such suspension should have been announced between July 13 and 29, while Harry Frazee was still openly negotiating to trade the pitcher. The wire asks that the suspension be raised to avoid inflicting considerable hardship on the Yankees. In conclusion, it said, "We make this request in the friendliest spirit, without, however, waiving our legal rights."

That sounds like a horseshoe in the glove. Mays will mean the difference between first and second division to the Yankees, and Colonels Ruppert and Huston are not going to lose his services without a battle. Harry Frazee openly declares that he believes the suspension was ordered to injure him. He claims that Johnson had a personal spite against him.

Colonel Huston was not anxious to discuss the suspension order last night.

"I am convinced that there must be some misunderstanding on the part of the president of the league," he said. "I would not protest against a matter of discipline. Colonel Ruppert and myself, I believe, always have shown that we are anxious to have discipline maintained in the game. We have the game and its interests at heart as much as anybody in it. We are waiting a reply to our wire from Mr. Johnson."

Mays Needed in Box

Mays is badly needed by the Yankees, as yesterday's game demonstrated. Shore will not be of much use to the team for some time to come. Pessimistic Yank followers believe that he may never be of a great deal of use. With the addition of Mays the Yanks would be in a strategic position to make a real battle for the pennant. The indefinite suspension practically spikes their chances to win back their lead.

This is not the first time that the throne of the Czar of Baseball was threatened. Harry Frazee led a fight against him sometime back, and came within one vote of evicting the Czar. For that reason, among others, Mr. Johnson and Mr. Frazee are not the dearest of friends.

It was loose talk on the part of the Czar that largely helped the defunct Federal League in getting a heavy money judgment against organized baseball. The Czar had uttered many dire threats as to what he would do to opponents of organized baseball, and his edicts were used at the trial with telling effect by the plaintiffs.

For some time the resentment against the rule of the Czar of Baseball has been developing. This Mays matter may mean the start of a movement that will have baseball, or at least the American League, run along more democratic lines, as befits the sport of a republic.

There are not many Czars left.

Ruppert Wires Johnson Protest of Delayed Act

Colonel Jacob Ruppert, half owner of the Yankees, last night sent the following telegram to President Ban Johnson:

B. B. Johnson, President American League, Fisher Building, Chicago.

In dealing for Mays New York felt that you must have been cognizant from press reports that three clubs of our league were negotiating for this man; also if you considered Mays's conduct called for any action on your part and was other than an internal affair with Boston club you would have acted during the period of July 13 to 29. Receiving no answer to our telegram of July 24, in reply to yours of even date, we felt you were being imposed upon, and therefore we continued our negotiations for the player.

The player reported to President Frazee on July 29 and was later transferred to New York. Therefore your action in suspending the player works such a terrible hardship on our club that we respectfully ask that you raise this suspension. We make this request in the friendliest spirit, without, however, waiving our legal rights.

— Jacob Ruppert

The success the team began to enjoy under Ruppert finally sparked sustained interest in the team in the New York press. W. O. "Bill" McGeehan of the New York Tribune *was one of the finest writers in what would later be recognized as a golden age of New York sports reporting.*

In July 1919, star pitcher Carl Mays of the Red Sox walked off the field in the middle of a game. AL president Ban Johnson wanted Boston owner Harry Frazee to suspend the pitcher. Instead, Frazee sold him to the Yankees. The deal precipitated a split in the American

League, leading the Yankees, Red Sox, and White Sox to enter into an alliance against Johnson's despotic reign. Known collectively as "the Insurrectos," over the next few seasons they tried to topple Johnson, whom McGeehan dubbed baseball's "Czar." Their efforts would ultimately prove successful and lead to the most important acquisition in club history — the purchase of Babe Ruth from Boston after the 1919 season.

PART II

MURDERERS' ROW

In 1914 Jacob Ruppert and Cap Huston emancipated the Yankees from the corrupt and cash-poor regime of Farrell and Devery. They gave the team a much-needed infusion of cash and, even more significant, a chance to win. AL President Ban Johnson had long promised to help the team acquire talent, but when he reneged, the Yankees entered into an alliance with the Red Sox and White Sox to topple the Czar. The fallout from that battle was a huge factor in the Yankees' purchase of Babe Ruth in December 1919.

With Ruth in the middle of the Yankee lineup, the pieces of a championship team rapidly fell into place, culminating in their first World Series win in 1923. Under the leadership of manager Miller Huggins and with first baseman Lou Gehrig hitting in tandem with Ruth, the first Yankee dynasty took shape.

It was also the golden age of New York sportswriting, as writers such as Ring Lardner, Heywood Broun, Damon Runyon, W. O. McGeehan, Grantland Rice, John Kieran, and others matched the Yankees' accomplishments on the field with stylish writing and reporting that made those performances legendary. They were a "Murderers' Row" of reporters whose groundbreaking efforts helped pull journalism out of the nineteenth century and into the modern era. They wrote without precedents, before clichés were recognized as such. Their work allowed Yankee fans to relive every moment of every season. Together, they created a shared history that fans could discuss and debate all winter long. And then, each season, spring returned, with the promise of more memorable moments yet to come.

W. O. McGeehan

··

RUTH'S PRESENCE UPSETS RIVALS IN LAST INNING

Babe Wields Bat and Griff's Minions Toss Off Game; Peck Makes Home Run

from *The New York Tribune*, April 27, 1920

Babe Ruth, supposed to be a pale and interesting invalid with his eleventh rib wrenched loose from its moorings, stalked out as a pinch hitter in the ninth inning at the Polo Grounds yesterday after the Yankees had tossed a ball game away to the Senators. His presence, like that of a somewhat overfed Banquo's ghost, so startled the Senators that they tossed the game right back at the Yankees. The final score was: Yanks, 3; Washington, 2.

The pastiming was considerably loose and ragged up to that time. The Yanks were leading by the length of Peckinpaugh's home run to the left field bleachers until the sixth, when Herbert Thormahlen let in two runs, entirely without assistance. He passed two Senators and threw the ball over Aaron Ward's head, letting the two men score.

Ward did most of the starring for the Yankees. He got three clean hits and a base on balls and he fielded beautifully. If he keeps the pace the management of the Yankees will rapidly discontinue sighing for J. Franklin Baker.

The melodrama in which the corpulent and ruddy ghost of Babe Ruth demanded a lot of the spotlight occurred early in the ninth. Meusel sent a fast one down to O'Neill, who juggled the ball long enough for the long-legged son of the Golden West to reach the first sack. Then came Ping Bodie, champion rock roller of Telegraph Hill, San Francisco. Ping punched a hit through center.

Babe in Uniform Again

In the mean time something that looked like a grizzly bear in the Yankee uniform crawled out of the dugout swinging three sticks in one paw. It was the Babe, who was supposed to be tossing on his cot of pain in the nearest hospital. He was just about to roll up to the plate when Miller Huggins halted him and let Ruel take his own turn at bat. Muddy was to have sent the runners along with a sacrifice, but he popped a puny little fly into the paws of Leif Erickson — Leif the Viking, of Pennsylvania Avenue, Washington, D.C.

Leif, the Viking, looked at Babe Ruth, meditatively swinging his triplet of bats, and Leif, the Red, seemed a little white around the gills.

"I thought hay ban a sick feller," muttered Leif the Red to Gharrity. "Hay don't look like hay ban sick feller." The Viking was visibly disconcerted.

The Babe then went to bat for Thormahlen and caught the second pitched ball and crashed a high one out in center. It was long and high enough to send Meusel and Bodie a base each further. "If hay ban sick, by yimminey, what can hay do when hay get well again?" mused Leif the Red. He was so disconcerted that he passed Aaron Ward and the bases were filled. The baleful presence of Babe Ruth also seemed to throw a scare into Gharrity, the Senator's catcher. Gharrity threw to catch Ping Bodie, who was doing an Italian spaghetti dance off second.

The throw went wide and wild into center field. Meusel cranked himself up and scooted across the plate with the run that tied. The Senators were rapidly disintegrating. Pipp shot a fast one down to O'Neill, who fumbled it and Ping Bodie came across with the winning run.

Pratt Has Busy Afternoon

Derrill Pratt had a busy time in the infield. The entire attack of the Washington crew seemed to be centered on his sector, but Derrill was equal to the occasion. He took sixteen chances and did not boot a single one, which came very close to the fielding record for one afternoon. Very few of the chances were soft ones either. Pratt's interest in baseball seems to have revived suddenly of late.

Peckinpaugh was the first of the Yanks to disconcert Eric the Red. Peck just naturally lifted one into the left field bleachers and it looked as though the Yankee hitting section had started the season's work.

Herbert Thormahlen, the left-handed, upset the frijoles all over the park in the sixth in a fit of spring wildness. Herbert passed Harris; then he passed Gharrity. This brought Eric the Red up to the bat. The Viking is vehement with the bat, but not particularly accurate. He took a few wild swings and laced the ball down to Thormahlen's feet.

Herbert came trundling up and picked up the ball with his left hand. He took careful aim at Aaron Ward, but the ball whizzed several yards high and to the right. By the time it was recovered two runs had crossed the plate.

The six thousand who witnessed this calamity continued to plead to the Yanks for a rally. The Yanks did not exactly rally in the ninth, but the Senators unrallied, so that the result was the same. The Babe, whose presence seemed to shoot the chills into the morale of the Senators, was rambling around the lot in early practice, but nobody suspected him to have any intention of bursting into the game.

Without taking his temperature or measuring his blood pressure, one is led to believe that the Babe will be back in the regular line-up in a few days. Anyhow, he will emerge once in a while to act as a scare crow while the Senators are with us.

When the Yankees first acquired Ruth, he was not quite yet the figure we remember today. Many people in baseball expected him to be a flash in the pan as a hitter, and there were knowing nods everywhere when he got off to a slow start in New York, then separated his ribs trying to wow fans during batting practice. But he soon turned his season around, and in this account McGeehan notes that Ruth's mere presence could change the game. That would remain true for a generation.

RING W. LARDNER

YANKEES FINALLY WIN; LANDIS DOUBTS LEGALITY

from the Bell Syndicate, October 12, 1923

POLO GROUNDS, NEW YORK, OCT. 11 — This article may sound kind of embarrassed, as I am writing it in the press box and they's a large crowd of beauty lovers standing in front of the screen, giving we newspaper boys a long and admiring look, and this in spite of the fact that a little ways off is seated two other movie queens, George Ade and Thomas Meighan. But will try and forget myself long enough to tell the fans that the score is said to of been 4 to 2 in favor of the Yankees, though it seems so improbable that Judge L — — s has called a meeting of the umpires and official scorers to go over the game inning by inning and see if it was legal.

They's a man in our crowd of admirers that says this is not the first time the Yankees ever win from the Giants but he has got a long gray beard and may be all through from a mental standpoint.

The thing that probably beat the Giants today, if the report is true that they were beaten, was the terror struck in their hearts by this man Pennock. Before the World Champions bat against a pitcher who they have never faced, Mr. McGraw makes them go to the library and look up all the books that bear on the subject. Well, they learned that Pennock is a man who has a country estate in Kennett Square, Pennsylvania, and when he ain't pitching he rides to hounds.

"What does it mean," asked Casey Stengel, "when it says a man rides to hounds?"

"All it means," replied Cozy Dolan, "is that you ain't going to hit against him."

A great many of the Giants, after witnessing Pennock's exhibition has made up their mind to spend the winter riding to hounds no matter what it is.

Will say in this connection that Great Neck is a great place for riding to hounds and practically every time I go out in my costly motor I run over a couple of them.

Last year I predicted that Babe Ruth was going to be the hero of the World Serious, and a good many people thought I meant the World Serious which I was then writing about. They must of been crazy.

Arthur Robinson says that the Babe is now two up on Cy Williams and Cy ain't got no chance to catch up this season unlest he can get some Shelby, Mont., banker to arrange a City Serious in Philadelphia.

Well, when Mr. Pennock took his turn in the Yankee batting practice indicating that he was going to pitch, Casey Stengel's dogs was heard to give a loud bark of relief, knowing they would not be sent on another long trip as long as a left-hander was working. The dogs was probably pulling for Pennock to last through the game, but Casey was not. The official announcement that Herb was going to start caused quite a discussion on the Giant bench. Some of the boys wanted to go up to bat without their bats, as the only Yankee left-hander they had ever faced before was Harry Harper.

The experts who had picked Arthur Nehf to work was greatly surprised when the well-known organist never even warmed up. Bentley and McQuillan worked out and in McQuillan's first inning it looked like the Yankees was the ones that might as well of left their bats on the bench, but after Hugh had throwed eight of the wildest balls ever seen to Dugan and Ruth somebody pointed out the plate to him and he made Meusel hit into a double play. By the time the next inning started the Giant hurler's control was so good that he hit Ward's bat right in the middle. He done the same thing to the Babe's big bludgeon in the fourth. If anybody had been riding on the ball Babe hit they could of got right on the elevated without climbing the stairs. Before this round was over word was sent to McQuillan from the clubhouse saying that his tub was ready. The Yankees was leading by three runs at the end of the fifth and the game began to look like an even bet with the Giants a slight favorite.

Along about this time it was announced that Mrs. Caroline Dorsey, the Traverse City, Mich., fan, was still in her seat at the Yankee stadium, thinking the game was being played there. It is thought that standing in line so long has infected the lady's mind, which wasn't so good to start with. It was even whispered that her ambition is to become a pinch base runner for the Yankees.

The monotony of the general situation was relieved somewhat in the Giant half of the sixth by the interspersal of a bit of football. With Youngs on first base, Emil Meusel tried to hit into a double play. Scott tossed the ball to Ward and forced Youngs, but Ward couldn't throw to first as Youngs was setting on him. The Yanks claimed interference, but the umpires refused to allow same, and for a time the fans thought he was the same party that refereed the Dempsey-Firpo fight.

Mr. Stengel's dogs began to whine in the eighth, when Manager McGraw sent Gowdy to bat for Cunningham, and they knew that Casey would have to work at least one inning. They were obliged to carry the old boy on two defensive trips, the second of which landed him under Ruth's long fly which would of been the Babe's third homer if he had aimed it pretty near any other direction.

After the game the writer visited the rival clubhouses to interview the rival managers.

"Mr. Huggins," I said, "have you anything to say about the game?"

But it seems that Mr. Huggins had left the clubhouse. So had Mr. McGraw.

Ring Lardner, who by 1923 had already earned a lasting reputation as one of America's foremost humorists and short story writers, began his writing career in the press box, covering baseball. When he chose to return to the game, his growing renown gave him the freedom to write about baseball in an unfettered way.

NEW YORK YANKEES 4, NEW YORK GIANTS 2

from *The New York World*, October 12, 1923

The Ruth is mighty and shall prevail. He did yesterday. Babe made two home runs and the Yankees won from the Giants at the Polo Grounds by a score of 4 to 2. This evens up the World Series with one game for each contender.

It was the first game the Yankees won from the Giants since October 10, 1921, and it ended a string of eight successive victories for the latter, with one tie thrown in.

Victory came to the American League champions through a change of tactics. Miller Huggins could hardly fail to have observed Wednesday that terrible things were almost certain to happen to his men if they paused any place along the line from first to home.

In order to prevent blunders in base running he wisely decided to eliminate it. The batter who hits a ball into the stands cannot possibly be caught napping off any base.

The Yankees prevented Kelly, Frisch and the rest from performing tricks in black magic by consistently hammering the ball out of the park or into sections of the stand where only amateurs were seated.

Through simplicity itself, the system worked like a charm. Three of the Yankees' four runs were the product of homers, and this was enough for the winning total. Aaron Ward was Ruth's assistant, Irish Meusel of the Giants also made a home run, but yesterday's show belonged to Ruth.

For the first time since coming to New York, Babe achieved his full brilliance in a World Series game. Before this he has varied between pretty good and simply awful, but yesterday he was magnificent.

Just before the game John McGraw remarked:

"Why shouldn't we pitch to Ruth? I've said before and I'll say again, we pitch to better hitters than Ruth in the National League."

Ere the sun had set on McGraw's rash and presumptuous words, the Babe had flashed across the sky fiery portents which should have been sufficient to strike terror and conviction into the hearts of all infidels. But John McGraw clung to his heresy with a courage worthy of a better cause.

In the fourth inning Ruth drove the ball completely out of the premises. McQuillan was pitching at the time, and the count was two balls and one strike. The strike was a fast ball shoulder-high, at which Ruth had lunged with almost comic ferocity and ineptitude.

Snyder peeked at the bench to get a signal from McGraw. Catching for the Giants must be a terrific strain on the neck muscles, for apparently it is etiquette to take the signals from the bench manager furtively. The catcher is supposed to pretend he is merely glancing around to see if the girl in the red hat is anywhere in the grandstand, although all the time his eyes are intent on McGraw.

Of course the nature of the code is secret, but this time McGraw scratched his nose to indicate: "Try another of those shoulder-high fast ones on the Big Bum and let's see if we can't make him break his back again."

But Babe didn't break his back, for he had something solid to check his terrific swing. The ball started climbing from the moment it left the plate. It was a pop fly with a brand new gland and, although it flew high, it also flew far.

When last seen the ball was crossing the roof of the stand in deep right field at an altitude of 315 feet. We wonder whether new baseballs conversing in the original package ever remark: "Join Ruth and see the world."

In the fifth Ruth was up again and by this time McQuillan had left the park utterly and Jack Bentley was pitching. The count crept up to two strikes and two balls. Snyder sneaked a look at the little logician deep in the dugout. McGraw blinked twice, pulled up his trousers and thrust the forefinger of his right hand into his left eye. Snyder knew that he meant: "Try the Big Bozo on a slow curve around his knees and don't forget to throw to first if you happen to drop the third strike."

Snyder called for the delivery as directed and Ruth half-topped a line drive over the wall of the lower stand in right field. With that drive the Babe tied a record. Benny Kauff and Duffy Lewis are the only other players who ever made two home runs in a single World Series game.

But was McGraw convinced and did he rush out of the dugout and kneel before Ruth with a cry of "Maestro" as the Babe crossed the plate? He did not. He nibbled at not a single word he has ever uttered in disparagement of the prowess of the Yankee slugger. In the ninth Ruth came to bat with two out and a runner on second base. By every consideration of prudent tactics an intentional pass seemed indicated.

Snyder jerked his head around and observed that McGraw was blowing his nose. The Giant catcher was puzzled, for that was a signal he had never learned. By a process of pure reasoning he attempted to figure out just what it was that his chief was trying to convey to him.

"Maybe he means if we pitch to Ruth we'll blow the game," thought Snyder, but he looked toward the bench again just to make sure.

Now McGraw intended no signal at all when he blew his nose. That was not tactics but only a head cold. On the second glance Snyder observed that the little Napoleon gritted his teeth. Then he proceeded to spell out with the first three fingers of his right hand: "The Old Guard dies, but never surrenders." That was a signal Snyder recognized, although it never had passed between him and his manager before.

McGraw was saying: "Pitch to the Big Bum if he hammers every ball in the park into the North River."

And so, at Snyder's request, Bentley did pitch to Ruth and the Babe drove the ball deep into right center; so deep that Casey Stengel could feel the hot breath of the bleacherites on his back as the ball came down and he caught it. If that drive had been just a shade to the right it would have been a third home run for Ruth. As it was, the Babe had a great day, with two home runs, a terrific long fly and two bases on balls.

Neither pass was intentional. For that McGraw should receive due credit. His game deserves to be recorded along with the man who said, "Lay on, Macduff," "Sink the ship, Master Ginner, split her in twain," and "I'll fight it out on this line if it takes all summer." For John McGraw also went down eyes front and his thumb on his nose.

Some of the sportsmanship of the afternoon was not so admirable. In the sixth inning Pep Youngs prevented a Yankee double play by diving at the legs of Ward, who was just about to throw to first after a force-out. Tack Hardwick never took out an opposing back more neatly. Half the spectators booed Youngs and the other half applauded him.

It did not seem to us that there was any very good reason for booing Youngs, since the tradition of professional baseball always has been agreeably free of chivalry. The rule is, "Do anything you can get away with."

But Youngs never should have been permitted to get away with interference. The runner on first ought to have been declared out. In coming down to second Youngs had complete rights to the baseline and the bag, but those rights should not have permitted him the privilege of diving all the way across the bag to tackle Ward around the ankles.

It was a most palpably incompetent decision by Hart, the National League umpire on second base. Fortunately the blunder had no effect on the game, since the next Giant batter hit into a double play in which the Giant rushline was unable to reach Ward in time to do anything about it.

Ruth crushed to earth shall rise again. Herb Pennock, the assistant hero of the afternoon, did the same thing. In the fourth inning, Jack Bentley toppled the slim Yankee left-hander into a crumpled heap by hitting him in the back with a fast ball. Pennock went down with a groan which could be heard even in the dollar seats. All the players gathered around him as he writhed, and what with sympathy and some judicious massage, he was up again within three or four minutes, and his pitching efficiency seemed to be in no wise impaired. It was, of course, wholly an accident, as the kidney punch is barred in baseball.

Entirely aside from his injury, Pennock looked none too stalwart. He is a meager athlete who winds up with great deliberation, as if fearful about what the opposing batter will do with the ball. And it was mostly slow curves that he fed to the Giants, but they did nothing much in crucial moments. Every now and then Pennock switched to a fast one, and the change of pace had McGraw's men baffled throughout.

Just once Pennock was in grave danger. It looked as if his three-run lead might be swept away in the sixth inning. Groh, Frisch and Youngs, the three Giants to face him at that point, all singled solidly. It seemed the part of wisdom to remove Pennock immediately after Youngs's single had scored Groh. Here Huggins was shrewd. He guessed wisely and stuck to Pennock.

Irish Meusel forced Youngs, and it would have been a double play but for Young's interference with Ward's throw. Cunningham, who followed, did hit into a double play, Scott to Ward to Pipp. The Giants' rally thus was limited to one run.

Their other score came in the second inning, when Irish Meusel drove a home run into the upper tier of the left field stands. It was a long wallop and served to tie the score at that stage of the game, as Aaron Ward had made a home run for the Yankees in the first half of the inning. Ward's homer was less lusty, but went in the same general direction.

In the fourth the Yankees broke the tie. Ruth began it with his over-the-fence smash, and another run came across on a single by Pipp, Schang's hit to right — which Youngs fumbled long enough to let Pipp reach third — and Scott's clean line hit to center. This is said to be Scott's last year as a regular and he seems intent on making a good exit, for, in addition to fielding spryly, he made two singles.

The defensive star of the afternoon was Joe Dugan, third baseman of the Yankees. He specialized on bunts. McQuillan caught him flat-footed with an unexpected tap, but he threw it on the dead run in time to get his man at first.

Again he made a great play against Kelly, first batter up in the last half of the ninth. Kelly just nicked the ball with a vicious swing and the result was a treacherous spinning grounder that rolled only half-way down to third. Dugan had to run and throw in conjunction this time, too, but he got his man.

For the Giants, Frisch, Youngs and Meusel batted hard, and Jack Bentley pitched well after relieving McQuillan in the fourth. He was hit fairly hard and he was a trifle wild, but the only run scored against him was Ruth's homer in the fifth.

As for the local color, the only bit we saw was around the neck of a spectator in a large white hat. The big handkerchief, which was spread completely over the gentleman's chest, was green and yellow, with purple spots. The rooter said his name was Tom Mix, but offered no other explanation.

Heywood Broun was a journalist who sometimes covered sports. The flamboyant, Harvard-educated Broun would make his lasting mark outside the world of sports in his influential general column, "As I See It," which appeared first in the World *and later in the* World Telegram and Post.

    Despite his many other accomplishments as a writer, many consider Broun's story on Game 2 of the 1923 World Series to be his best work. Next up is Grantland Rice's report on the same event. Though Broun's account is less showy, it is no less effective, since it reflects his reportorial skills as much as his writing skills.

YANKEES WIN WORLD'S SERIES, TAKING 6TH GAME, 6–4, AS GIANT PITCHERS BLOW UP IN 8TH INNING

Come from Behind, Clinch $1,000,000
Contest When 2 Hurlers Pitch 12 Balls Wide
with Bases Full. Ruth's Homer Record One.
Meusel's "$50,000 Hit" Saves Babe's Fame
After He Strikes Out in Crisis

from *The New York Tribune,* October 16, 1923

The Yankees rode through the storm at last, to reach the shining haven where the gold dust for the winter's end lies ankle-deep in the streets.

Trailing by three runs at the end of the seventh inning of the world's series game yesterday, with Art Nehf in supreme command of their waning destinies, they came through shadows as black as the heart of Stygia to find for the first time the radiant sunlight of a championship.

For the third straight afternoon the aroused Yankees beat the Giants, this time by 6 to 4, in a ball game that reeked with drama from a thousand open pores.

Greatest of the Series

There have been great games before in this amazing series, but nothing even to approach the melodramatic upheaval that brought the Yankees to triumph in the eighth frame. For in this eighth inning there were massed and concentrated the fall of Rome, the destruction of Carthage, the feast of Belshazzar, the rout of Cyrus, the march of Attila, the wreck of the *Hesperus* and the Chicago fire.

Almost every element that tends to churn human emotions into a froth and start the pulse jumping sideways struck the scene in this wild and woolly inning before the last Yankee was retired. There has been nothing like it in a pastime that has rung in sudden changes upon 10,000 themes. Nothing quite like it through a year of drama that in almost every branch of sport has lifted the human scalp up and down like flapjacks tossed by the camp cook in the heart of the piney woods.

When the rally ended, which carried the Yankees from defeat to victory, there was hardly a thumping heart in the park that wasn't pumped dry of blood as the crowd sank back, limp and exhausted from the nerve-wrecking strain.

The crash came with the startling suddenness of a simoon across the Indian Ocean, where the simoon has its lair. When the Yankees came to bat in the eighth the Giants were leading 4 to 1, with Art Nehf in one of his most brilliant moods. With the exception of a pass to Babe Ruth in the fourth Nehf had retired sixteen Yankees in unbroken order, rolling them back as some great cliff would turn back the summer's surf. They were breaking in vain against his speed, curves and control, while Giant batsmen were nicking Herb Pennock from round to round with an even, steady bombardment led by the spectacular Frisch.

Nehf Cracks Under Strain

Outside of Babe Ruth's home run in the first, a wallop that broke two records, and Ward's single in the second Nehf had allowed nothing like a hit. But as the finish drew near only his steel-spun nerve was holding him up. His face was beginning to show signs of the crushing strain, as he came in after the seventh white and drawn. But he had held Yankee hitters in such complete subjection to his wiry left wrist that no one looked for anything approaching the debacle that followed. Ward was the first to face Nehf in the eighth, and he popped out. He was the twelfth Yankee in succession that had been turned back from first.

With Ward out Schang singled, the first Yankee hit since the second inning. But it was not until Deacon Scott followed with another smashing punch to safe terrain that the crowd came to its feet with the call of the wild. There was then the scent of carnage in the air, the indefinable something that tips off the approaching hurricane.

Drama in the Eighth

The weary Nehf, now completely fogged, pitched four successive balls to Hofmann, who had supplanted Pennock at bat. By now, with the bases filled and only one out, the crowd was a seething cauldron of riot and action, great stuff for a mob scene picture of the French Revolution. Nehf's last stand was one of the tragedies of sport. From the heights of the conqueror he had dropped within three minutes to the rocks below, as if fate had pushed him from the ledge just as he was crossing the final gap. With his control still broken he then passed Joe Bush, batting for Whitey Witt, forcing Schang over the plate, and leaving the bases still full.

Eight successive balls ended Nehf's work for the year. He came from the field with bowed head, wiping the grimy sweat from his eyes with his gloved hand, moving as a man walks to the guillotine or the chair.

You can imagine the scene at this moment, with Rosy Ryan standing in the box as Joe Dugan came to bat. Ryan, picking up where Nehf left off, added another pass without throwing a strike, forcing in another run. Nehf and Ryan together had now missed the plate twelve times in a row — one of the most amazing lapses of control ever seen in any game, from the bush to the big tent. Twelve balls without a strike may not be a record, but it isn't far away.

Still the drama grew in tensity. For here was Babe Ruth at bat, with the bases filled and two runs needed to win — Ruth standing "amid the alien corn," as Keats once put it, yearning "for home."

And it was here that Ryan for a moment almost saved the day. Ruth took two vicious cuts, fouled and missed. The next was a ball. Then Ryan, coming up on his toes, broke over a fast, deep curve ball that also came near breaking Ruth's heart. The home-run maker, lashing with full power, struck empty October air as the ball broke a full foot below his whistling mace for the third strike.

Ruth Strikes Out

Oh, what a fall was that, my countrymen! No wonder here that Giant rooters arose en masse with the shrill clamor of the tribe, as Yankee rooters, dumfounded by the sudden turn, caught their throats with shaking hands. For there were now two out, and if Ryan could only retire Bob Meusel the game was safe, after all, with the Giants still a run beyond. Ruth, after the greatest world's series ball he had ever played, was almost as broken and dejected as Nehf as he stalked back to the dugout, knowing that if Meusel failed the king would be a goat within the few tickings of a watch.

But Ryan for the moment had pitched his soul away to strike out Ruth. Meusel, amid the reverberating clamor of the multitude, ripped a sharp bounder through the box.

The ball dropped just beyond the Giant's reach and scampered on to center field as Haines, running for Hofmann, and Johnson, running for Bush, scored with waving arms.

The $50,000 Blow

This $50,000 blow broke up the battle with all further doubt removed when Cunningham's throw to third bounded past Groh and Dugan also crossed the plate with the fifth run of the famous round.

This was the eighth run of the series that Meusel had driven in, breaking all world series records. And it was the richest hit a ball player ever made.

The Yankees, beaten almost to a pulp, through their own fighting rally and the collapse of Giant pitching, had come from far behind to reach at last the portals guarded by the Giants since 1921. They had been forced to weather more than one howling gale, but they had come to port.

After this Sad Sam Jones, no longer sad, stopped the Giant attack through the last two frames with a confident precision that was beyond all doubt. But the Giants after that heart-ripping eighth inning had little soul for battle. A moment or two before they were advancing on their way to the seventh game, with the series tied. Only a breath or two back they had a ball game won and salted away, all set and ready for the final autumn drive to kale and glory.

Giant Crowns in Dust

And then within a rushing minute or two they were flat upon their backs, with all signs of life extinct, no longer the proud champions of a ball-playing world. Their crowns were in the dust and mud of the field. The two-year growth of laurel had faded and dried to the last sprig, all in one fatal inning of disaster and destruction.

As Meusel's hit drove in the winning run the loudest yelp of triumph came from the throat of Babe Ruth. For Ruth also had just escaped imminent disaster and despair. Up to his appearance at bat in the eighth, with the bases full, he had been one of the shining stars. By his home run in the first he had broken two records with three home runs for one world series and four home runs for all world series time. No other toiling athlete had ever reached either mark. That was something.

In addition, he had broken a world series record by drawing eight passes. He had led both teams in runs scored, with eight important tallies harvested from the field. He had batted .368, played brilliantly in the field and run the bases like another Cobb.

And then upon this resplendent showing a heavy shadow was about to fall. History and the crowd look closest to the final move. And when he struck out in the eighth with the bases filled and a hit needed to tie and win, all his achievements since April buds came up through winter snows would have been forgotten if Meusel's hit hadn't saved the game.

Such is baseball and the fame or infamy thereof, and no one knows it better than Ruth. There is no crown so great that in a twinkling it can't be changed into the hollow horns of the derided goat.

Ruth had done his full share; had broken three records, had been a six-game star — but that one immortal collapse in the eighth, with the bases full, would have been one of the main chapters of his life story if Meusel had failed for the third out, leaving the Giants still ahead.

As it was, the strike-out was only an episode, for success doesn't check back on what might have been. That is for the solace of the beaten alone.

For the first seven innings the Giants had the battle in their arms. Ruth socked Nehf in the first for the smashing homer that traveled like a flying shell into the upper right field stands. The Giants came back promptly and knotted the count on hits by Groh, Frisch and Youngs.

Then Nehf, pitching faultless ball, and again backed up by the swift and sure Giant defense, moved along the even tenor of his way. Frank Frisch, especially, was the wonder of the gray and sunny afternoon. Frisch not only made three hits, scored two runs and helped to drive in another, but was the golden headed kid of fortune around the infield.

Frisch's Miracle Catch

In addition to a brace of other star plays he went into right field for Dugan's fly in the fourth for the greatest single play of the series. His speed was so great that he ran out from under his hat and, with his hair blowing, finally leaped forward to take the ball on a miracle catch that swept the crowd up with a stand-shaking uproar. No one believed he had a chance even to get near the ball and when he brought it down, with his back to the plate, the tribute paid was well deserved. The all-star defensive play of Frisch and Nehf alone broke up more than one near rally, and the combination seemed to be quite enough until the somber tidings of the haunted eighth fell upon Giant ears.

After scoring in the first the Giants came back for another when Frisch opened the fourth with a single, to score later on Cunningham's punch. There was still more sorrow for the Yankees when Frank Snyder walloped a home run to the left field stands in the fifth. And when Frisch tripled and scored in the sixth, giving the Giants four runs and a big lead, the last Yankee chance looked about as large as the point of a needle.

When the flurry in the eighth opened Miller Huggins began concentrating his attack, making no fewer than four shifts to get full value for the drive at hand. It had seemed before this inning that the Giants, having discovered that matter was on the verge of submerging mind, had suddenly adopted the Yankee system of socking the ball and leaving the rest of it to fate.

Yet something went astray, for the Giants, making ten hits to the Yankees' five, were crumpled into a shapeless mass. The Yankees crossed their opponents by scoring six runs on five hits, which is bound to be a boost for something beyond mere brute force.

Yankees Real Champions

There can be no other answer in the face of the verified returns. When a team can be outbatted by two to one and still win it is not riding exclusively on the Brawn Special, with the Mental Urge tossed into the sink. The box-score refutes a number of points brought up earlier in the war.

Whether by force of brawn or brain the Yankees are the new world's champions, with every laurel deserved. They out-hit the Giants, out-pitched them and matched their great defensive play with equal skill by Dugan, Scott, Ward and Pipp — an infield that made only one error in six games.

For nearly half a century Grantland Rice was America's best-known and most beloved sportswriter. He came to New York in 1911, and his column and reporting were eventually syndicated nationwide. While Rice's florid, highly descriptive, and dramatic style would not remain in vogue forever, there was no one better at presenting a sporting event as a life-or-death drama.

The perfect subject for Rice was Babe Ruth, a player whose achievements made even the most ornate writing seem understated. The 1923 World Series was Ruth's coming-out party as he led the Yankees to their first world championship. Rice gave his readers the Ruth we have come to know today, the larger-than-life mythical figure like no one else in baseball history. But Rice was not the only writer in New York to make Ruth his subject. Many outdid themselves trying to capture his remarkable performance.

JOHN KIERAN

FROM "SPORTS OF THE TIMES"

from *The New York Times*, October 2, 1927

Some four months ago or more there was printed in this column a versified query: "Was there ever a guy like Ruth?" From time to time Yankee rooters suggested the reprinting of the query, and now that Babe Ruth has answered it a recital of the old question may be in order. Here it is:

A Query

You may sing your song of the good old days till the phantom cows
    come home;
You may dig up glorious deeds of yore from many a dusty tome;
You may rise to tell of Rube Waddell and the way he buzzed them
    through,
And top it all with the great fast ball that Rusie's rooters knew.
You may rant of Brouthers, Keefe and Ward and half a dozen more;
You may quote by rote from the record book in a way that I
    deplore;
You may rave, I say, till the break of day, but the truth remains the
    truth:
From "One Old Cat" to the last "At Bat," was there ever a guy like
    Ruth?

He can start and go, he can catch and throw, he can field with the
    very best.
He's the Prince of Ash and the King of Crash, and that's not an idle
    jest.
He can hit that ball o'er the garden wall, high up and far away,

Beyond the uttermost picket lines where the fleet-foot fielders
   stray.
He's the Bogey Man of the pitching clan and he clubs 'em soon and
   late;
He has manned his guns and hit home runs from here to the
   Golden Gate;
With vim and verve he has walloped the curve from Texas to
   Duluth,
Which is no small task, and I beg to ask: Was there ever a guy like
   Ruth?

No Answer Needed

As a matter of fact, there was never even a good imitation of the
Playboy of Baseball. What this big, good-natured, uproarious lad
has done is little short of a miracle of sport. There is a common ax-
iom: They never come back. But Babe Ruth came back twice. Just
like him. He would.

It takes quite a bit of remembering to recall that the great home-
run hitter was once the best left-handed pitcher in baseball. When
he was a member of the Boston Red Sox team he set a record
of pitching twenty-nine scoreless innings in world's series competition.

Then he started to slip and everybody said the usual thing:
"Good-bye Forever!" (copyright by Tosti).

Babe gathered in all the "Good-byes" and said: "Hello, everybody!
I'm a heavy-hitting outfielder."

And he was. He set a league record of twenty-nine home runs in
1919 and then he came to New York and took the cover off the siege
gun.

The Heavy Firing

That was Ruth's first come-back. A mild one. Others had done that,
and the Babe yearned to be distinguished even from a chosen few.
He wanted to be the One and Only. He nearly knocked the American League apart with fifty-four home runs in 1920, and in 1921 he
set the record at fifty-nine circuit clouts for the season.

"It will stay there forever," prophesied the conservatives.

For five years the record was safe enough. In his bland and child-like way the Babe fell afoul of disciplinary and dietary laws, with the result that he was barred from the diamond for lengthy stretches on orders from Judge Landis, Miller Huggins and the Ruth family physician.

He set the record of fifty-nine home runs when he was 27 years old. In the following years he failed to come within hailing distance of his high-water mark, and once again everybody said: "Good-bye Forever!" (copyright by Tosti).

A Change in Tune

The Babe's answer was: "Say au revoir, but not good-bye!" And G. German Ruth was as right as rain. It was "Au revoir" for five seasons, and in the sixth season the big boy came back with a bang!

Supposedly "over the hill," slipping down the steps of Time, stumbling toward the discard, six years past his peak, Babe Ruth stepped out and hung up a new home-run record at which all the sport world may stand and wonder. What Big Bill Tilden couldn't do on the tennis court, Babe Ruth has done on the diamond. What Dempsey couldn't do with his fists, Ruth has done with his bat. He came back.

Put it in the book in letters of gold. It will be a long time before any one else betters that home-run mark, and a still longer time before any aging athlete makes such a gallant and glorious charge over the come-back trail.

And in Conclusion

You may rise and sing till the rafters ring that sad and sorrowful strain:
"They strive and fail — it's the old, old tale; they never come back again."
Yes, it's in the dope, when they hit the slope they're off for the shadowed vale,
But the great, big Bam with the circuit slam came back on the uphill trail;
Came back with cheers from the drifted years where the best of them go down;

Came back once more with a record score to wear a brighter
  crown.
My voice may be loud above the crowd and my words just a bit
  uncouth,
But I'll stand and shout till the last man's out: There was never a
  guy like Ruth!

*In 1927 what would arguably become the greatest team in baseball his-
tory was surrounded by an equally great roster of sportswriters as Rice
and McGeehan were joined by the most talented group of reporters to
ever cover one team at one time. Their influence on precisely how the
1927 Yankees would be judged by history cannot be overstated. To a
great degree, the 1927 Yankees are still considered the best because the
writers at the time said so, and said so more eloquently than any subse-
quent statistical analysis.*

John Kieran first wrote for the New York Times *and then the* Herald Tribune *before returning to the* Times *in 1927 to author the paper's first signed column, "Sports of the Times." The 1927 Yankees provided ideal subject matter, and Kieran made the most of it.*

LARDNER LOST HIS SHIRT ONCE; IT IS ON PIRATES NOW

Humorist and Pittsburgh Manager Served
Terms in Bush Together

from The Bell Syndicate, October 4, 1927

PITTSBURGH, OCT. 3 — Well, friends, you can see for yourselves that I am
back in the city where I lost my shirt just two years ago and swore at
the time that I would never come here again, but it is the inalienable
right of every free born, partly white American citizen to change
their mind, if any, especially when one's dear public demands it.

Furthermore, this is one World's Series which I am interested in
personally and my nerves have been so shattered during the last
couple weeks that I can't risk the lives of my wife and kiddies by listening with them to the play-by-play account over the radio. On Friday, the 23d of September, I sat in front of the loud speaker while
somebody at WNYC reported the third battle between the Giants
and Pittsburgh, and when Freddy Lindstrom broke up the game
with a hit that hopped over three or four of the Waner boys' heads I
kicked our darling dog Peter through a costly plate glass window
and called the parrot everything but Polly. If any of my little ones
had been in the room I would have knocked them for a Chicago
count, and the madam herself would not have escaped without her
quota of contusions.

Bush Leagues with Bush

No doubt you are in a fever to know the reasons for this renewal of
the baseball rabies in a torpid old stiff like the undersigned. Well,

last spring before the season opened, I wagered a pretty penny at odds of 3 to 1 that Pittsburgh would win the pennant and another pretty penny at even money that Pittsburgh would beat out the Giants. But that ain't nowheres near the half of it. Pittsburgh's present manager and I broke into the national pastime in the same league, the same year, and I have always felt toward him the way you feel toward whoever shared with you the griefs and mortifications of harassed saphood.

Veteran ball players in that league, the Central, used to take inhuman advantage of Donie Bush's unsophistication and mine and kid us to such an extent that we almost wept together evenings into steins of South Bend's best beer. That was twenty-two years ago, when the hick shortstop was nineteen years old and the hick reporter twenty. Which would make him forty-one at the present writing and me forty-two; that is, if we hadn't aged ten years apiece since last April. Jack Hendricks, whose Cincinnati Reds scrunched St. Louis Thursday, had the best ball club in that Central League and Bush would have been a member of it if Jack hadn't been blessed with Champ Osteen, one of the greatest of minor league shortstops.

Boston Made Mistake

Just the same I claim credit for first calling a big league scout's attention to Donie. The scout was George Huff, athletic director at the University of Illinois and ivory hunter for the Boston Red Sox. George had an engagement one afternoon at Notre Dame, but I persuaded him to come out to the South Bend ball park and take a look at Bush. It was Donie's bad day. Hitting three times left-handed and three times right-handed, he amassed one home run, two triples and three singles. George wired that night to John I. Taylor, who owned the Boston Club. John I. wired back that he was perfectly satisfied with the shortstop he had. Which was reasonable enough, his shortstop being Heinie Wagner.

Donie was drafted by Detroit, sent to Indianapolis for a year's seasoning, and then recalled by Hughey Jennings. He had several run-ins with Ty Cobb. I met him in Chicago one time and asked him what the trouble was.

"Nobody in the world," said Donie, "can get along with that so-

and-so. He's driving me crazy. He's handed me twenty-six signs to remember, and if I miss one, he rides me. He's a so-and-so!"

"I'm supposed to be writing a story about him for the *American Magazine*," I said.

"Well, then," said Donie, "you're writing about the greatest ball player that ever lived or ever will live."

And he proceeded to give me 150 words of instances of Ty's superiority over all other ball players, past, present and to come.

That reminds me. I telephoned John Heydler last Thursday morning and asked him what would happen if the Thursday's game between St. Louis and Cincinnati had to be called off on account of wet grounds.

Hopes Pirates Win

"I'm glad you brought that up," said John. "I suppose you didn't think I had enough to worry me already. Well, if the game is called off, St. Louis, which has no game scheduled for Friday, will insist on playing Cincinnati Friday morning. Pittsburgh will protest and it will be up to the Board of Directors. And while you are looking for trouble, I may as well tell you that this pennant race is likely to end with three clubs tied for first place. In that event, there will be a series of three-game series before the World's Series and the next time you want to play golf you can tee up on all snowdrifts."

For the benefit of those who have just tuned in, the club that is going to oppose Pittsburgh in this world's series is the New York American League club. I am going to bet on them, a very small percentage of my winnings. And I hope I lose, but please don't repeat that to the Babe or Mr. Huggins. It's a tough series to guess. You can't tell how the Yankees will act in a regular ball game after playing exhibition games all season. Anyway, I have decided that the only way to keep a shirt in a world's series is to keep it on, and this shirt is going to remain right where it is till the series is over. So may the best club win quick.

Even as Lardner's fame as a writer expanded, most notably owing to his baseball-based "Alibi Ike" series, he periodically continued to cover baseball and annually gave his unique take on the World Series. He knew when to quit, however: the 1927 World Series was the last he covered as a journalist.

DAMON RUNYON

RUTH CLOUTS HOMER IN N.Y. 4-3 TRIUMPH

Hugmen Equal Record with Four Straight;
Pirate Hurler Makes Hefty Peg in Ninth Round

from The Universal Service, October 9, 1927

YANKEE STADIUM, NEW YORK, OCT. 8 — In the midst of chills and fevers of baseball drama up at the Yankee Stadium this afternoon, there suddenly came a sort of "plop" and the World Series of 1927 ended in what you might call an anti-climax, with the New York Yankees the victors in four straight games over the Pittsburgh Pirates.

It was like getting all lathered up over a tense, nerve-wiggling dramatic scene, and then having the low comedian step out and whack somebody over the noggin with a bladder, for with the score a tie at three, all in the last half of the ninth, the bases loaded with Yanks, and two out, John Miljus of Pittsburgh tore off a wild pitch that scored Earl Combs from third, giving the Yanks the fourth and last game by a score of 4 to 3.

It is the second time in modern baseball history that a club has won four consecutive games in a World Series. The Boston Braves, under George Stallings, did it in 1914, against the Philadelphia Athletics. The Giants won four games from the Yanks in a series of 1921, but a fifth was tied. Its exploit against the National League champions undoubtedly establishes Miller Huggins' 1927 club as one of the greatest of all time.

Almost Funny!

It was an almost ludicrous wind-up in view of the events of the ninth inning. The Yanks had the bases packed with no outs when John Miljus, who had relieved the be-spectacled Carmen Hill as the

Pittsburgh pitcher, struck out the slugging Lou Gehrig and long Bob Meusel. The Pittsburgh rooters in the crowd of 60,000 were fervently imploring him to do the same to "Poosh 'em up Tony Lazzeri" when Miljus banged away with a pitch that eluded John Gooch's clutch.

The Pirate catcher just touched it with his gloved hand, and the ball bounded over toward the Pirate bench out of which poured the Pittsburgh utility men as Combs came tearing in from third with the other two Yankee runners, Koenig and the mighty Ruth, in motion.

Crowd Pours on Field

The crowd from the boxes and the lower stands immediately swept over the field, cheering wildly, and John Miljus, who had almost been a hero, worked his way through the mob, swinging his pitching glove dejectedly over by the Yankee bench. The New York players were fighting their way out of their dugout while the fans reached eager hands for them.

The fans seemed particularly anxious to grab the large mitts of Mr. George Herman Babe Ruth, whose second home run of the series, a drive into the right field bleachers in the fifth, apparently stowed the game away right then and there. The Bambino's smash scored Koenig ahead of him, giving the Yanks a lead of 3 to 1. It was Ruth who drove in the first run, too, a tally which tied an early score by the Pirates.

And for that matter, the shadow of the mighty Babe fell athwart the Pittsburghers throughout the game today, for it was John Miljus' anxiety in pitching to him in that ninth that put Combs on third. At the time Ruth came up, Combs was on second and Koenig on first, with no one out. Miljus couldn't pass Ruth under the circumstances, and he tried to put too much on the ball in pitching to him. Thus his first toss became a wild pitch and the runners advanced. Then Ruth was purposely walked, and Miljus set the stage for his own defeat.

Some hands reached out, too, for the horny fist of Farmer Wilcy Moore, who finally got credit for a victory in the series. You know Waite Hoyt got the official brackets for the game that Farmer Moore finished up for him in Pittsburgh. Of the forty-seven games in which Farmer Moore figured during the season of 1927, he started but few. Today he pitched all the way, though the Pirates clouted him rather freely.

"Butter fingers," as the kids used to call 'em, kept the Pirates in the game until the last of the ninth. Old Wilcy Moore, himself, and "Poosh 'em Up" Tony Lazzeri fumbled the ball about in the seventh, letting the Pirates up to a tie, and for the moment annulling that mighty swat by the Bambino in the fifth. But perhaps it was just as well, because it produced the finish that gave the lie to the tradition that there's nothing new in baseball. This was brand new for a World Series, anyway.

Under the grandstand Mr. Egg-Bert Barrow, the genial business manager of the Yanks, joined his tears with those of Mr. Harry M. Stevens. After the game, the former weeping for the $217,000 that he must turn back to the clients because there will be no Sunday game, and the latter brooding over the lost hot-dog traffic of today. For a couple of innings it looked as if the fumbles of Wilcy Moore and Lazzeri would be worth about $108,500 apiece to the Yanks.

Damon Runyon began his sportswriting career in 1911 with the New York American, *and for most of the next two decades he was one of the central figures in the press boxes of New York, covering games and writing columns with consummate skill and originality. But Runyon was always drawn to more colorful subjects — Broadway, gangsters, and New York nightlife. In 1929 he wrote the first of his Broadway stories and capped his newspaper career with an even more successful one as a writer of fiction.*

THE OLD YANKEE

from *The Oakland Tribune*, September 26, 1979

The old Yankee slouched in a chair. A spider web was fixed inside a light fixture near his head. A leftover meal, crusted by time, sat on a table behind him. Dust and clutter filled the room, loneliness permeated it.

"We're more or less hermits, my wife and I," said Mark Koenig, shortstop on the famous 1927 Yankees' Murderers' Row. "We don't have many friends and very few visitors."

He looked around the unkempt house, otherwise shaded and cooled by the woodsy atmosphere of this tiny Sonoma County town where Jack London's life burned out at 40.

"This used to be a nice house, but now it's a mess. I can't do it anymore," said Koenig. "My wife has had two hip operations and is in a wheelchair. She has become . . . imbecilic. She wets the bed every night. I have to clean it up.

"I've had a cataract operation in my right eye. I've got back problems. I'm 75. My legs feel leaden all the time. Ah, it's no use talking."

It's easier to remember. Deep in the recesses of his mind, the sound of thousands cheering echoes faintly and long-ago World Series flags wave at Yankee stadium.

"Babe Ruth? He was a big, overgrown kid, that's all he was," said Koenig. "I don't think he read any books. He didn't know the difference between Robin Hood and Cock Robin. He was just interested in girls and drinking and eating.

"But what a beautiful swing he had, even when he struck out. And I never saw him drop a fly ball. He was a good fielder, pretty fast for his size, even with his pipestem legs.

"We never saw much of Ruth during the season. He had his private room on the road. But Ruth, [Bob] Meusel and I used to go to a place called Jimmy Donahue's in Passaic, N.J. There'd be long tables filled with food and waiters would run up the stairs from the bar below with steins of beer. We had some wonderful times."

It was the Roaring Twenties, and no figure, perhaps other than Lindbergh, is more remembered from that dapper, flapper period than Ruth. The Babe was a king in layman's garments.

"Babe stood up the queen of the Netherlands," Koenig recalled. "They were supposed to meet on the courthouse steps in Minneapolis, but Babe didn't show up. He didn't give a darn about anything.

"The Yankees had an infielder named Mike McNally. He heard Babe was going to be in the Follies after the season, so he asked him for a couple of Annie Oakleys. Babe said, 'Sure, I'll get you two of the swellest blondes in the show.'"

Lou Gehrig was the Pride of the Yankees, Ruth the Pulse of the Yankees. They posed often, Ruth's arms around the younger, socially correct Gehrig. Yet, they weren't friends, we are told.

"That's not true," Koenig declared. "Oh, they might have had their differences, but that's all.

"Gehrig was a nice kid. Never said much. Benny Bengough and I had an apartment, One hundred eighty-first and Broadway. Gehrig was there three or four times a week. Meusel and I used to go to his home. Gehrig's mother and father, what dinners they put on. Oh, boy.

"Meusel was one of my best friends, so was [Herb] Pennock. Meusel was very quiet . . . drank a lot."

Koenig and Tony Lazzeri were the Yankees' shortstop and second baseman during the 1926–27–28 pennant years. Poosh 'Em Up Tony once scared the daylights out of his double-play partner.

"Lazzeri had epileptic fits, but never on the ball field," Koenig recalled. "He'd be standing in front of the mirror, combing his hair. Suddenly, the comb would fly out of his hand and hit the wall.

"One morning in Chicago, he had a fit. He fell on the ground and started foaming. I didn't know what to do, so I ran out the door without a stitch of clothing on to get Waite Hoyt, who was a mortician in the off-season.

"Lazzeri recovered, but that's what killed him, you know. He had a fit, fell down the stairs, and broke his neck."

Ty Cobb was nearing the end of his unparalleled career when Koenig broke in with New York. Time hadn't blunted the Georgia Peach's bat or his abrasive personality.

"I didn't have no use for Cobb," said Koenig. "I remember facing Lil Stoner in Detroit, when Cobb was the manager. Stoner had a beautiful curve and he got two by me right away. For some reason, I turned and winked at Gehrig near the batting circle.

"Sure enough, Stoner throws me a fastball on the next pitch and I hit it into the right-field stands. As I'm running around the bases, I see Cobb in the outfield holding his nose and waving his arms up and down at Stoner. Cobb was a miserable man."

Trains and games. Life was fun when the Yankees first clickety-clacked down baseball's tracks toward becoming the game's greatest dynasty.

"The train cars were air-cooled," remembered Koenig. "Just as well, because St. Louis was 110 in the shade. There was a colored place downtown with great big racks of ribs. We knew where to get some home brew too. We'd go sit in the boxcar, drink beer, and gnaw on ribs. Then we'd fire the empty bottles at the telegraph poles.

"I was with Cincinnati [1934] when they became the first team to fly. Jim Bottomley and I wouldn't fly. We took the train. I never flew as a player."

The Yankees had incredible talent — Ruth, Gehrig, Earl Combs, Lazzeri, Meusel, Pennock, Hoyt, Joe Dugan. Manager Miller Huggins scribbled out a lineup card, leaned back, and watched the fireworks. He expected and got results and didn't worry about such minutia as curfews and drinking.

"There were no rules on the Yankees about having to be in your room by midnight," said Koenig. "We used to come in at 3 or 4 in the morning and the elevator guy would say, 'Gee, I just took a load up.'

"We stayed at this beautiful hotel in Washington, where ambassadors walked around with ribbons on their chests. We came in one morning at 2, wanting to take a swim. The clerk said they were draining the pool. That did it. [Johnny] Grabowski took off his clothes and dove in. He came up with a big bump on his head."

The tiny man in charge looked the other way.

"Huggins was the best manager I ever played for," said Koenig. "He understood human nature. He never bawled anybody out. When sports writers were saying 'Koenig's got to go,' he called me in and said, 'Listen, as long as I want you to play, you're going to play.' He gave me confidence.

"When I joined the Giants [1935], Bill Terry had rules where you had to be in your room by 11 p.m., you had to get permission to go out to eat. Terry was a lousy manager. If you had a bad day at the plate, he wouldn't even talk to you."

Mark Anthony Koenig was born in San Francisco. Hardly a day of his youth passed that he wasn't playing at Big Rec in Golden Gate Park.

His first professional contract was with Moose Jaw, Saskatchewan. He was 17. Then came Jamestown, Des Moines, and St. Paul, where he homered off Lefty Grove in the Little World Series. The Yankees bought him up the following year, 1925.

"I was a small cog in a big machine," said Koenig of his parceled slice of fame. "The Yankees could have had a midget at shortstop. I was a lousy infielder, I made a lot of errors. I had small hands and we didn't have the butterfly nets that fielders wear today. I did have a powerful arm."

Koenig and Meusel were the goats of the 1926 World Series. Each made an error in the seventh game as the Cardinals scored three unearned runs in the fourth inning to win 3–2. Of course, the game is remembered more for Grover Cleveland Alexander's staggering out of the bullpen to strike out Lazzeri.

"Alexander has whisky bottles hidden all over the hotel during the Series, like behind the potted palms," said Koenig. "He was a drunkard. He struck out Lazzeri on a bad pitch. The ball was outside."

Koenig hit .271, .285, .319, and .292 during his four full seasons in the Yankee pinstripes. His batting average in three Series was .125, .500 (tops in the 1927 Series), and .158. New York won four straight from both Pittsburgh and St. Louis the next two years after losing to the Cardinals in 1926.

The 1927 Yankees generally are considered the greatest team in baseball history. Koenig doesn't see it as all that cut-and-dried.

"There have been other great teams, but we did have a great aggregation," he said. "You'll never see another Ruth. He hit 60 home runs that year and Gehrig 47. And there were just a few good long-ball hitters then.

"I batted second in the lineup behind Combs. We didn't have to run, not with that kind of hitting. We could be six runs down in the eighth and still win. I was on third base with a triple when Ruth hit his sixtieth against Washington's Tom Zachary.

"Our pitching made us, though. We had Pennock, Hoyt, Dutch Ruether, Urban Shocker, and Wilcy Moore, who was the best relief pitcher you ever saw. He had one of the first good sinker balls. He'd go in with three men on, they'd never score."

Koenig's fielding problems finally made him expendable in 1930, when he was traded to Detroit. The Tigers thought he needed eyeglasses and tried to convert him to a pitcher.

By 1932, he was in the minors. His career appeared about over. Then a gun shot resurrected his career.

"Billy Jurges of the Cubs was shot by some girl in a hotel room," said Koenig. "So the Cubs bought me. When I joined the club, we were six games behind St. Louis. I had a heckuva month and a half, batting .353, and we won the pennant."

Despite his contribution, Koenig was voted a half-share by his Cub teammates as they prepared to meet the Yankees. Ruth was incensed by Chicago's treatment of his former teammate.

Both teams came through the same tunnel before the first game. Ruth was waiting when the Cubs emerged.

"He called them penny pinchers and misers," said Koenig.

Supposedly, Ruth's anger prompted that historic moment when he did or didn't point to the fence before clubbing a home run off Charlie Root.

"He pointed kind of like this," said Koenig, waving his arm quickly. "But you know darn well a guy with two strikes isn't going to say he'll hit a home run on the next pitch.

"But I wouldn't put it past him. He would come into the dugout some days and say, 'I feel good. I think I'll hit one.' And, by God, he always did."

Koenig didn't actually clarify whether Ruth called his shot. It doesn't matter. Let us forever think that he did.

Koenig looks like he has worn the same soiled T-shirt for two weeks. His pants are baggy, and he needs a shave — the hair on his neck is so long, it has curled.

"It was a good life," he said of his baseball career. "I put in 17 years of professional ball [12 in the majors, .279 lifetime batting average]. I got into five World Series, made some extra dough."

He retired in 1936 after two years with the Giants, bought two gas stations in San Francisco, and later worked for a brewery. He married a second time and eventually moved to Glen Ellen, located on Highway 12 between Sonoma and Santa Rosa.

"I have one daughter. She lives on an olive-almond ranch in Orland. She comes down once in a while to help out, but this place needs a thorough cleaning. I never see any of my grandchildren and I was good to them when they were young."

No one stays young forever, however. Nothing is eternal.

"There's only about five of us 1927 Yankees left . . . Hoyt, Bob Shawkey, Dugan, George Pipgras, Ray Morehart," he said. "I write to Hoyt and Dugan, but if you don't write to them, they never write to you. . . ."

Koenig looked at the floor, counting the ghosts.

"Meusel is dead, Combs is dead, Ruth is dead, Gehrig is dead, Lazzeri is dead, Pennock is dead. Oh, my God."

Then a voice from the other room. "Who you talking to out there?"

Koenig excused himself. A few minutes later, he wheeled in his wife, stopping her in front of the crusty food on the plate. She began eating.

The work he can't keep doing started all over again.

Stripped of sentiment, this bittersweet portrayal of Yankee infielder Mark Koenig offers a rare glimpse of the world of baseball in an earlier era. Despite their remarkable record, the 1927 Yankees would be a team touched by tragedy: a number of key figures, among them manager Miller Huggins, pitcher Urban Shocker, and Lou Gehrig, would die before their time. In a sense, Newhouse's award-winning story serves as an elegy for the entire team.

JAMES R. HARRISON

....

YANKEES WIN SERIES, TAKING FINAL, 7 TO 3; RUTH HITS 3 HOMERS

New York Team Sets Record of Eight Straight
by Beating the Cards Fourth Time in Row.
Bottles Thrown at Ruth. St. Louis Fans Angry
After His Second Homer — Makes Great
Catch to End Game. Second Victory for Hoyt.
Gehrig and Durst Also Make Home Runs —
Total Receipts for Series $777,290.

from *The New York Times*, October 9, 1928

ST. LOUIS, OCT. 9 — Establishing records that will live as long as the game itself, scaling a baseball Matterhorn where no other foot had ever trod before, the Yankees made it four in a row over the Cardinals today, 7 to 3, as Babe Ruth, for the second time in his incredible career, hit three homers in one world's series game.

For the second successive year this super team of supermen defeated its National League rivals in four straight games to build for itself a monument that still will be standing when the names of Ruth and Gehrig and Huggins are mellow memories out of the distant past.

And to climax his marvelous career, to reach the greatest heights ever attained by any ball player, George Herman Ruth did again today what no other man had done even once. Three times he drove the ball over the right-field bleachers. He finished with the highest world's series batting average on record, .625; while his co-partner and protégé, Lou Gehrig, hit one homer to set a new series record for runs driven in — nine.

Game Is Unparalleled

This was a game unparalleled in baseball history, not merely because, for the first time in that history, a team had won its second world's series in four straight games. Not merely because Ruth hit three homers for the second time in his career or because Gehrig drove in his ninth run. Not merely because the Yankees hammered out five homers in one game and set a new mark.

No, it was unparalleled mainly because it saw the Yankees rising triumphantly to overcome the greatest obstacles that might face a world's series team. Because it saw George H. Ruth and the badly crippled New Yorkers reach the very climax of their greatness to do deeds that will be remembered as long as the game lives. If there was any lingering doubt, if anywhere in this broad land there were misguided souls who believed that Babe Ruth was not the greatest living ball player, they should have seen him today.

They should have seen him hooted and hissed, come to the plate three times, twice against Wee Willie Sherdel and once against the great Pete Alexander, and send three mighty drives whistling over that right-field pavilion.

They should have seen him swaggering and waving a friendly fist at the world as he romped out to left field — the play boy of baseball — to be greeted by a barrage of pop bottles thrown by a few sportsmen who thought that the Babe had been struck out in the seventh, a moment before he clouted his second homer to tie the score. Misguided sportsmen who could not appreciate the incredible feats of this incredible man.

Try to Spoil Catch

They should have seen him at the very end of the game as he drove an injured knee forward at top speed, dashing down the foul line and past the field boxes to make a one-handed catch while St. Louis partisans threw paper and programs at him to blind his vision.

They should have seen him, that great catch completed, continue to run in, holding the ball aloft in his gloved right hand — the picture of triumph and glee and kindly defiance of the whole world.

It was thus that the world's series of 1928 passed into history — with Ruth triumphant, with Ruth rampant on a field of green, with

Ruth again stranger than fiction and mightier than even his most fervent admirers had dreamed he would be.

"The king is not dead, long live the king!" they might have shouted as this amazing play boy, this boisterous soul, in the great hour of his career, added new records to a list already stretching ten years back into baseball history.

Path Strewn with Flowers

They threw bottles and programs and newspapers at him today, did a few small-souled St. Louis fans, but as he ran from the field his path was strewn with the invisible flowers of invisible persons who know real baseball greatness when they see it.

Overshadowed by Ruth were even the other heroes of this Yankee ball team which started the series as the under dog and ended it as the greatest world's series team of all time.

Overshadowed was Henry Louis Gehrig — Gehrig who today tied Ruth's record of four homers in one series and set a new mark for runs driven in. Overshadowed was little Miller Huggins, who now is tied with John McGraw and Connie Mack in number of world's championships — three. Overshadowed was Waite Hoyt, who won his second game from the Cardinals, and Tony Lazzeri and all the other soldiers of this immortal battalion.

No, this game was the Ruth and nothing but the Ruth. So was the series, in which, besides his homerun feats, he established a new record for runs scored with nine and record for runs scored in one series with nine and for homers in his nine series with thirteen and tied Joe Harris's mark of twenty-two total bases in one series. Except that Ruth hit his in four games and Harris in seven.

Drama in the Seventh

The seventh inning was one of the greatest in world's series annals. Hoyt, thanks to two errors in the fourth inning, was on the short end of a 2–1 score when that inning dawned. Wee Willie Sherdel, though roughly handled by the Yanks, had escaped extinction so far.

The only run off him had been Ruth's first homer in the fourth round. The game little southpaw threw a curve a half foot inside the plate. It was not a ball to swing at, but Ruth isn't human. He smacked it clear over the right-field bleachers without even touching that structure.

At the outset of the seventh Koenig popped to Maranville. Then Sherdel planted two strikes across the plate and had G. H. Ruth in a bad way. Immediately after the second strike Sherdel tried a quick return, tried to sneak the ball over while Ruth, his head turned, was exchanging quips and bright repartee with Catcher Earl Smith.

The sneak delivery was right across there, but Umpire Charley Pfirman refused to call it. He ruled that such a delivery was illegal in a world's series and was upheld by the three other umpires, who pointed out to the Cards that such a ruling had been agreed upon before the series and that both teams had been notified.

None the less, the Cardinals squawked bitterly. McKechnie and his lieutenants, sergeants and buck privates streamed out from the bench, exuding perspiration and indignation. They were joined at the plate by nine other Cardinals, led by Fordham Frank Frisch. The squawking was loud and enthusiastic. The general verdict was that Mr. Pfirman, if he ever took the blindfolded cigarette test, wouldn't need a bandage.

But though the Cardinals howled and the crowd joined in, the umpire's verdict stood. It was still two and nothing on the Babe. The next was a ball outside. Ball two was also off the plate. Then Sherdel wound up again and threw a slow curve outside.

With no perceptible effort, with an easy swing, the Bambino met the ball and knocked it toward the right-field bleachers. The crowd gasped and then groaned as the ball, flying high and never losing momentum, cleared the roof of the pavilion. Through a narrow aperture at the back you could see a white speck fall and then disappear into the great open spaces of Grand Boulevard.

As he went around the bases Ruth was triumph itself. Mockingly he waved his hand at the crowd. As he passed second base he sent a salute to his friendly enemies in the left-field bleachers. He turned toward home still waving a mocking and derisive hand at a crowd too stunned to give this feat the ovation it deserved.

Tried to Catch King Asleep

So they had tried to sneak a third strike over on Ruth, eh! They tried to catch the king asleep, did they! Must have been afraid to throw it when he was looking, for see what happened when he was.

And then, in the wake of Babe Ruth, came the Yankee attack, the New York shock troops, fierce and dauntless, fast moving and hard hitting. Look out, the Yanks are coming!

On the second ball pitched by Willie Sherdel, Gehrig came back with that big bat of his and hammered a homer to the roof of the right-field stand, close to the foul line. Ruth had tied the score, Gehrig had put his team ahead. What a pair! What men! Between them they had made this world's series a shamble, a source of humiliation and sorrow for the National League, which in eight straight games against this unbelievable Yankee team had met nothing but one-sided defeat.

And again the terrible Yankees swung into double trot and leaped into action. Meusel jabbed a single to left and Wee Willie Sherdel, protesting in vain, was taken out of the box — Willie Sherdel, who in four games against the Yanks had pitched well but had never won.

From the bullpen came Grover Cleveland Alexander, not so awe-inspiring as he had been two years ago when he shuffled in from another bullpen to stave off a Yankee attack.

Old Alex had some tough breaks today. Lazzeri raised a fly to left field which Hafey lost in a blinding October sun. Chick ran away from the ball instead of toward it, and Orsatti though making a game try, got only his finger-tips on the leather.

This synthetic two-bagger advanced Meusel to third, and then Robertson, batting for Dugan, grounded to Frisch, who tried to nab Meusel at the plate but was too late.

With Lazzeri on third, one out and the Yanks two runs ahead, Huggins pulled out Bengough. There was a commotion on the Yankee bench and then out strode a straight, graceful figure of a man, a trimly built fellow who admits no rivals in the centre-field business. In other words, Earl Combs, the Kentucky Rosebud.

Graceful Act by Huggins

This was the Combs who hurt his wrist and was put out of the series before it started, whose loss, it was feared, might wreck the Yankees' chances. Here he was now, coming in at the last moment — a graceful act on the part of Miller Huggins.

There didn't seem to be anything wrong with Earl's batting eye.

He steamed a line drive to right with old-time vigor. Harper made a nice catch, but Lazzeri scored from third with the fourth run of as exciting an inning as was ever played.

Now the Yanks were three runs ahead, and after Hoyt had cut down the Cards in their half the Hugmen added two more in the eighth. Durst began it with a drive into the right field bleachers — the fourth Yankee homer. Alexander wasn't getting much on the ball.

When Ruth came up Alex threw a called strike and then essayed a curve on the inside corner. What a foolish mistake! What bad control by a man who was one of the masters of control! For the Babe met this ball squarely and drove it again to right, and, to show you how badly the Babe was slipping, this ball only hit on the roof of the pavilion. The big boy was certainly starting to slump.

Incidentally, all three homers were hit off curve balls on the inside of the plate. If an American League pitcher ever did such a thing three times in one afternoon, he would be given away to the South Norwalk club.

"I got two more 'cousins' to add to my list — Sherdel and Alexander," said the Babe after the game. "Cousins" is baseball slang for a pitcher easy to hit. All the St. Louis pitchers are cousins of G. Herman, for it was at Sportsman's Park, two years ago, that he hit three homers in one game.

Though rapped for eleven hits, Hoyt pitched a careful and capable game and justified the claim that he is in the front rank of right-handed pitchers. His support was not good; in fact, for six innings the Yanks were far from impressive. Their fielding was mediocre and they had plenty of chances to score, but were feeble in the pinches. However, they are an old and steady team; they have been through the mill and enjoy unbounded confidence in themselves, and they never looked like a beaten team.

This team has something that every great person has — whether a great athlete or a great actor, or a great lawyer, or a great business man. It has a certain intangible something, a confidence, almost cockiness, that it is the best team on earth. It has poise, aplomb, insouciance — a calm, sure faith in itself that shines forth and is radiated to the other team and the enemy crowd.

Cards Awed and Beaten

In this series the Cardinals were awed and beaten before they had swung a bat.

What a series it was, too; a gay, joyous romp for the American League, which is brimming with pride over the Yankees — and with some amazement, too, it must be admitted. Surely the junior circuit, founded twenty-eight years ago by Ban Johnson, had its biggest day this afternoon as its Yankee envoys scored their eighth successive victory over the older organization, to beat the former record by two.

And equally so, it was a day of bitterness and regrets for the National League, which could not even give the Yanks a run for their money in two successive Octobers.

In their hour of defeat the Cardinals need sympathy more than censure and so we shall not dwell on their shortcomings and failures. Naturally, they gave their best. Today, in a desperate effort to inject new life and new blood into his team, Bill McKechnie benched Taylor Douthit and Jimmy Wilson, sending Ernie Orsatti to centre and Earl Smith behind the plate.

It was rather tough on Wilson to be taken out at this late date after he had been worn down to a shadow by the nerve-wracking task of catching almost every game the Cards have played since June.

Company for the Cards

The Cardinals' great trouble was that they could not stop Ruth and Gehrig. In this great sorrow they have plenty of company, the company of seven American League clubs, including the Athletics.

The Cardinals played even worse ball than the Pirates last October and that is the only barb we care to shoot at them. Not another team in baseball could have beaten the Yanks in this series, so why pick on the poor old Cardinals, who are now down and out and have received all the kicks that the human system can assimilate in any given space of time?

Anyway, what the Yanks have done in their last two world's series has been incredible and superhuman. They can't be weighed and measured by ordinary standards as long as they have two fiends in human form like G. Herman Ruth and H. Louis Gehrig, by far the two greatest ball players ever on one team.

Always we will remember Babe Ruth today — as he ran around the bases after those three homers, as he picked up pop bottles in left field and kidded with the crowd before turning his back on that menacing throng. But particularly we shall remember him as he looked when he charged along the foul line and in front of the field boxes — 230 pounds of the best ball player that ever lived — swerving in toward the wooden railing, his gloved right hand outstretched and his legs pounding while fans stood up and pelted paper missives at him.

Holds the Ball Aloft

Then we shall remember how he caught that baseball incredibly and held it up for the world to see in his right hand. Of all our baseball memories that shall be the clearest-etched and most unforgettable. Ruth, indomitable, unconquerable, triumphant. An amazing man, this George Herman Ruth.

The Cardinals had a grand opening in the first inning, but what is a little thing like an opening to the Cards? With one out, Ruth, blinded by the sun, let High's easy fly fall safely for a two-bagger, but Hoyt fanned Frisch at three and two, walked Bottomley and then stopped Hafey on a feeble grounder to the box.

More St. Louis ineptness in the second. Smith singled with one gone. McKechnie flashed the hit-and-run sign, but Hoyt threw that particular pitch at Maranville's head and Smitty was out standing up at second, whereupon the Rabbit socked a double to right, Meusel playing in none too well, but Sherdel bounded to Gehrig.

Finally the Cards scored a run. To open the third Orsatti planted a fly in short centre and by daring base running made two bases. Paschal should have had him at second. High caught the Yanks off guard and beat out a bunt, and Frisch contributed a sacrifice fly which scored Orsatti. Bottomley and Harper, the latter striking out, chloroformed a promising rally.

The Cards worked hard for that tally and the Yanks made theirs with a minimum of labor. The Babe led off in the fourth in an admirable fashion, sending a liner whistling over the right field stand.

The count was two balls and one strike and Sherdel would have been satisfied to make it four and nothing. He slipped a curve six inches inside the plate — a bad ball obviously — but Ruth stepped away from it and nailed the ball half way down his bat and gave it a long ride.

Sherdel followed by walking Gehrig, Meusel flied deep to Orsatti, Lazzeri singled to left — his first hit of the series — but Dugan and Bengough were unable to come through with assistance.

Koenig was a Santa Claus in the fourth and made the Cards a present of a run. After Smith had singled he was forced by Maranville. Koenig had a sure double play in sight but made the wildest wild throw on record, heaving the ball into the lap of a spectator fifteen rows back in the grand stand. Maranville, of course, went to second.

Sherdel flied to centre, and with Orsatti at bat the Yanks baited a trap for Maranville. The idea was for Bengough to return the ball to Hoyt, who would wheel quickly and throw to Koenig, who meanwhile would have sneaked up behind Maranville.

Koenig Misses Signal

The thing worked perfectly except that Koenig missed the signal and failed to do any sneaking. And so when Hoyt turned and threw, there was no Yankee at second and the pill, naturally enough, went on to centre field while Maranville churned for the plate and scored.

Hoyt and Paschal singled with none out in the fifth, but the Yanks couldn't move a wheel. Koenig popped to Frisch, Ruth grounded to Bottomley, Gehrig walked and Meusel forced out Columbia Lou.

Again in the sixth the first two Yankees, Lazzeri and Dugan, hit singles, but the next three worthies were a total loss.

You know all about the riotous doings of the seventh frame. In the eighth Cedric Durst whaled a homer into the right field stand and Ruth did likewise.

The Cardinals scored once in the ninth with the consent of Mr. Hoyt, who let Martin, who ran for Smith, run wild on the bases and score on a single by High.

The paid attendance for today was 37,331, bringing the total paid attendance for the four games to 199,075, which is short of the total for four games last year. The total receipts were $777,290. The receipts for today were $161,902.

Although John Kieran held the top spot in the Times*'s sporting section, James Harrison gave the newspaper a strong voice on the daily beat. In contrast to the hyperbole that marked the reportage of most other New York papers, Harrison's clear, cogent, understated accounts of the World Series made the* Times*'s sports stories a must-read.*

BREATH BY BREATH AT THE POLO GROUNDS

from *The New York Times*, October 7, 1936

The Yanks made a bad start. Frank Crosetti broke his bat hitting a pop fly to Phi Beta Kappa Whitehead. If Fred Fitzsimmons could break a Yankee bat with each pitch the Yanks would soon be reduced to desperate straits.

The Giants were a trifle slow getting under way, which is to say that Joe Moore didn't hit the first ball safely. It was the third twister served up by Lefty Gomez that Jo-Jo looped to left field for a single.

Daredevil Dick Bartell dilly-dallied around the plate until Don Vernon evidently became tired of looking at him and passed him to first base. Two on, none out. If Bill Terry hadn't bunted, the nearest policeman would have taken him outside and ordered him destroyed. At that, Bill is so lame that a couple of kindly turfmen were fingering their guns ever since the series started.

Handsome Hank Leiber looked over four wide ones in a row. That filled the bases, and Mel Ott sent two mates home with a double that flirted with the right-field foul line all the way to the fence.

Men on second and third and one out. The situation was still promising, but the promise was broken when Gus Mancuso fouled to Rolfe. The Giants might have made a million runs, more or less, if they hadn't wasted so much time hitting flies to the third baseman.

There were two out in the Yankee segment of the second when Twinkletoes Selkirk foisted a foot race on the baseball crowd. Ott and Leiber looked like Jack Lovelock and Archie San Romani as they chased his tripe to the Giant bullpen.

Jake Powell thought he had a base on balls, but Umpire Harry Geisel ordered him to stay where he was, at the plate. This was no favor to Fred Fitzsimmons. Jake wafted the next one into the upper left-field stands. That loud knock tied the score.

Farewell to Fitz

The Yanks hopped on Fitz for a run in the third on singles to left by Rolfe and DiMaggio and a long fly to right by Gehrig. But what happened in the fourth wasn't Fitz's fault. Due to advancing age, Travis Jackson was playing his usual stationary defense at third base and Powell and Lazzeri took mean advantage of the old gent. They rattled a couple of grounders through there for base hits.

Of course, Gaffer Jackson made a move to halt those bounders. If he had moved a little faster it might have been called a snail's pace. Two on, one out. Don Vernon Gomez astonished the multitude by poling a looping single to left that brought Powell clattering over the plate. When Crosetti flied out it seemed that Old Fitz, stout fella, might survive the storm, but that very annoying Red Rolfe rifled a hit to right and Lazzeri rode home, to make the score 5–2. Bill Terry waved Fitz to the showers and called in Slick Castleman. There were those in the stands who thought that Terry should have put Fitz at third and sent Jackson to the showers.

A spectator was carried out of the upper stand in the fifth inning. A gendarme who helped in the cortege said that the victim was a regular Giant fan who dropped in a dead faint when Mel Ott hit a homer into the left-field stands, of all places.

Slick Castleman turned the Yankee sixth into a fanning bee. He whiffed Powell, Lazzeri and Gomez in a row.

The strategy of Bill Terry in the seventh tangled up the batting order so much that most of the bewildered spectators tore up their score cards and put the rest of the game on the cuff.

One in the Seventh

The tragedy for the Giants could be set down in a single phrase — to wit: One in the seventh. It might have been written, "Won in the seventh," which is the sad part of it.

The score was 5–3 when Daredevil Dick Bartell doubled to left and came in on Terry's single to center that DiMaggio fumbled long enough to let Memphis Bill reach second. None out, score 5–4, Handsome Hank Leiber up, big enough to carry a trunk under each arm. Terry ordered Big Hank to put down a little bunt. In other words, Terry was trying for a tie instead of going for the game right there.

Leiber bunted, as ordered, and the Giants made no more runs that inning, though Terry called in everybody except Eddie Brannick and Horace Stoneham to help him some. The inning wound up with Mark Koenig looking at a third strike with the bases filled.

Lefty Gomez was withdrawn in the confusion and Johnny Murphy finished the game for the Yankees. It didn't matter much, but the spectators from the Bronx gave their neighborhood acquaintance a friendly cheer.

It was a ball game until they let Dick Coffman into it in the ninth. Of course, the Giants were losing, but they were sinking slowly. Coffman speeded up the game. The way those Yankees tore around the bases was scandalous.

Then Master Gumbert came in and he made Coffman look pretty good. The Yanks began to run around twice as fast.

What did the Yankees care if they ran themselves ragged? They can sleep today and dream of the world series cheques that K. M. Landis is about to sign in their favor.

In the last analysis the trouble with the Giants in the series was the same trouble that so many football teams claim they encounter. They played too tough a schedule.

PART III

A TALE OF TWO JOES

Manager Joe McCarthy took command in 1932, and outfielder Joe DiMaggio joined the team in 1936, just as the skills of first baseman Lou Gehrig began to erode under the insidious effects of the disease that now bears his name. Under the two Joes, the Yankee dynasty entered its golden age, dominating the American League both before and after World War II. In an era that looked for heroes, DiMaggio seemed ready-made. His unparalleled achievements on the field, culminating in his historic 56-game hitting streak, and underscored by victory after victory, gave the press license to create a hero.

Yet during this period the Yankees were not without challenges to their supremacy. Before the war the Yankees won on pure talent — no other team in baseball could keep up. But the war would take its toll on the team, and afterwards the Red Sox in the American League and the Dodgers and Giants in the NL all took aim at the dynasty. The Yankees were no longer a team of stars, but a team of role players like Phil Rizzuto. They learned to play together as a unit, every player contributing, in order to win. The mighty Yankees had to struggle to maintain their dynasty as McCarthy moved on after the 1946 season, replaced by Casey Stengel, and DiMaggio's skills slowly gave way to advancing age. They didn't always win anymore, but that only made victory more dramatic and precious.

After the war changing attitudes in American society rightfully challenged baseball's color line, and the reporting on the game became more serious. Radio and television coverage allowed more fans to see the games themselves, relieving the writer of the responsibility to describe each play in detail. So the press began to focus on details that fans still couldn't see, smaller moments that revealed larger truths. The writer's work didn't necessarily begin and end with the game anymore. Writers such as Red Smith expanded the notion of what sportswriting was and what it could be as style began to be as important as the subject.

NO ORDINARY JOE

from *The Miami Herald,* August 27, 1995

Fifty-six games do not tell the whole story.

Joe DiMaggio's record-setting 56-game hitting streak in the summer of 1941 defines him. It is one of the great feats of American sport, and one of the least likely to be duplicated. The essence of DiMaggio's character — his unmatched ability to perform under pressure — is embodied in the day-to-day challenge of the streak. The rest of his on-field accomplishments — ten pennants and nine world championships in thirteen seasons with the New York Yankees, three MVP awards, two batting titles and two home-run crowns — are ancillary to the tangible reality of baseball's great unbroken record.

Yet even more amazing than the record itself is the fact that such a remarkable, sustained performance against unlikely odds was nothing new to Joe DiMaggio.

In 1933, in his first full season of professional baseball, 18-year-old Joe DiMaggio, only a day or two away from being dropped from the team, began a hitting streak that lasted through *61* consecutive games, salvaging his own career and saving the Pacific Coast League from ruin. It made him a hero. And he has been that hero ever since.

But details of this first streak, like those of most of his early career, are little known. DiMaggio has never been eager to tell his own life story. Since participating in a few ghost-written profiles in the late 1940s, he has agreed to only a handful of brief, highly controlled interviews since then. When he deigns to meet with a reporter, questions usually must be submitted in advance to his attorneys, and certain topics — most notably Marilyn Monroe — are strictly off-limits.

Today, DiMaggio makes his official residence in South Florida, close by his attorneys in Hollywood. He moved here from San Francisco several years ago in order to take advantage of the weather and the tax laws. He has spurned offers in excess of $2 million to spill his guts in a "tell-all" autobiography. The streak of his own silence is nearly as extraordinary as any record he set on the baseball field.

DiMaggio was raised in a poor fishing family in San Francisco's North Beach neighborhood. His standard biographies dismiss his minor-league experience as a no-sweat prelude to his major-league ascendancy: Joe played a few games for the San Francisco Seals of the Pacific Coast League at the end of the 1932 season, became an immediate star the following year, hit in 61 consecutive games, and ended up in the Yankees' starting lineup in 1936.

As usual, the truth is not quite so pat. Like Joe, each of his older brothers — Tom, Mike, and Vince — preferred playing baseball to fishing. Tom and Mike were forced to abandon the game to take over their father's fishing boat, but once Vince started picking up a few extra dollars playing ball, the brothers all encouraged Joe to play. He quit school at age 16 and became, in effect, a full-time baseball player. Over the next year and a half he played hundreds of games for at least a half-dozen teams in the semi-pro leagues that were everywhere in San Francisco.

In the meantime, brother Vince had been signed by the Seals, and in September of 1932 recommended his younger brother as a late season fill-in. Joe appeared at shortstop in the last three games of the season, hit an unimpressive .222, and made an error.

That winter, DiMaggio played in the Seals Winter League, did well, and was invited to spring training. He hit everything in sight, but threw every ground ball he fielded into the bleachers.

It was the Depression, as much as his own skill, that won DiMaggio a place on the Seal roster. Attendance was down everywhere in the Pacific Coast League. Money was tight. It was cheaper to keep Joe DiMaggio than a veteran player.

The Seals opened at home against Portland, and neither Joe nor Vince, who had a sore arm, played in either of the first two games. In the eighth inning of the series' third game, the Seals trailed 6–4. With right fielder George Thomas scheduled to bat, Seal manager

Ike Caveney called for Joe DiMaggio to pinch-hit. He flew out, and the Seals failed to score.

In the top of the ninth, Caveney sent Joe DiMaggio to right field, a position he had never played. He received no chances in one inning of work. The Seals lost, 6–4. After the game, the Seals released four players, including Vince DiMaggio. The cuts saved Seal owner Charley Graham over $1,200 a month.

Now there was room in the Seals lineup for Joe DiMaggio. Caveney already knew Joe could run and hit. If he could play the outfield, he could help the team. If he couldn't, it was still early in the year. DiMaggio could be cut loose and the Seals would be out only a few hundred dollars.

In the fourth game of the season, DiMaggio started in right field and hit sixth. Although he was hitless in the 3–1 Portland win, he ranged far and wide in the outfield, collecting five putouts. He wasn't always pretty, but he got to the ball. Portland, aware of DiMaggio's lack of experience, gave his arm an early test.

The erratic shotgun that DiMaggio wielded in the infield proved more accurate from the outfield, and he gunned down two Portland baserunners. Right field was his, at least until he stopped hitting or started dropping fly balls. DiMaggio and Coast League were a perfect match. He was able to live at home, and as Vince's brother he was spared much of the hazing endured by most rookies. The official league ball was livelier than that used in the major leagues or in many other minor leagues. The PCL had a well-deserved reputation as the most offensive-minded circuit in baseball. The rabbit ball helped young hitters like DiMaggio build confidence.

Joe got off to a fast start. He hit in eight of the next nine games, going 14–38, a robust .368, and was moved from right field to center. On April 16, he cracked his first professional home run, off veteran Portland pitcher Herm Pillette.

Then Joe cooled, hitting only .250 for the remainder of the month. The Seals were even worse. Desperate to stop their slide, they re-signed Vince DiMaggio on April 26. Vince temporarily pushed Joe from the fifth spot in the batting order to second, and Joe moved back to right field as Vince took over in center. Still, the Seals ended April in last place, a pitiful 9–18.

Playing alongside his brother, Joe regained some of the consistency and power he had demonstrated over the first two weeks of the season. In early May, *The Sporting News* even took note of DiMaggio's auspicious start. "Joe Demaggio [*sic*], the 17-year-old outfielder signed by the San Francisco Seals, is creating quite a furore [*sic*]," wrote an unnamed correspondent. "This hard-hitting kid seems to have no weakness at the plate and he knows how to play the outfield much better than more experienced flychasers. . . . He has a right wing that propels the horsehide like a bullet shot from a rifle. . . ."

But when the Seals failed to improve, they decided that two DiMaggios were a luxury they couldn't afford. On May 8, Vince was again cut loose. Joe had hit over .300 with Vince in the lineup. With Vince gone, Joe struggled. He bounced back and forth between right field and center, and was inconsistent at the plate.

In midmonth, he slumped terribly, going a pitiful 6–48 over 12 games. Worse, in the previous three weeks he collected only one extra-base hit. His average tumbled below .250. That didn't count for much in the potent PCL. Of the 82 players in the league who had played more than 15 games, 53 were hitting above .300. DiMaggio was 76th, ahead of only six other hitters. He was clearly in danger of playing himself out of the league.

It didn't help that the PCL was on the brink of collapse. The Depression was wreaking havoc with the minor leagues. A wet, cold spring on the West Coast kept fans away. The Seals were losing money each day. According to *The Sporting News,* San Francisco's wholesale release of veterans sparked complaints among other league members of the Seals' "indifference," a charge that struck at the integrity of the league.

PCL owners wanted to disband, pay off players for the balance of the season, and re-form in 1934. But Baseball Commissioner Judge Kenesaw Mountain Landis indicated that if the league suspended operations, he'd make all the players free agents, even if they were paid for the season. Landis' threat kept the league going.

The rumors of a shut-down couldn't have helped DiMaggio's confidence. He was a rookie, he was struggling, and it appeared as if the league was about to fold. Established veterans might have been able to hook on with other clubs, but rookies hitting like DiMaggio faced an uncertain future.

The owners prayed for good weather. And a miracle. They got

both. As the weather warmed with the beginning of summer, something remarkable happened. Just as the league reached its nadir, and his own performance reached its low point, Joe DiMaggio did something extraordinary.

Beginning in the second game of a double-header against first-place Portland on May 28, he did the kind of thing heroes do. The 18-year-old DiMaggio, the youngest and one of the worst hitters in the league, smacked out a double, then proceeded to collect at least one base hit in each of the next 60 games. For the first time, DiMaggio demonstrated his singular talent: He played best when all seemed lost. When the streak ended, the fortunes of the San Francisco Seals, the Pacific Coast League, and Joe DiMaggio were secure.

After an off-day, Joe followed with his best performance of the year, as he went 3-for-6 in the first game of a double-header with Seattle, including a 10th-inning double to cement a 10–8 Seal win, and 3-for-4 in the second game, knocking in three runs and scoring three with a single, triple and home run.

In four of the next five games he smacked two hits, including two home runs. When the Seals returned home to face Oakland, DiMaggio kept hitting and the club started playing .500 ball.

There were still rough edges to DiMaggio's game. On June 15, his streak in its infancy, legendary baseball writer Abe Kemp of the *San Francisco Examiner* remarked after two DiMaggio errors that "Joe appears able to drop fly balls and home runs with equal ease."

DiMaggio's streak nearly ended five days later, as the Seals' Jimmy Zinn and the Missions' Johnny Babich squared off in a pitchers' duel. As the game entered the eighth inning, there was no score and DiMaggio was hitless. But Funk doubled and DiMaggio followed with a long drive off the left-field fence for a triple, knocking in the game's only run and extending his streak to 19.

Eight years later, in game 40 of DiMaggio's 56-game hitting streak, Babich gained some notoriety when he publicly promised to stop Joe by not throwing him any strikes. In DiMaggio's second at-bat, Babich worked the count to 3–0 before he was nearly castrated by a line-drive base hit between his legs on a pitch Babich meant to be ball four. Babich's pre-game pronouncement in 1941 might have been inspired by his recollection of the DiMaggio triple eight years before.

The following day DiMaggio's ninth-inning base hit again proved the difference in another Seals win. Joe was now the big bat in the Seals' lineup. Over his last 20 games, he had scored 18 runs and knocked in 21.

After DiMaggio went 2–4 and 1–4 in a double-header split with the Missions on June 25, the press finally took note of the streak as Kemp wrote that DiMaggio "hit safely in his 29th and 30th straight game," then added, "Joe has a long and tortuous path to weave before he can approach the [49-game] Coast League Record of Jack Ness." But from that day on, DiMaggio's streak was public knowledge.

Kemp followed with a cautious analysis of the young player. He wrote "Joe De Maggio [*sic*] is a greatly improved hitter. He now hits the ball where it is pitched, and that is the secret of collecting base hits, at least one of the secrets. Joe, however, gives fans heart failure the ways he goes after fly balls. His position in the outfield reminds you of a quarterback squatting behind the lines barking the signals."

By July 3, DiMaggio had lifted his batting average to .321. As pleased as he may have been with his own performance, he must have been doubly pleased to learn that brother Vince, his sore arm now healed, had returned to the PCL with Hollywood.

As Joe's streak reached 40 games, only nine games short of Ness' mark, he became the object of increased attention. Attendance at Seals games started to rise and the press starting filling in DiMaggio's background. They called him "Dead Pan Joe" in reference to his demeanor and one-word answers to questions.

In game 40 of the streak, DiMaggio again averted disaster. Hitless entering the eighth inning against Hollywood pitcher Tom Sheehan, DiMaggio worked the count to 3–2 before whistling a letter-high fastball to left-center field. Vince, playing center for Hollywood, tried desperately to cut the drive off, but it fell just out of reach and Joe pulled in at second for a double.

The build-up was intense as DiMaggio approached Ness' record of 49 games, but Joe still wasn't of much help to the press. Abe Kemp even published an interview with Joe in which DiMaggio's responses consisted only of shrugs and nods. The press translated DiMaggio's recalcitrance into such praiseworthy traits as humility and determination, both characteristics that have remained a part of DiMaggio's image to this day.

He tied Ness' mark on July 13 in Seals Stadium versus Los Angeles. In his first at-bat, Joe blooped the first pitch off pitcher Fay Thomas into center field. His next time up he homered on the first pitch, then collected a single to go 3–5. The Seals still lost, 8–2.

Joe shattered the record the next night to stretch his streak to 50 games. Ten thousand fans, the Seals' largest crowd of the season, turned out on "Joe DiMaggio Night" and saw DiMaggio single in his first appearance to set a new PCL record, then lash out three doubles to finish 4-for-5 in a 7–6 Seal win. After the game, San Francisco Mayor Angelo Rossi presented DiMaggio with a watch, and the following evening DiMaggio was feted at the Milano Theater in North Beach and received a silver loving cup in recognition of his achievement as a "Son of Italy." The Italian community in San Francisco was following DiMaggio's performance with tremendous fervor. The fisherman's son was becoming a hero, whether he wanted the homage or not.

With Ness' record out of the way, the press set its sights on Joe Wilhoit's minor-league hitting streak record of 69 games, set in 1919. DiMaggio's streak was at 53 games when the Seals headed to Sacramento for a seven-game series against the league's best pitching staff.

DiMaggio had little trouble extending the streak to 55 in the first two games of the series. But in game 56, he twice reached on errors before lining a clean single off former Seal pitcher Bill Hartwig.

Joe now appeared to be pressing. Collecting a hit every game in relative obscurity was one matter; doing so as an object of adoration was something else. He hadn't had an extra-base hit in a week and was having trouble making solid contact. On July 21, he stretched the streak to 57 games on an easy ground ball that eluded Sacramento shortstop Ray French. On July 22, DiMaggio lucked out again on another sixth-inning ground ball to French. French, normally a fine fielder and later selected as a member of the all-time PCL All-Star team, let the ball roll between his legs for DiMaggio's only hit of the day. The Associated Press reported that while the hit was "legitimate . . . [it] was of the variety which are questionable to the spectators."

During a double-header on July 23, DiMaggio's brinkmanship continued. In the ninth inning of game one, DiMaggio beat out a hit on a swinging bunt against a cooperative Sacramento infield. In game two, DiMaggio again lucked out. Hitless entering the ninth inning, he drove a hard grounder to deep short. Ray French again failed to field the ball cleanly and DiMaggio reached first without drawing a throw. *Sacramento Bee* sports editor Steve George, the official scorer, gave DiMaggio a hit.

After each game with a borderline hit, irate fans, some of whom wanted to see the streak continue — legitimately — and others who hoped to see it end, stormed the press box. After game two police had to escort George safely from the park.

The scorers were not entirely to blame for the questionable legitimacy of DiMaggio's performance over that July week. Seals games had been drawing larger and larger crowds. Opposing players were well aware of DiMaggio's importance to the financial health of the league. They wanted the streak to continue. A little help was not out of the question. While opposing infields gave DiMaggio a break by playing deeper than normal, the strategy didn't hand him a base hit. DiMaggio still had to hit the ball. He was skilled enough to turn the small allowance to his advantage.

Back in San Francisco on July 25, DiMaggio continued to press, not collecting a hit until the Seals fortuitously exploded for eight eighth-inning runs in a 12–4 win. The streak was at 61 games.

The next day, July 26, Caveney moved DiMaggio from the clean-up position to lead-off, hoping the change would give the young slugger an additional at-bat.

Facing Oakland pitcher Ed Walsh Jr., son of eventual Hall-of-Famer Ed Walsh Sr., a star for the Chicago White Sox three decades earlier, DiMaggio was hitless in his first four at-bats.

With the score tied 3–3 entering the ninth inning, Joe was scheduled to hit fourth. Seal first baseman Frank Fenton opened the ninth inning with a hard ground ball to short, but it rolled suspiciously between the infielder's legs and Fenton dashed all the way to second, conveniently removing the possibility of a double play that could end the inning before DiMaggio got one last chance to hit. Frank Bottarini carefully sacrificed Fenton to third. Walsh then intentionally walked pitcher Jimmy Zinn to set up the double play.

DiMaggio stepped to the plate, and the Seals Stadium crowd rose and gave him a long ovation. Walsh wound up, threw, and DiMaggio lifted a fly ball toward right field.

The crowd started to roar, but their cheers faded as Oak right fielder Harlan Pool drifted back. He caught the ball 30 feet short of the fence. Fenton tagged and crossed the plate with the winning run. The Seals won, 3–2. Even as the streak ended at 61 games, DiMaggio revealed another trait: He sacrificed himself and gave his team a victory.

When the streak began on May 28, Joe DiMaggio was unknown to all but the most attentive fan of PCL baseball. He was apparently overmatched, and in danger of being released. By the time the streak ended, DiMaggio was a household name on the West Coast, a bona fide star, the greatest drawing card in the league, and publicly acclaimed its savior.

In two short months, DiMaggio's life changed dramatically. Moreover, in those two months he learned lessons that would later prove invaluable in the midst of another streak. Until the very end, the pressure did not affect his performance. It never did again.

This DiMaggio would be no regular Joe. He was a hero.

Only one player in baseball history, at any level, has ever had two hitting streaks in excess of 55 games — Joe DiMaggio. In addition to his 61-game streak for the San Francisco Seals of the Pacific Coast League, he hit in 56 straight games for the Yankees in 1941. Many of the qualities that would later be attributed to him by New York sportswriters were already in evidence when the young DiMaggio came out of nowhere to become the greatest prospect in baseball.

BREAKING UP THE YANKEES

The Time — December. The Place — The
Geltmore Hotel, New York. The Characters —
President Harridge, Club Owners and Managers
of the American League, and Baseball Writers

from *Baseball Magazine*, December 1939

President Harridge — We are gathered here, gentlemen, to discuss plans for trying to loosen the stranglehold of the Yankees ball club on the American League. The seven other club members —

A Baseball Writer — You mean the seven other club victims —

President Harridge — Are determined to do something about the pennant races in our league, now that the Yanks have won four consecutive flags.

A Baseball Writer — What pennant races in the American League?

Another Baseball Writer — Yeah — if you can see any recent pennant races in the American League I can see some yacht races in the Mohave desert.

President Griffith — And something's got to be done to have an annual pennant race in our loop, instead of our annual pennant parade.

President Briggs — Quite right. Who wants to see the Yanks always winning?

President Barrow — Well, I'm broad-minded. I've no objection to it.

President Harridge — But four consecutive Yankee flags is too much!

Manager McCarthy (placidly) — Not for us, Mr. President.

President Harridge — Well, are there any suggestions?

President Griffith — Yes. I suggest breaking up the New York Yankees.

Manager Vitt — And I got a swell suggestion for doing it, Mr. President.

President Harridge — And what is your swell suggestion, Mr. Vitt?

Manager Vitt — I suggest that this Joe DiMaggio be traded to our Indians. He's the egg that's been mainly responsible for breaking up all the other clubs in our loop. And with him on our club, I'll guarantee that he'll break up the Yankees' club, as well.

President Briggs — But what good would that do our Detroit Tigers?

Manager Vitt — Not very much. Especially if your Detroit Tigers decided to pitch to the guy with the bases loaded.

A Baseball Writer — I thought Joe Cronin had the Yankees broken up when his Red Sox beat 'em five straight games last season.

Another Baseball Writer — At least Joe McCarthy seemed all broken up about it. His lead was reduced to six games. And anytime Joseph's club isn't leading by at least ten games, he thinks something's wrong.

Manager Cronin (disgustedly) — Yeah, when we beat the Yanks five straight I thought I had the right idea about breaking 'em up. But heck! They copped the flag by 17 games. And if we'd of beat 'em ten straight, I hate to think how many games they would of copped the flag by.

President Harridge — Have you a suggestion about how to keep the Yankees from always being at the top of the league, Mr. Barnes?

President Barnes, of St. Louis (wearily) — What difference does it make to us, Mr. President, who's at the top of the league? When we're nearly always at the bottom of the league anyway?

President Griffith (determinedly) — Well, we're determined to do something about this Yankee situation in Washington.

A Baseball Writer — And about the only place anything can be done about this Yankee situation seems to be in Washington. The Supreme Court might declare Ed Barrow and Joe McCarthy unconstitutional.

Another Baseball Writer — Or President Roosevelt might veto Joe

DiMaggio and Red Ruffing. Why don't you gents write your congressmen?

A Baseball Writer — Yeah — they oughta be able to get the Yanks indicted or something for restraint of baseball trade.

President Harridge — Have you any suggestions regarding this Yankee situation, Mr. Briggs?

President Briggs — I'd suggest that if the Yanks would trade pitching staffs with us it might balance the loop, as well as our club.

Manager Vitt (brightly) — The loop could be balanced without making the Yanks trade off a single player, Mr. President.

President Griffith (ironically) — Sure — by the simple expedient of shooting President Barrow and Manager Joe McCarthy.

Manager Vitt — That would be quite unnecessary, if quite justified, Mr. Griffith. Simply play Ed Barrow in center-field, instead of in the Front Office; and have Joe DiMaggio manage affairs in the Front Office, instead of massacre pitchers in the batter's box. And play Joe McCarthy instead of Joe Gordon at second-base; and let Joe Gordon instead of Joe McCarthy manage the ball club. That would be a nice change for them.

Manager Jimmy Dykes — To say nothing of the rest of the league.

President Tom Yawkey — But isn't the Yankee problem one of too much player talent through too many player-farm clubs, Mr. President?

President Harridge (thoughtfully) — That, Mr. Yawkey, is problematical.

Manager Jimmy Dykes — No, Mr. President — it's alphabetical.

President Harridge — Alphabetical, Mr. Dykes!

Manager Jimmy Dykes — Sure. The d —— Yankees have too many d —— D's on their d —— ball club. And if you'd make 'em trade off DiMaggio, Dickey and Donald, the loop, as well as the alphabet, would be balanced.

Manager Mack (reflectively) — Don't you think that perhaps Night Baseball might be the solution of the whole problem, Mr. President?

President Harridge — You suggest making the Yankees play Night Baseball, Mr. Mack?

Manager Mack — Yes, Mr. President — without the Night Baseball lights.

President Barnes — Perhaps, Mr. President, merely a change in our baseball schedule would be all that's necessary to adjust this matter.

President Harridge — You mean to shorten the schedule, Mr. Barnes?

President Barnes — I mean you could even eliminate the schedule, where these Yanks are concerned, for all of me, Mr. President.

Manager Jimmy Dykes (thinking deeply) — Why not start the schedule in December, instead of April, Mr. President?

President Harridge (in surprise) — But that, Mr. Dykes, would force our ball clubs inside!

Manager Jimmy Dykes — Exactly. Then these Bronx Bombers would hafta play "inside" baseball, insteada hitting the ball all over the next county.

A Baseball Writer — Speaking of indoor games, Mr. President, why not have your clubs play Bingo, instead of Baseball? At least then the Yankees wouldn't have the numbers of all your other clubs.

Another Baseball Writer — For that matter, Bill, why not have a schedule of pinochle games, instead of baseball games? That would give the other players a chance. You can always shuffle the cards, if you can't shuffle the Yankees.

A Baseball Writer — Sure. And guys like DiMaggio and Dickey would have more trouble getting "round-trips" in pinochle games than in baseball games.

A Newspaper War Correspondent — If you must restrain these Yankees, Mr. President, why don't you just put an embargo on them?

Manager Cronin — Well, I wish somebody would put something on 'em — if it's only a jinx or a Gypsy Curse.

President Harridge (severely) — Gentlemen, gentlemen! Order! Order!

All the Baseball Writers — Make mine the same!!!!

President Harridge — Let's not descend to mere levity. This is a serious meeting. And it's getting entirely out of hand!

The Others (in unison) — Well, so are these blink-blank Yanks!!!!

The oldest argument in the game is that Yankee dominance is bad for baseball. Over the years, as in this tongue-in-cheek account, the call to "break up the Yankees" has become as predictable and familiar as spring training.

RICHARDS VIDMER

....

MAGIC NUMBERS

from *The New York Herald Tribune*, July 19, 1941

Sixty . . . Sixty-one . . . Fifty-six . . .

Over the span of the last fifteen years the Yankees have created considerable chaos among the statisticians who compile and keep the baseball records. They have shattered, collectively and individually, a double handful of marks. But three figures kept the public's pulses pumping as they were being made, turned the fidgeting fans' attention from the pennant races to the spectacular sideshows and created interest across the country.

One was Babe Ruth's home-run splurge in the season of 1927. Another was Ben Chapman's sensational base-stealing exploits in 1931. And the third was Joe DiMaggio's hitting streak which came to an end under the bright lights of Municipal Stadium in Cleveland on Thursday night.

These three remarkable achievements furnished the longest sustained thrills the big leagues have known in more than twenty years. Each one held the headlines day after day. Each mark was followed in the making by the baseball world at large.

Back in 1927 the first thing the average fan looked for was the summary of the Yankees' box score. Had Ruth hit another homer? How many did that make? Steadily and surely he swung his big bat across the campaign. Closer and closer he drew to his own record of fifty-nine, made six years before. Seldom two days went by without a homer by the Babe, and it became such a routine matter that the reporters following the Yankees in general and Ruth in particular made up pools in the press box each day.

Nine slips of paper would be put in a hat, each bearing a number representing an inning. Nine dollars would be collected and the numbers drawn. As soon as Babe hit another homer the holder of the winning inning would collect and pot and nine more slips would be made out. The turnover was terrific.

Babe moved into the final month needing seventeen homers to top his old mark. It was a big order, but he filled it on the final day with an echoing wallop off Tom Zachary for his sixtieth homer of the year.

Three Threaten Record

Three others have approached that amazing record since, but none has been able to equal it. Hack Wilson, of the Cubs, hammered out fifty-six homers in 1930, Jimmy Foxx, of the Athletics, hit fifty-eight in 1932 and Hank Greenberg hit fifty-eight in 1938. But somehow none of them caused the sensation as he neared the record that Ruth did when he made it. Perhaps the baseball public just felt no one could equal the Babe.

Chapman's base-stealing exploits caused almost as much hysteria, however, in 1931. Long before the fleet-footed flier from Birmingham, Ala., arrived on the scene Ty Cobb had stolen ninety-six bases in a season, but that was back in 1915. Bob Beacher, of the Reds, had stolen eighty, but that was in 1911. Sam Rice, of the Senators, stole sixty-three in 1920, but not since then had anything even approaching Ben's base running been seen around the big league circuit.

In the intervening ten years the game had settled down to a slugging match. Home runs were the vogue and base stealing was almost a lost art. But Chapman came up to the Yankees with wings on his feet and thrilled the fans across the country with his daring dashes from first to second and second to third, sometimes from third to home.

It got so that the crowds gathered less to see the Yankees play than to see the Alabama Express run. A new tenseness came into every game when he got on base, and Chapman's sideshow stole the spotlight from the main attraction. His speed became so widely discussed that foot races were put on before several games to test his fleetness. Other clubs entered challenges against him, but Ben beat 'em all.

He didn't set a record; didn't even approach Cobb's mark made sixteen years before, but he held the headlines and the sixty-one bases he stole brought him a lot of personal satisfaction in that he stole one more base that year than the number of homers Babe hit in his best campaign.

Curtain on Another Show

And ten years later along came DiMaggio to stage another Yankee sideshow that for a couple of months has held the headlines. Interest grew as the Yankee Clipper hit safely day after day and approached the modern mark set by George Sisler in 1922. Lost in the consecutive hitting streak of Joe DiMaggio was the rapid rise of the Yankees toward the league leadership. The first question wasn't whether the Yankees had won or lost, but whether Joe had made his daily hit — and how many.

When he reached and passed Sisler's record of hitting safely in forty-one consecutive contests, the tension was terrible. When he reached and passed the ancient record of Wee Willie Keeler, who hit safely in forty-four straight games back in 1897, it was just a matter of how long Joe could keep it up.

The show closed Thursday night when in his last time at bat he grounded into a double play and was held hitless for the first time after hitting safely in fifty-six consecutive contests. But he held the sustained interest of the fans across the country for two months, just as Babe Ruth did across the 1927 season and Ben Chapman four years later.

The Yankees, it seems, aren't content with furnishing most of the main fireworks, they have to put on an added attraction every now and then.

Richards Vidmer brought more than his writing skills to the ballpark — he was an accomplished athlete and once played minor league baseball under a pseudonym, giving his work a unique air of authority. The rakish sportswriter began his career with the Washington Herald *before joining the* Times *and then the* Herald Tribune, *where he succeeded Bill McGeehan.*

JOE McCARTHY'S TEN COMMANDMENTS FOR SUCCESS IN BASEBALL

circa 1940

1. Nobody ever became a ballplayer by walking after a ball.
2. You will never become a .300 hitter unless you take the bat off your shoulder.
3. An outfielder who throws in back of a runner is locking the barn after the horse is stolen.
4. Keep your head up and you may not have to keep it down.
5. When you start to slide, slide. He who changes his mind may have to change a good leg for a bad one.
6. Do not alibi on bad hops. Anybody can field the good ones.
7. Always run them out. You never can tell.
8. Do not quit.
9. Do not fight too much with the umpires. You cannot expect them to be as perfect as you are.
10. A pitcher who hasn't control hasn't anything.

Before joining the Yankees as manager in 1931, Joe McCarthy had already earned a reputation as one of the best managers in baseball while leading the Chicago Cubs. Baseball was his life, and in McCarthy's view, there was a right way to play the game. McCarthy wasn't a teacher — major leaguers were supposed to know how to play and behave.

He was the first to recognize a "Yankee tradition" and hold his players to that standard. Over time, as Ruth's skills and influence on the club waned, under McCarthy the Yankees would develop a reputation as baseball's consummate professionals.

RE: PIPER DAVIS AND ART WILSON OF BIRMINGHAM

1947

Re: Piper Davis and Art Wilson of Birmingham. Davis is 32 they tell me and Wilson is about the same age. Wilson has a finger off of his throwing hand. They are both good ball players. The St. Louis Browns scouted Davis in 1946, took option on him, then wanted to send him to Elmira. He wanted to go to the Browns so they released their option on him. If he wasn't good enough for the Browns two years ago I don't believe he could make it with the Yankees now.

There isn't an outstanding Negro player that anybody could recommend to step into the big league and hold down a regular job. The better players in Negro baseball are past the age for the big leagues. Several years ago I could have named several players that could more than hold their own in the big leagues. In fact, several would have been stars but now I know of not one that would stick. If they come up with certain named players please advise me and I will give you the low down on them. As I previously stated, there are no outstanding Negro players at this time.

I am aware of how these committees apply the pressure on the big leagues to hire one or perhaps two players. If you hire one or two, then they will want you to hire another one. There will be no compromise with them and they are mostly bluff.

They put the pressure on Yankee Stadium about two years ago to let Semler, Negro owner of the Black Yankees, promote the games in there. I am sure you know what has happened since the stadium was taken from Gottlieb and given to Semler. Semler is out of baseball, owes plenty of bills etc., but the pressure was put on the officials of the stadium and everybody lost money because Semler wasn't big enough for the job and this may have been a big factor in the failure of the Negro National League.

Hank Rigney of Toledo promotes all the Negro games in Sportsman's Park for the Browns. He is a white man. The Negros in St. Louis tried to get the park themselves. They got city and state officials to intercede for them but Bill DeWitt told them he was satisfied with Rigney and if any Negro games were played Rigney would promote them unless they wanted to put up a $5,000.00 guarantee. That was the last of these would be promoters but they made a big bluff and a lot of noise.

This document is apparently a Yankee scouting report on Negro League infielders Artie Wilson and Piper Davis. Precisely how it got into the files at the National Baseball Hall of Fame is a mystery. Yet as a statement of baseball's unwillingness to integrate, it is chilling for its candor.

After Jackie Robinson broke the color line in 1947, the Yankees, under George Weiss and Larry MacPhail, gave lip service to the topic. Denigrating the abilities of every black player they looked at, they signed only a few to appease pressure groups. Even after Elston Howard became the Yankees' first black major leaguer in 1954, the ball club remained slow to embrace black players in the organization.

PLAYED LIKE SEMI-PROS, DODGERS AGREE; DiMAGGIO ALIBIS REISER'S ERROR

Brooklyn Grateful Scene Switches to Ebbets Field. Stadium Shadows Bothered Shotton's Squad as Much as Bombers' Playing; Lombardi Thinks He Can Win if Given Another Chance

from *The New York Herald Tribune*, October 2, 1947

Joe DiMaggio, pillar of Yankee society, sat quietly in his cubicle in the Yankee dressing room yesterday after the second game of the World Series, untouched by the cries of congratulations that were being tossed back and forth across the dormitory.

DiMaggio had removed his shirt and sat puffing at a cigarette as his mates generated enthusiasm all around him. It is difficult to suggest to DiMaggio that he played a great game. After a while it becomes redundant because it is a DiMaggio habit.

"That was pretty tough on Pete Reiser out there, wasn't it, Joe?" asked a reporter.

"It's always like that in the fall," Joe answered. "It gets a lot darker around home plate and a haze settles in the background. It's no cinch to see a fly ball coming out of the shadows."

"Did it bother you at all?" some one asked.

Two Is Lucky Combination

DiMaggio looked up with a friendly grin. He seemed to like the idea of answering that one.

"Don't worry about the old boy," he said, referring to himself. "I've been playing in this park a long while."

The other players were shouting at each other with a spontaneity born of a two-game winning streak in the World Series.

"Nice goin', fellas, nice goin'," yelled Chuck Dressen.

"Two down and two to go," cried George Stirnweiss.

"What's the winning combination, Tommy?" said some one to Tommy Henrich.

"Combination's two," answered Henrich and every one who was listening released a chuckle.

There were handshakes along with the cries of victory. In fact, the Yankees were so pleased with themselves they even congratulated Yogi Berra, the catcher, who should have been playing with the Dodgers considering the mistakes he made.

Among Berra's indiscretions were a wild throw, on which he drew an error, a slow throw on which Pee Wee Reese stole second and a repugnance toward standing beneath a fly ball which fell at his feet in front of the plate.

Yanks in Gay Mood

To be truthful the Yankees were in such a gay mood that they were willing to let any one have a selection of seats for the sixth and seventh (if necessary) games at the Stadium. They don't think they'll have to be there for those games.

In the Brooklyn dressing room, Burt Shotton was confronted with the dual task of encouraging his players and satisfying reporters.

"They beat us and we don't like it," he said. "We got a lot of bad breaks and we set most of them up ourselves. What more can I say?"

Hugh Casey was dressing quietly near Shotton. Some one said: "That was a tough one?"

"That wasn't tough," Casey replied. "We just played like a bunch of semi-pros, that's all."

Vic Lombardi, the little left-hander, who had been knocked out in the fifth, was already in civilian clothes.

"I think I can beat them if I get another start," he said. "I had to bear down too much in the early innings."

Schacht Learns New Tricks

Most of the Dodgers, especially Reiser, who had experienced so much trouble in center-field, dressed without saying a word. Every one seemed happy about playing at Ebbets Field today.

Outside in the hall, Al Schacht, baseball's clown prince, appeared.

He had been visiting the Yankee dressing room to congratulate the winners.

"The Dodgers were trying to steal your act out there today, weren't they, Al?" asked a fan.

"They did," said Schacht emphatically. "It would take me a month to learn all those gags."

The Dodgers wouldn't have offered much argument, had they overheard. They were trying to save their strength for the next argument with the Yankees anyway.

The integrated Dodgers quickly became the greatest threat to the Yankees' dominance. Although Brooklyn wouldn't win a World Series until 1955, their battles with the Yankees became legendary. Nearly forgotten today, Bob Cooke was an integral part of the sports department of the Herald Tribune. *Under Stanley Woodward, who served as sports editor from 1937 through 1948, the* Herald Tribune's *sports department was easily the best of the era.*

LAVAGETTO DOUBLE IN 9TH BEATS BEVENS, YANKS 3-2

from *The New York Daily News*, October 4, 1947

Out of the mockery and ridicule of "the worst World Series in history," the greatest baseball game ever played was born yesterday. They'll talk about it forever, those 33,443 fans who saw it. They'll say: "I was there. I saw Bill Bevens come within one out of the only Series no-hitter; I saw the winning run purposely put on base by the Yankees; I saw Cookie Lavagetto send that winning run across a moment later with a pinch-hit double off the right-field wall — the only hit, but big enough to give the Brooks the 3–2 victory that put them even-up at two games apiece."

And maybe they'll talk about the mad minute that followed — the most frenzied scene ever erupted in this legendary spot called Ebbets Field. How some of the Faithful hugged each other in the stands; how others ran out to the center of the diamond and buried Lavagetto in their caresses; how Cookie's mates pushed the public off because they themselves wanted the right to swarm all over him; how Cookie, the man who had to plead for his job this Spring, finally fought his way down the dugout steps — laughing and crying at the same time in the first stages of joyous hysteria.

Elsewhere in the park, another man was so emotionally shaken he sought solitude. That was Branch Rickey, the supposedly cold, calloused business man. He sat down in a room just off the press box and posted a guard outside the door.

After 10 minutes of nerve-soothing ceiling-staring, Rickey wanted to talk about the finish — but he started a little earlier than that.

He flashed back to the top half of the frame, when Hughie Casey had come in with the bases loaded and one out, and got Tommy Henrich to hit a DP ball on the first serve. "Just one pitch, and he's the winning pitcher of a World Series game," Branch chuckled. "That's wonderful."

Rickey then turned to his favorite subject. "It was speed that won it," he said. This tickled Rickey because it had been the speed of Al Gionfriddo which saved the game. They had laughed at Gionfriddo when he came to the Brooks back in June in that $300,000 deal with the Pirates. They had said: "What did Rickey get that little squirt for; to carry the money in a satchel from Pittsburgh?" And they had added, "He'll be in Montreal in a couple of weeks."

But here it was World Series time, and "little Gi" was still around. Suddenly he was useful. Furillo was on first with two out. Carl had gotten there just as eight Brooks before him had — by walking. A couple of these passes had led to the Brooks' run in the fifth, and had cut New York's lead down to 2–1.

That's the way it still was when Gionfriddo went in to run for Furillo, and Pete Reiser was sent up to swing for Casey. Only now Bevens was just one out away from having his bronze image placed among the all-time greats in Cooperstown. He got the first out in the ninth on a gasp provoker, a long drive by Bruce Edwards which forced Johnny Lindell up against the left wall for the stretching grab. Furillo walked and Spider Jorgensen fouled meekly to George McQuinn, who was white as a sheet as he made the catch.

One out to go. Soon the count was 2–1 on Pete. Down came the next pitch — and up went a feverish screech. Gionfriddo had broken for second. Yogi Berra's peg flew down to second — high, just high enough to enable Gi to slide head-first under Phil Rizzuto's descending tag.

The pitch on which Gionfriddo went down had been high, making the count on Reiser 3-and-1. Then came the maneuver that makes Bucky Harris the most second-guessed man in baseball. The Yankee pilot signaled Berra to step out and take an intentional fourth ball from Bevens.

The cardinal principle of baseball had been disdained. The "winning run" had been put on — and Eddie Miksis ran for the sore-ankled Reiser.

The Brooks had run out of lefty pinch-hitters. But a good right-side swinger, a clutch money player like Lavagetto didn't get to be a 14-year man by being able to hit only one kind of chucking.

On the first pitch, Harris' guess still looked like a good one. Cookie swung at a fast ball and missed. Then another fast one, slightly high and toward the outside. Again Lavagetto swung. The ball soared toward the right corner — a territory seldom patronized by Cookie.

Because of that Tommy Henrich had been swung over toward right-center. Frantically Tommy took off after the drive, racing toward the line. He got there and leaped, but it was a hopeless leap. The ball flew some six feet over his glove and banged against the wooden wall. Gionfriddo was tearing around third and over with the tying run.

The ball caromed under Henrich's legs. On the second grab, Henrich clutched it and, still off balance, hurried a peg to McQuinn at the edge of the infield. The firstsacker whirled desperately and heaved home — but even as he loosed the ball, speedy young Miksis was plowing over the plate with a sitting slide, a big grin on his puss. Eddie, just turned 21, last week, sat right on home plate like an elated kid. For what seemed like much more than the actual three or four seconds, Miksis just sat there, looked at his mates and laughed insanely.

That's when God's Little Green Acre became bedlam. The clock read 3:51, Brooklyn Standard Time — the most emotional minute in the lives of thousands of Faithful. There was Lavagetto being mobbed — and off to the side, there was Bevens, head bowed low, walking dejectedly through the swarming crowd and completely ignored by it. Just a few seconds earlier, he was the one everybody was planning to pat on the back. He was the one who would have been carried off the field — the only pitcher ever to toss a no-hitter in a Series.

Now he was just another loser.

Dick Young spearheaded a new style of baseball reporting. He dropped the stylistic flourishes of his forebears in favor of a more straightforward, hard-boiled, and combative style of writing. Young also was one of the first writers to go behind the scene, reporting on clubhouse mat-

ters and the inner workings of the front office as much as the game on the field. For more than five decades writing for the Post, *the* Daily News, *and* The Sporting News, *Young was a must-read for baseball fans.*

PHIL RIZZUTO

....

HALL OF FAME INDUCTION SPEECH

Hall of Fame, July 31, 1994

Holy Cow! (*applause*) Oh, my voice is gone. Wait a minute, I have had problems with my voice. Never had this before. I mean I'm so nervous about being up here that I think it's like psychosomatic. My voice is — if you can hear me and understand me fine. If not, you're lucky that I don't have to go through all the pennants and World Series that the Yankees won — be here until next Wednesday. But I want to tell you I want to congratulate Murphy with the "golden tonsils," Lefty, whose record speaks for itself, and Leo "The Lip" who was my type of manager. The only thing was that he would get on me every once in a while in some of the World Series, and he'd like to find out something personal about you. This doesn't even sound like me. I can't — anyway, Durocher's favorite with me in the World Series was when I'd pop one up. He'd say, "Home run in an elevator shaft" (*laughter*), but he was a great man. And I'll tell you the only reason that I'm here today, believe it or not, is because of you fans, my family, my relatives and all my friends. (*applause*) Wait a minute. No, really I think you put so much pressure on them, kept sending in those petitions and saying, "He should be in the Hall of Fame," and actually my records paled with all these great Hall of Famers behind me, and that "Huckleberry" Lou Brock, he keeps calling me a rookie. (*laughter*) I'm the oldest living rookie in the Hall of Fame. (*laughter*) I mean, you talk about it taking a long time to get here, Steve, but anyway I had to write a few things down because I really was dreading this speech, and I wrote down something that says, "What baseball means to me."

Now I've been so lucky with the help of the man upstairs, and my family and friends, to be with the Yankees for 54 years with the same organization (*applause*), and baseball has made it possible for me to support my family, send them through college and meet people and go to places that we never would have had a chance to do. Actually, my whole life up to this moment has been baseball and it's flashing by me so quickly. I'm going to try and tell it as quickly as it's flashing by me because when I was a little kid in Brooklyn (*applause*) — no — I tell you it was a great spot. Pee Wee knows all about that, but when I say all the people that really helped me — my high school coach, Al Kuhnich, taught me how to bunt. Without knowing how to bunt, I'd have never made it to the big leagues.

Paul Kritchell, a Yankee scout, signed me up to Stengel and Bill Terry told me I was too small to play baseball and that was a big break for me. My first two managers in the first three years were Ray White, who went to the same high school I did, and he took me over kids that were a lot better than I was, and you gotta know somebody just like that. Bill Meyer, who was my manager at Kansas City for two years, is one of the great little managers and he taught me a lot about baseball.

The greatest manager I ever had was Joe McCarthy, "Old Marse Joe." But we had so many — I mean these great World Series. I know I'm — this is typical of me. I started at the end and go back to the middle and then the beginning and I really — I'm trying to get this down. When I was a kid playing in the streets of Brooklyn, all those days trying to — wanting to be a ball player and if I had never been a ball player I don't know what would have happened to me. A lot of nights I'd wake up in a cold sweat thinking, had I not been a major league ball player, what would I have done for a living? Because everything I tried to do turned bad. I tried to run a snowblower and I stuck my hand in and cut my fingers off. I mean, I'm lucky I can turn on the car and know how it runs and if I open the refrigerator and it's not right in front of me I don't know what I'm looking for. I mean, it's really terrible. (*laughter*) But when I talk about being a kid playing on the streets of Brooklyn, I mean we played everything that was possible, stick ball, rock ball, box ball, paddle ball. Pee Wee never heard of any of these things because he was shooting marbles down in Louisville. (*laughter*) But those were great games and it was great for our hand–eye coordination. So we broke a couple of windows and my mother, God bless her, said, "Look, get a cover off a baseball." It was tough to get a baseball number one, but we got one — cover broke off. She filled it full of rags and we were able to play on the street and you could throw curve balls and I think that helped me as much as all the spring training and all the practice in the minor leagues.

Now, if people are understanding this speech, just raise your hand or else your . . . (*laughter*) Well, my family knows me, so they raised their hands. But I'll never forget when the Yankees finally signed me to a contract and they sent me to Bassett, Virginia, in 1937. I'd never been away from home. My father took a twenty dollar bill and pinned it to my undershirt. (*laughter*) He said, "You gotta watch out for those guys on the trains" (*laughter*), and the Yankees gave me a nice seat, no sleeper, sat all the way to Bassett, Virginia. But it was a beautiful trip because we went through Washington, D.C. Stopped in Richmond, Virginia, the first taste of southern fried chicken. I tell you it was delicious, but they gave me — Hey, White, what's that stuff that looks like oatmeal? (*laughter*) Grits, grits! (*laughter*) No, they gave . . . they gave me these grits and I didn't know what to do with them, so I put them in my pocket. (*laughter*) I had no idea what — but anyway, then we got to Bassett. Now Bassett was a town of 1,600, counting the cows. I got off the train and there was no town there. I'm looking around at mountains just like the beautiful mountains and then the train pulled away and there was the town. A little drug store, a theatre that was only open two days a week and a drug store, and that was the town of Bassett. The sheriff met me there, Sheriff Coots, whom I used to have breakfast with every morning and he took me to the boarding house where we stayed, and don't forget I was making $75.00 a month at this time, saving money, sending half of it home to my mother. In those days, oh it's no sense talking about that. (*laughter*) I mean these kids today wouldn't remember that, but you could get a steak for 35¢ and all you could eat. But that was my — and yet only one thing happened to me in Bassett. No, I — listen any time you want to leave just leave because this is absolutely going no where. (*laughter*) But — no, I stepped in what they call a gopher hole down there. I stepped — I hurt my leg and I played on it for about two weeks and the manager and trainer, Ray White, used to pound my leg and rub it, which was the worst thing as we found out, and finally after about ten days an old umpire who lived down there — had umpired in the major leagues — would umpire on weekends down there. He told Ray, you better take this kid to a hospital. He took me to Roanoke, Virginia, which was about a hundred miles away, and little Dr. Johnson just felt my leg. He said, "You need an operation immediately. How can I get a hold of your mother?" Because I was under age and they had to get . . . He called my mother and said, "I gotta operate on your son." He operated on me and I had gangrene. Now this is very unbelievable — if he hadn't operated, I'd only have one leg. Someway I would have found a way to play baseball with that one leg. But what I'm getting at is how lucky you have to be. I've got one of these flies. (*laughter*) No, but anyway — no anyway I woke up the next morning and my mother was there and my brother who is here today, Freddie, and he fainted from the ether and was in the next bed. I didn't know where the hell I was when I woke up. (*laughter*) And so anyway he had to cut part of the muscle out of my leg because it was infested with gangrene, and actually that was a break for me because I used to be so fast when I was a kid. I'd run by the ground balls and this slowed me up just enough so that I could make the ball. (*laughter*) I only got a couple of more of these. (*laughter*) No but — when I was in New York at the time that I played for the Yankees, when I finally came up, I mean it was baseball universe. I mean the Dodgers were there, the Giants were there, the Yankees were there. You could walk down any street in Brooklyn and New York and never miss an inning or a pitch. Somebody had the radio on all the way down the block, and it was just, you know, it was so great, the baseball was so great. The rivalry was so great with the Dodgers, the Giants just one year, but the rivalry with the Dodgers was really exceptional. It's unfortunate we beat them every year but that one year that (*laughter*) — that one year they lucked out. We figured we'd better let them win one or they're going to leave town and they left town anyway. (*laughter*)

Well, I want to tell you something that we had, I mean, we had the best team, you know, and it wasn't that money could buy. In those days, we didn't make any money. What a club we had. We'd win the pennant close to the Fourth of July and then we'd relax and just get in the World Series, and in those days we made more money from the World Series checks than we did in our salary for the year. That was supposed to be a joke. (*laughter*) All right, anyway, when you've got your team — I mean it went right down the line too. When I joined the Yankees, they had Keller, Henrich and DiMaggio in the outfield, Rolfe at third, Gordon at second, Dickey behind the plate, Ruffing, Gomez, Murphy, Bonham, all those great pitchers. I mean, it was unbelievable and I was just happy to be at the right spot at the right time. Sounds like I'm in Yankee Stadium with that echo coming back to me, but anyway, Frank Crosetti was just about ready to hang up his spikes and I got in here and all I had to do is make a few double plays, beat out a bunt. Crosetti looked toward me — had to get hit with a pitch so it wouldn't hurt. (*laughter*) All the little things and I just collect that World Series check and I mean we just — so great. And my voice is starting to go. I would like to introduce my family before it does go on the blink or . . . Of course number one is my pride and joy. I mean, Steve mentioned the fact that baseball wives should get a medal every day for what they put up with when we're home and when we're on the road and the groupies following us and the (*laughter*) — not me — wait a minute — no, no, no, but no, I want to tell you some of the things that Cora did for me.

In 1946, after I came back from three years in the service, they started to throw curve — I couldn't hit a curve ball. I came back and I figured my career was over and then the Paschal boys came up from Mexico and they were flashing $10,000 bills around and they got Stirnweiss and myself — put us in a Cadillac, went under the bridge by the Yankee Stadium and they said, "If you leave right now, we'll give each one of you $10,000, a new Cadillac, but you gotta go down there and call Mr. McCarthy from down in Mexico." So I went home and told Cora. I said, "Let's pack, let's go to Mexico." Well, we were going to get apartment buildings. We wouldn't pay taxes, which turned out to be wrong. I mean the . . . (*laughter*) but anyway, Cora says, "If you go to Mexico, you go without me." But you know what she turned down? Don't forget, after the war you couldn't get stockings, you couldn't get girdles, you couldn't get butter. She didn't need a girdle, I'll tell you that. (*laughter*) She's pretty well built (*laughter*) but that — I would have gone but she and Larry MacPhail had the Yankees that time. Lee is here today, his son, and Larry said they had bugged Paschal's room and they said — came to George and I and said, "We want you to testify against them because this way we can get them out of . . ." I said, "I'm not going to testify, they want to give me more money." I mean, I was wrong — I mean it was the wrong approach, I know, because he suspended George and me for a couple of days, but then they left — the Paschals left town and George and I got a raise after that. So that was one of the better things, many better things and my wife. And another one — the other one was it happened before this. See the way I jump around, it's ridiculous. (*laughter*)

When I was in the Navy — you believe me in the Navy? I used to get sea sick on the ferry and people (*laughter*) — the people on the ship used — on the ferry ship used to say, "You're going to protect us? You're going to war?" It was very embarrassing. (*laughter*) But when we — all of a sudden a blanket order came down. Pee Wee and I were in our glory down in Norfolk then, and a blanket order, all athletes overseas. Now they didn't teach us anything but how to make our bed and I know over there you didn't have to make a bed where we were going, because they gave me old clothes that were camouflaged. They gave me a bag that had a rifle in it with all these rounds of ammunition which I gave away on board ship. I found out I could have been court-martialed on that later on. (*laughter*) So we're walking to the gangplank and I got my sea bag on my shoulder and I see a phone over there and the line is being held up, and speaking of lines as I jump round again, I made up my mind I would never stand in another line again when I got out of service. I don't know what that's got to do with the story, but I got to the phone. I called Cora up. I said, "Listen, Cora, I got a chance to go over the hill." I said, "They're going to New Guinea in the Philippines, and I don't want to go," and she said — and she said, "If you go, I won't be here when" — well, no, it wasn't quite that strong. But she said, "If you go, you don't go with my blessings." So I went back on ship and again [it] was a great thing because I didn't get killed over there and I got seasick every day.

Just one quick story. I was on board ship, I was on board ship 30 days. I was sick for 30 days. They found out I had chronic seasickness. One day there are planes flying overhead and the siren goes "To your battle stations." I didn't move. The captain came and said, "You get up there — you'll get court-martialed." I said, "That would be the best thing that happened — that or throw me overboard."

(*laughter*) So they put me off the ship, but unfortunately it was in New Guinea. I thought I'd see a lot of Italians there, but that's not what — that . . . (*laughter*)

Well, wait a minute. No, I played with and against the greatest — I mean, that era of baseball was absolutely the best. Now it's great for the monies they're paying now. I mean, I'd like to play just one year a while, but — now wait a minute. Oh, you figured the teams — the team that I mentioned and Ted Williams and those great teams and — played against Jimmie Foxx and Hank Greenberg. I mean, all those great players and — baseball, to me it's been my whole life. I mean, thank God for baseball. (*applause*)

You know, I got a note here about Joe DiMaggio and Lefty Gomez teaching me about room service. They — I never knew you could, in a room, pick up the phone and order room service and get your food sent up, and now I do it all the time. I mean, I never go downstairs. I tried it with Cora after we came home but she wouldn't — she didn't — no room service. But I do — still on that — I got a — I've got to mention — I've got to get these flies out of here. (*laughter*) I want to introduce my bride, Cora Rizzuto, right there — come on. (*applause*) I mean, like Steve said, when you're away on these long road trips, and we had three-week road trips back then. One of the kids would have the measles. I wouldn't be there. Another fall off a bike and get stitches in their chin. I wasn't there, and one of the ones — my oldest daughter, Patricia Rizzuto — Patricia. (*applause*) And then the next one is Cindy, Cynthia Rizzuto, Cindy. (*applause*) And then Penny, (*applause*) Penny Rizzuto, and the apple of my eye, Scooter. (*applause*) There he is, and Scooter's wife, Anne. (*applause*) Jennifer, Patty's daughter, one of my granddaughters, and that middle huckleberry right in the front, Margaret Carolina. (*applause*)

All right, this is it. Oh no — wait a minute. I got (*laughter*) I forgot my whole career as an announcer. But I think that's, that's best forgotten, because Howard Cosell told me the first week — he says, "You'll never last." He says, "You look like George Burns and sound like Groucho Marx." (*laughter*) So 38 years later I'm doing it my way and still here in broadcasting but . . . (*applause*) And they were right — I says, "You don't hear the score often or the game too often," but I think all my friends who like to have their name mentioned in the restaurants — I get a free meal. White knows that I do it that way and (*laughter*) — but I mean, I enjoy the game like that and that's why I was blessed with having — just like I had great partners on the radio as — you know — as my broadcast partners. Mel Allen I started with and of course, the guy who I did the greatest with and felt more at ease with, and had more fun with, was White. White was over there. He was introduced before. (*applause*) He didn't leave, did he? White — there he is. But I mean, really you're great. Now I got Murcer. Took me a while to learn that Oklahoma easy language, but now he's got it down pat and he's an excellent broadcaster. You know, it's a funny thing. Murcer and Mantle both came up as short-stops. You know, when Mickey came up — now this is ridiculous. I'm going from the end of my career back to the — you know, when Mantle came up I had my bags packed because I had heard about Mantle. He could out run a rabbit and hit the ball out of the moon — over the moon, over the moon, and I had won the MVP that year before and I had — I really thought they'd trade me but I saw Mickey trying to field grounders. He and Murcer were the same. As soon as I saw them try to field grounders, and they had to clear the — in back of the first baseman, had to get all of the people out of the stands because they were hitting them. (*laughter*) So they put Mickey in the outfield. He never played the outfield. They gave him a pair of sun glasses. He put them down. The first ball hit to him hit him right on the head. (*laughter*) But he turned out to be a pretty outstanding outfielder. What a ball player. (*applause*) Why, he could have won every award if he had two good legs.

Well, I'm on the last page. What — no, no — wait a minute. Take my time. No, really, you people have me but — all right — I mean, I'd stay up out here all day if my voice was good, no kidding. (*applause*)

Why don't all you huckleberries go back to the hotel? (*laughter*) Pee Wee is the first one to jump up. No, if you want to let these old timers go back to the hotel, go ahead and I'll just talk to the kids. Anyone wants to leave out there, (*laughter*), go ahead. I'll tell you, they take so many foul balls in . . . George Grande.

No, seriously, I better not, but — oh, I got them coming up on the last page. I got one now. This real dear friend of mine, Ruby Sabetino. Now, you know — ends in a vowel, any name that ends in a vowel I'll give a birthday to, but I wish a happy birthday and get well soon because Ruby is a little bit under the weather. She couldn't make the trip, and the canolis came last night and this morning. (*applause*) A day without the canolis is like a day without sunshine. I got to get off here. If one of you guys would just come and drag me physically off. I just . . . (*laughter*) No really, I just want to say, I have been the luckiest man in the world, and I talk about my family. I talked about my baseball career, broadcasting — is really — I'm embarrassed to get my paycheck. Not too embarrassed. I'll go and get it, but it's such an easy job. I mean — this guy White and the Murcer and Coleman and Seaver — I mean Seaver — unbelievable with Seaver. He should be someplace and he's sittin' up here. He should be out broadcasting games. He could be the Commissioner or the President of the American League or the National League. (*applause*) No, I'm telling you, he is a lot like White. They think things out before they say anything. No, my bride again told me that the reason I got in so much trouble — when you get a thought it's supposed to travel through your brain. You got a little trap door back here and then you say, "Should I or shouldn't I?" Okay, and you drop the thing. She says my trap door is open constantly so whatever I say could come out before I can think about it (*laughter*) and that's how I do get in trouble. But I really — the broadcast partners I have had, Mel Allen, the greatest voice of the Yankees, right on down the line. Every one of them that — and all the ball players I've played with — all the teammates I had, without them we wouldn't have gotten all those — I mean, after the DiMaggio era and Henrich and Berra, we had Mantle, the Bauers, the Woodlings, and Yogi, and who else?

I mean, we had — oh, on third base — wait a minute. All my third basemen had to be alert for any ball hit in a hole. I tried to teach these young kids today ball hit in the hole. Backhanded — throw it to the third baseman, let him throw the guy out. Of course, you know you've got them going away and the same way with the second baseman. For Brown, Dr. Bobby Brown, who's leaving the American League presidency in a little while, was at third. He had the great arm. Billy Johnson had a great arm, Andy Carey, another one who had a great arm, Gil McDougald. They were all — McDougald, outstanding ball player. Could play any position, Hall of Fame.

What? Oh, Clete Boyer? Well, I didn't play with Clete Boyer. No,

Clete Boyer is not dead. (*laughter*) Do you have the — when Bob came into the stadium, who did he tell it? Came into the stadium and he saw me and he was mad. He said, "I thought you were dead?" I said, "I'm not dead." He said, "I sent you a card, send it back to me." (*laughter*)

No, listen, one thing I want to do and no, I don't want to hear any boos on this now. A man who wants to win so badly that — and has been so wonderful to my family and myself and all the Yankee ball players — I just want to say thanks, George Steinbrenner. Thank you very much for all your help. (*applause*)

And I don't say that because I lead the league in days, I have had more days and always George comes through. As a matter of fact, I was supposed to have a day on August 13th. The strike came up and I said, "Hot dog, I won't have a day." George moved the day to the 9th. (*laughter*) So now we're going to have another day for me. But let me, let me just read this. I just want to — this is the only thing that I put down, that I wrote down.

I want to thank all of you who have been — let's see now — I don't want to start — I don't want to start crying. Now everybody comes up here — cries. I know it's not too bad if you do cry but you know all of you have been there for the most wonderful lifetime that one man can possibly have, and I just want to say, God bless all of you, and God bless this wonderful game that they call baseball.

Thank you very much. (*applause*)

Of all the players who have ever worn pinstripes, perhaps none is more beloved than Hall of Fame shortstop Phil Rizzuto. He set the table for the Yankee dynasty from 1941 to 1956, underscoring Yankee power with his defense and speed. Ty Cobb considered him one of the few players of the modern era who would have been a star during the Dead Ball Era.

After his playing career ended, Rizzuto, a Brooklyn native, endeared himself to New York fans as a broadcaster. His entertaining, meandering style of storytelling, punctuated by his signature call "Holy Cow!" and captured perfectly in his induction speech, made Yankee broadcasts worth listening to even when the team wasn't worthy of the attention.

THE SILENT SEASON OF A HERO

from *Esquire*, July 1966

"I would like to take the great DiMaggio fishing," the old man said. "They say his father was a fisherman. Maybe he was as poor as we are and would understand."

— Ernest Hemingway, *The Old Man and the Sea*

It was not quite spring, the silent season before the search for salmon, and the old fishermen of San Francisco were either painting their boats or repairing their nets along the pier or sitting in the sun talking quietly among themselves, watching the tourists come and go, and smiling, now, as a pretty girl paused to take their picture. She was about 25, healthy and blue-eyed and wearing a turtleneck sweater, and she had long, flowing blonde hair that she brushed back a few times before clicking her camera. The fishermen, looking at her, made admiring comments, but she did not understand because they spoke a Sicilian dialect; nor did she understand the tall gray-haired man in a dark suit who stood watching her from behind a big bay window on the second floor of DiMaggio's Restaurant that overlooks the pier.

He watched until she left, lost in the crowd of newly arrived tourists that had just come down the hill by cable car. Then he sat down again at the table in the restaurant, finishing his tea and lighting another cigarette, his fifth in the last half hour. It was 11:30 in the morning. None of the other tables was occupied, and the only sounds came from the bar, where a liquor salesman was laughing at something the headwaiter had said. But then the salesman, his brief-case under his arm, headed for the door, stopping briefly to peek into the dining room and call out, "See you later, Joe." Joe DiMaggio turned and waved at the salesman. Then the room was quiet again.

At 51, DiMaggio was a most distinguished-looking man, aging as gracefully as he had played on the ball field, impeccable in his tailoring, his nails manicured, his 6-foot-2 body seeming as lean and capable as when he posed for the portrait that hangs in the restaurant and shows him in Yankee Stadium, swinging from the heels at a pitch thrown 20 years ago. His gray hair was thinning at the crown, but just barely, and his face was lined in the right places, and his expression, once as sad and haunted as a matador's, was more in repose these days, though, as now, tension had returned and he chain-smoked and occasionally paced the floor and looked out the window at the people below. In the crowd was a man he did not wish to see.

The man had met DiMaggio in New York. This week he had come to San Francisco and had telephoned several times, but none of the calls had been returned because DiMaggio suspected that the man, who had said he was doing research on some vague sociological project, really wanted to delve into DiMaggio's private life and that of DiMaggio's former wife, Marilyn Monroe. DiMaggio would never tolerate this. The memory of her death is still very painful to him, and yet, because he keeps it to himself, some people are not sensitive to it. One night in a supper club, a woman who had been drinking approached his table, and when he did not ask her to join him, she snapped:

"All right, I guess I'm *not* Marilyn Monroe."

He ignored her remark, but when she repeated it, he replied, barely controlling his anger, "No — I wish you were, but you're not."

The tone of his voice softened her, and she asked, "Am I saying something wrong?"

"You already have," he said. "Now will you please leave me alone?"

His friends on the wharf, understanding him as they do, are very careful when discussing him with strangers, knowing that should they inadvertently betray a confidence, he will not denounce them but rather will never speak to them again; this comes from a sense of propriety not inconsistent in the man who also, after Marilyn Monroe's death, directed that fresh flowers be placed on her grave "forever."

Some of the older fishermen who have known DiMaggio all his life remember him as a small boy who helped clean his father's boat, and as a young man who sneaked away and used a broken oar as a bat on the sandlots nearby. His father, a small mustachioed man known as Zio Pepe, would become infuriated and call him *lagnuso,* lazy, *meschino,* good-for-nothing, but in 1936 Zio Pepe was among those who cheered when Joe DiMaggio returned to San Francisco after his first season with the New York Yankees and was carried along the wharf on the shoulders of the fishermen.

The fishermen also remember how, after his retirement in 1951, DiMaggio brought his second wife, Marilyn, to live near the wharf, and sometimes they would be seen early in the morning fishing off DiMaggio's boat, the *Yankee Clipper,* now docked quietly in the marina, and in the evening they would be sitting and talking on the pier. They had arguments, too, the fishermen knew, and one night Marilyn was seen running hysterically, crying, as she ran, along the road away from the pier, with Joe following. But the fishermen pretended they did not see this; it was none of their affair. They knew that Joe wanted her to stay in San Francisco and avoid the sharks in Hollywood, but she was confused and torn then — "She was a child," they said — and even today DiMaggio loathes Los Angeles and many of the people in it. He no longer speaks to his onetime friend, Frank Sinatra, who had befriended Marilyn in her final years, and he also is cool to Dean Martin and Peter Lawford and Lawford's former wife, Pat, who once gave a party at which she introduced Marilyn Monroe to Robert Kennedy, and the two of them danced often that night, Joe heard, and he did not take it well. He was possessive of her that year, his close friends say, because Marilyn and he had planned to remarry; but before they could she was dead, and DiMaggio banned the Lawfords and Sinatra and many Hollywood people from her funeral. When Marilyn Monroe's attorney complained that DiMaggio was keeping her friends away, DiMaggio answered coldly, "If it weren't for those friends persuading her to stay in Hollywood, she would still be alive."

Joe DiMaggio now spends most of the year in San Francisco, and each day tourists, noticing the name on the restaurant, ask the men on the wharf if they ever see him. Oh, yes, the men say, they see him nearly every day; they have not seen him yet this morning, they add, but he should be arriving shortly. So the tourists continue to walk along the piers past the crab vendors, under the circling sea gulls, past the fish-'n'-chip stands, sometimes stopping to watch a large vessel steaming toward the Golden Gate Bridge, which, to their dismay, is painted red. Then they visit the Wax Museum, where there is a life-size figure of DiMaggio in uniform, and walk across the street and spend a quarter to peer through the silver telescopes focused on the island of Alcatraz, which is no longer a federal prison. Then they return to ask the men if DiMaggio has been seen. Not yet, the men say, although they notice his blue Impala parked in the lot next to the restaurant. Sometimes tourists will walk into the restaurant and have lunch and will see him sitting calmly in a corner signing autographs and being extremely gracious with everyone. At other times, as on this particular morning when the man from New York chose to visit, DiMaggio was tense and suspicious.

When the man entered the restaurant from the side steps leading to the dining room, he saw DiMaggio standing near the window, talking with an elderly maître d' named Charles Friscia. Not wanting to walk in and risk intrusion, the man asked one of DiMaggio's nephews to inform Joe of his presence. When DiMaggio got the message, he quickly turned and left Friscia and disappeared through an exit leading down to the kitchen.

Astonished and confused, the visitor stood in the hall. A moment later Friscia appeared and the man asked, "Did Joe leave?"

"Joe who?" Friscia replied.

"Joe DiMaggio!"

"Haven't seen him," Friscia said.

"You haven't *seen* him! He was standing right next to you a second ago!"

"It wasn't me," Friscia said.

"You were standing next to him. I saw you. In the dining room."

"You must be mistaken," Friscia said, softly, seriously. "It wasn't me."

"You *must* be kidding," the man said angrily, turning and leaving the restaurant. Before he could get to his car, however, DiMaggio's nephew came running after him and said, "Joe wants to see you."

He returned, expecting to see DiMaggio waiting for him. Instead, he was handed a telephone. The voice was powerful and deep and so tense that the quick sentences ran together.

"You are invading my rights. I did not ask you to come. I assume you have a lawyer. You must have a lawyer, get your lawyer!"

"I came as a friend," the man interrupted.

"That's beside the point," DiMaggio said. "I have my privacy. I do not want it violated. You'd better get a lawyer. . . ." Then, pausing, DiMaggio asked, "Is my nephew there?"

He was not.

"Then wait where you are."

A moment later DiMaggio appeared, tall and red-faced, erect and beautifully dressed in his dark suit and white shirt with the gray silk tie and the gleaming silver cuff links. He moved with his big steps toward the man and handed him an airmail envelope unopened that the man had written from New York.

"Here," DiMaggio said. "This is yours."

Then DiMaggio sat down at a small table. He said nothing, just lit a cigarette and waited, legs crossed, his head held high and back so as to reveal the intricate construction of his nose, a fine sharp tip above the big nostrils and tiny bones built out from the bridge, a great nose.

"Look," DiMaggio said, more calmly, "I do not interfere with other people's lives. And I do not expect them to interfere with mine. There are things about my life, personal things, that I refuse to talk about. And even if you asked my brothers, they would be unable to tell you about them because they do not know. There are things about me, so many things, that they simply do not know. . . ."

"I don't want to cause trouble," the man said. "I think you're a great man, and . . ."

"I'm not great," DiMaggio cut in. "I'm not great," he repeated softly. "I'm just a man trying to get along."

Then DiMaggio, as if realizing that he was intruding upon his own privacy, abruptly stood up. He looked at his watch.

"I'm late," he said, very formal again. "I'm 10 minutes late. You're making me late."

The man left the restaurant. He crossed the street and wandered over to the pier, briefly watching the fishermen hauling their nets and talking in the sun, seemingly very calm and contented. Then, after he turned and was headed back toward the parking lot, a blue Impala stopped in front of him and Joe DiMaggio leaned out the window and asked, "Do you have a car?" His voice was very gentle.

"Yes," the man said.

"Oh," DiMaggio said. "I would have given you a ride."

Joe DiMaggio was not born in San Francisco but in Martinez, a small fishing village 25 miles northeast of the Golden Gate. Zio Pepe had settled there after leaving Isola delle Femmine, an islet off Palermo where the DiMaggios had been fishermen for generations. But in 1915, hearing of the luckier waters off San Francisco's wharf, Zio Pepe left Martinez, packing his boat with furniture and family, including Joe, who was one year old.

San Francisco was placid and picturesque when the DiMaggios arrived, but there was a competitive undercurrent and struggle for power along the pier. At dawn the boats would sail out to where the bay meets the ocean and the sea is rough, and later the men would race back with their hauls, hoping to beat their fellow fishermen to shore and sell it while they could. Twenty or 30 boats would sometimes be trying to gain the channel shoreward at the same time, and a fisherman had to know every rock in the water, and later know every bargaining trick along the shore, because the dealers and restaurateurs would play one fisherman off against the other, keeping the prices down. Later the fishermen became wiser and organized, predetermining the maximum amount each fisherman would catch, but there were always some men who, like the fish, never learned, and so heads would sometimes be broken, nets slashed, gasoline poured onto their fish, flowers of warning placed outside their doors.

But these days were ending when Zio Pepe arrived, and he expected his five sons to succeed him as fishermen, and the first two, Tom and Michael, did; but a third, Vincent, wanted to sing. He sang with such magnificent power as a young man that he came to the attention of the great banker, A. P. Giannini, and there were plans to send him to Italy for tutoring and the opera. But there was hesitation around the DiMaggio household and Vince never went; instead, he played ball with the San Francisco Seals and sports writers misspelled his name.

It was DeMaggio until Joe, at Vince's recommendation, joined the team and became a sensation, being followed later by the youngest brother, Dominic, who was also outstanding. All three later played in the big leagues, and some writers like to say that Joe was the best hitter, Dom the best fielder, Vince the best singer, and Casey Stengel once said: "Vince is the only player I ever saw who could strike out three times in one game and not be embarrassed. He'd walk into the clubhouse whistling. Everybody would be feeling sorry for him, but Vince always thought he was doing good."

After he retired from baseball Vince became a bartender, then a milkman, now a carpenter. He lives 40 miles north of San Francisco in a house he partly built, has been happily married for 34 years, has four grandchildren, has in the closet one of Joe's tailor-made suits that he has never had altered to fit, and when people ask him if he envies Joe he always says, "No, maybe Joe would like to have what I have." The brother Vincent most admired was Michael, "a big earthy man, a dreamer, a fisherman who wanted things but didn't want to take from Joe, or to work in the restaurant. He wanted a bigger boat, but wanted to earn it on his own. He never got it." In 1953, at the age of 44, Michael fell from his boat and drowned.

Since Zio Pepe's death at 77 in 1949, Tom at 62, the oldest brother — two of his four sisters are older — has become nominal head of the family and manages the restaurant that was opened in 1937 as Joe DiMaggio's Grotto. Later Joe sold out his share, and now Tom is the co-owner with Dominic. Of all the brothers, Dominic, who was known as the "Little Professor" when he played with the Boston Red Sox, is the most successful in business. He lives in a fashionable Boston suburb with his wife and three children and is president of a firm that manufactures fiber cushion materials and grossed more than $3,500,000 last year.

Joe DiMaggio lives with his widowed sister, Marie, in a tan stone house on a quiet residential street not far from Fisherman's Wharf. He bought the house almost 30 years ago for his parents, and after their deaths he lived there with Marilyn Monroe. Now it is cared for by Marie, a slim and handsome dark-eyed woman who has an apartment on the second floor, Joe on the third. There are some baseball trophies and plaques in the small room off DiMaggio's bedroom, and on his dresser are photographs of Marilyn Monroe, and in the living room downstairs is a small painting of her that DiMaggio likes very much; it reveals only her face and shoulders and she is wearing a wide-brimmed sun hat, and there is a soft, sweet smile on her lips, an innocent curiosity about her that is the way he saw her and the way he wanted her to be seen by others — a simple girl, "a warm, big-hearted girl," he once described her, "that everybody took advantage of."

The publicity photographs emphasizing her sex appeal often offend him, and a memorable moment for Billy Wilder, who directed her in *The Seven-Year Itch*, occurred when he spotted DiMaggio in a large crowd of people gathered on Lexington Avenue in New York to watch a scene in which Marilyn, standing over a subway grating to cool herself, had her skirts blown high by a sudden wind blow. "What the hell is going on here?" DiMaggio was overheard to have said in the crowd, and Wilder recalled, "I shall never forget the look of death on Joe's face."

He was then 39, she was 27. They had been married in January of that year, 1954, despite disharmony in temperament and time; he was tired of publicity, she was thriving on it; he was intolerant of tardiness, she was always late. During their honeymoon in Tokyo an American general had introduced himself and asked if, as a patriotic gesture, she would visit the troops in Korea. She looked at Joe. "It's your honeymoon," he said, shrugging, "go ahead if you want to."

She appeared on 10 occasions before 100,000 servicemen, and when she returned, she said, "It was so wonderful, Joe. You never heard such cheering."

"Yes, I have," he said.

Across from her portrait in the living room, on a coffee table in front of a sofa, is a sterling-silver humidor that was presented to him by his Yankee teammates at a time when he was the most talked-about man in America, and when Les Brown's band had recorded a hit that was heard day and night on the radio.

> From Coast to Coast, that's all you hear
>   Of Joe the One-Man Show.
> He's glorified the horsehide sphere,
>   Jolting Joe DiMaggio . . .
> Joe . . . Joe . . . DiMaggio . . . we
> want you on our side . . .

The year was 1941, and it began for DiMaggio in the middle of May after the Yankees had lost four games in a row, seven of their last nine, and were in fourth place, five and a half games behind the leading Cleveland Indians. On May 15, DiMaggio hit only a first-inning single in a game that New York lost to Chicago 13–1; he was barely hitting .300, and had greatly disappointed the crowds that had seen him finish with a .352 average the year before and .381 in 1939.

He got a hit in the next game, and the next, and the next. On May 24, with the Yankees losing 6–5 to Boston, DiMaggio came up with runners on second and third and singled them home, winning the game, extending his streak to 10 games. But it went largely unnoticed. Even DiMaggio was not conscious of it until it had reached 29 games in mid-June. Then the newspapers began to dramatize it, the public became aroused, they sent him good-luck charms of every description, and DiMaggio kept hitting, and radio announcers would interrupt programs to announce the news, and then the song again: "Joe . . . Joe . . . DiMaggio . . . we want you on our side . . ."

Sometimes DiMaggio would be hitless his first three times up, the tension would build, it would appear that the game would end without his getting another chance — but he always would, and then he would hit the ball against the left-field wall, or through the pitcher's legs, or between two leaping infielders. In the forty-first game, the first of a doubleheader in Washington, DiMaggio tied an American League record that George Sisler had set in 1922. But before the second game began, a spectator sneaked onto the field and into the Yankees' dugout and stole DiMaggio's favorite bat. In the second game, using another of his bats, DiMaggio lined out twice and flied out. But in the seventh inning, borrowing one of his old bats that a teammate was using, he singled and broke Sisler's record, and he was only three games away from surpassing the major-league record of 44 set in 1897 by Willie Keeler while playing for Baltimore when it was a National League franchise.

An appeal for the missing bat was made through the newspapers. A man from Newark admitted the crime and returned it with regrets. And on July 2 at Yankee Stadium, DiMaggio hit a home run into the left-field stands. The record was broken.

He also got hits in the next 11 games, but on July 17 in Cleveland, at a night game attended by 67,468, he failed against two pitchers, Al

Smith and Jim Bagby, Jr., although Cleveland's hero was really its
third baseman, Ken Keltner, who in the first inning lunged to his
right to make a spectacular backhanded stop of a drive and, from
the foul line behind third base, threw DiMaggio out. DiMaggio received a walk in the fourth inning. But in the seventh he again hit
a hard shot at Keltner, who again stopped it and threw him out.
DiMaggio hit sharply toward the shortstop in the eighth inning,
the ball taking a bad hop, but Lou Boudreau speared it off his shoulder and threw to the second baseman to start a double play and
DiMaggio's streak was stopped at 56 games. But the New York Yankees were on their way to winning the pennant by 17 games, and the
World Series too, and so in August, in a hotel suite in Washington,
the players threw a surprise party for DiMaggio and toasted him
with champagne and presented him with his Tiffany silver humidor
that is now in San Francisco in his living room. . . .

Marie was in the kitchen making toast and tea when DiMaggio
came down for breakfast; his gray hair was uncombed but, since he
wears it short, it was not untidy. He said good morning to Marie, sat
down, and yawned. He lit a cigarette. He wore a blue wool bathrobe
over his pajamas. It was 8:00 A.M. He had many things to do today
and he seemed cheerful. He had a conference with the president of
Continental Television, Inc., a large retail chain in California of
which he is a partner and vice-president; later he had a golf date,
and then a big banquet to attend, and, if that did not go on too long
and if he were not too tired afterward, he might have a date.

Picking up the morning paper, not rushing to the sports page,
DiMaggio read the front-page news, the people problems of 1966;
Kwame Nkrumah was overthrown in Ghana, students were burning
their draft cards (DiMaggio shook his head), the flu epidemic was
spreading through the whole state of California. Then he flipped inside through the gossip columns, thankful they did not have him in
there today — they had printed an item about his dating "an electri-
fying airline hostess" not long ago, and they also spotted him at dinner with Dori Lane, "the frantic frugger" in Whisky à Go Go's glass
cage — and then he turned to the sports page and read a story about
how the injured Mickey Mantle may never regain his form.

It happened all so quickly, the passing of Mantle, or so it seemed;

he had succeeded DiMaggio, who had succeeded Ruth, but now there was no great young power hitter coming up, and the Yankee management, almost desperate, had talked Mantle out of retirement, and on September 18, 1965, they gave him a "day" in New York during which he received several thousand dollars' worth of gifts — an automobile, two quarter horses, free vacation trips to Rome, Nassau, Puerto Rico — and DiMaggio had flown to New York to make the introduction before 50,000: it had been a dramatic day, an almost holy day for the believers who had jammed the grandstands early to witness the canonization of a new stadium saint. Cardinal Spellman was on the committee, President Johnson sent a telegram, the day was officially proclaimed by the Mayor of New York, an orchestra assembled in the center field in front of the trinity of monuments to Ruth, Gehrig, Huggins; and high in the grandstands, billowing in the breeze of early autumn, were white banners that read: "Don't Quit, Mick," "We Love the Mick."

The banner had been held by hundreds of young boys whose dreams had been fulfilled so often by Mantle, but also seated in the grandstands were older men, paunchy and balding, in whose middle-aged minds DiMaggio was still vivid and invincible, and some of them remembered how one month before, during a pregame exhibition at Old-Timers' Day in Yankee Stadium, DiMaggio had hit a pitch into the left-field seats, and suddenly thousands of people had jumped wildly to their feet, joyously screaming — the great DiMaggio had returned, they were young again, it was yesterday.

But on this sunny September day at the stadium, the feast day of Mickey Mantle, DiMaggio was not wearing No. 5 on his back or a black cap to cover his graying hair; he was wearing a black suit and white shirt and blue tie, and he stood in one corner of the Yankees' dugout waiting to be introduced by Red Barber, who was standing near home plate behind a silver microphone. In the outfield Guy Lombardo's Royal Canadians were playing soothing, soft music; and moving slowly back and forth over the sprawling green grass between the left-field bullpen and the infield were two carts driven by grounds keepers and containing dozens and dozens of large gifts for Mantle — a 6-foot, 100-pound Hebrew National salami, a Winchester rifle, a mink coat for Mrs. Mantle, a set of Wilson golf clubs, a year's supply of Chunky Candy. DiMaggio smoked a cigarette, but cupped it in his hands as if not wanting to be caught in the act by teen-aged boys near enough to peek down into the dugout. Then, edging forward a step, DiMaggio poked his head out and looked up. He could see nothing above except the packed, towering green grandstands that seemed a mile high and moving, and he could see no clouds or blue sky, only a sky of faces. Then the announcer called out his name — *"Joe DiMaggio!"* — and suddenly there was a blast of cheering that grew louder and louder, echoing and reechoing within the big steel canyon, and DiMaggio stomped out his cigarette and climbed up the dugout steps and onto the soft green grass, the noise resounding in his ears, he could almost feel the breeze, the breath of 50,000 lungs upon him, 100,000 eyes watching his every move, and for the briefest instant as he walked he closed his eyes.

Then in his path he saw Mickey Mantle's mother, a smiling woman wearing an orchid, and he gently reached out for her elbow, holding it as he led her toward the microphone next to the other dignitaries lined up on the infield. Then he stood, very erect and without expression as the cheers softened and the stadium settled down.

Mantle was still in the dugout, in uniform, standing with one leg on the top step, and lined on both sides of him were the other Yankees who, when the ceremony was over, would play the Detroit Tigers. Then into the dugout, smiling, came Senator Robert Kennedy, accompanied by two tall curly-haired assistants with blue eyes, Fordham freckles. Jim Farley was the first on the field to notice the Senator, and Farley muttered, loud enough for others to hear, "Who the hell invited *him?*"

Toots Shor and some of the other committeemen standing near Farley looked into the dugout, and so did DiMaggio, his glance seeming cold, but he remained silent. Kennedy walked up and down within the dugout, shaking hands with the Yankees, but he did not walk onto the field.

"Senator," said Yankees' manager Johnny Keane, "why don't you sit down?" Kennedy quickly shook his head, smiled. He remained standing, and then one Yankee came over and asked about getting relatives out of Cuba, and Kennedy called over one of his aides to take down the details in a notebook.

On the infield the ceremony went on, Mantle's gifts continued to pile up — a Mobilette motorbike, a Sooner Schooner wagon barbecue, a year's supply of Chock Full O' Nuts coffee, a year's supply of Topps Chewing Gum — and the Yankee players watched, and Maris seemed glum.

"Hey, Rog," yelled a man with a tape recorder, Murray Olderman, "I want to do a 30-second tape with you."

Maris swore angrily, shook his head.

"Why don't you ask Richardson? He's a better talker than me."

"Yes, but the fact that it comes from you . . ."

Maris swore again. But finally he went over and said in an interview that Mantle was the finest player of his era, a great competitor, a great hitter.

Fifteen minutes later, standing behind the microphone at home plate, DiMaggio was telling the crowd, "I'm proud to introduce the man who succeeded me in center field in 1951," and from every corner of the stadium, the cheering, whistling, clapping came down. Mantle stepped forward. He stood with his wife and children, posed for the photographers kneeling in front. Then he thanked the crowd in a short speech, and, turning, shook hands with the dignitaries standing nearby. Among them now was Senator Kennedy, who had been spotted in the dugout five minutes before by Red Barber, and been called out and introduced. Kennedy posed with Mantle for a photographer, then shook hands with the Mantle children, and with Toots Shor and James Farley and others. DiMaggio saw him coming down the line and at the last second he backed away, casually, hardly anybody noticing it, and Kennedy seemed not to notice it either, just swept past, shaking more hands. . . .

Finishing his tea, putting aside the newspaper, DiMaggio went upstairs to dress, and soon he was waving good-bye to Marie and driving toward his business appointment in downtown San Francisco with his partners in the retail television business. DiMaggio, while not a millionaire, has invested wisely and has always had, since his retirement from baseball, executive positions with big companies that have paid him well. He also was among the organizers of the Fisherman's National Bank of San Francisco last year, and, though it never came about, he demonstrated an acuteness that impressed those businessmen who had thought of him only in terms of baseball. He has had offers to manage big-league baseball teams but always has rejected them, saying, "I have enough trouble taking care of my own problems without taking on the responsibilities of 25 ball players."

So his only contact with baseball these days, excluding public appearances, is his unsalaried job as a batting coach each spring in Florida with the New York Yankees, a trip he would make once again on the following Sunday, three days away, if he could accomplish what for him is always the dreaded responsibility of packing, a task made no easier by the fact that he lately had fallen into the habit of keeping his clothes in two places — some hang in his closet at home, some hang in the back room of a saloon called Reno's.

Reno's is a dimly lit bar in the center of San Francisco. A portrait of DiMaggio swinging a bat hangs on the wall, in addition to portraits of other star athletes, and the clientele consists mainly of the sporting crowd and newspapermen, people who know DiMaggio quite well and around whom he speaks freely on a number of subjects and relaxes as he can in few other places. The owner of the bar is Reno Barsocchini, a broad-shouldered and handsome man of 51 with graying wavy hair who began as a fiddler in Dago Mary's tavern 35 years ago. He later became a bartender there and elsewhere, including DiMaggio's Restaurant, and now he is probably DiMaggio's closest friend. He was the best man at the DiMaggio-Monroe wedding in 1954, and when they separated nine months later in Los Angeles, Reno rushed down to help DiMaggio with the packing and drove him back to San Francisco. Reno will never forget the day.

Hundreds of people were gathered around the Beverly Hills home that DiMaggio and Marilyn had rented, and photographers were perched in the trees watching the windows, and others stood on the lawn and behind the rose bushes waiting to snap pictures of anybody who walked out of the house. The newspapers that day played all the puns — "Joe Fanned on Jealousy"; "Marilyn and Joe — Out at Home" — and the Hollywood columnists, to whom DiMaggio was never an idol, never a gracious host, recounted instances of incompatibility, and Oscar Levant said it all proved that no man could be a success in two national pastimes. When Reno Barsocchini arrived, he had to push his way through the mob, then bang on the door for several minutes before being admitted. Marilyn Monroe was upstairs in bed. Joe DiMaggio was downstairs with his suitcases, tense and pale, his eyes bloodshot.

Reno took the suitcase and golf clubs out to DiMaggio's car, and then DiMaggio came out of the house, the reporters moving toward him, the lights flashing.

"Where are you going?" they yelled.

"I'm driving to San Francisco," he said, walking quickly.

"Is that going to be your home?"

"That is my home and always has been."

"Are you coming back?"

DiMaggio turned for a moment, looking up at the house.

"No," he said, "I'll never be back."

Reno Barsocchini, except for a brief falling-out over something he will not discuss, has been DiMaggio's trusted companion ever since, joining him whenever he can on the golf course or on the town, otherwise waiting for him in the bar with other middle-aged men. They may wait for hours sometimes, waiting and knowing that when he arrives he may wish to be alone; but it does not seem to matter, they are endlessly awed by him, moved by the mystique, he is a kind of male Garbo. They know that he can be warm and loyal if they are sensitive to his wishes, but they must never be late for an appointment to meet him. One man, unable to find a parking place, arrived a half hour late once, and DiMaggio did not talk to him again for three months. They know, too, when dining at night with DiMaggio, that he generally prefers male companions and occasionally one or two young women, but never wives; wives gossip, wives complain, wives are trouble, and men wishing to remain close to DiMaggio must keep their wives at home.

When DiMaggio strolls into Reno's bar, the men wave and call out his name and Reno Barsocchini smiles and announces, "Here's the Clipper!" — the "Yankee Clipper" being a nickname from his baseball days.

"Hey Clipper, Clipper," Reno had said two nights before, "where you been, Clipper? . . . Clipper, how 'bout a belt?"

DiMaggio refused the offer of a drink, ordering instead a pot of tea, which he prefers to all other beverages except before a date, when he will switch to vodka.

"Hey, Joe," a sports writer asked, a man researching a magazine piece on golf, "why is it that a golfer, when he starts getting older, loses his putting touch first? Like Snead and Hogan, they can still hit a ball well off the tee, but on the greens they lose the strokes."

"It's the pressure of age," DiMaggio said, turning around on his barstool. "With age you get jittery. It's true of golfers, it's true of any man when he gets into his 50s. He doesn't take chances like he used to. The younger golfer, on the greens, he'll stroke his putts better. The older man, he becomes hesitant. A little uncertain. Shaky. When it comes to taking chances, the younger man, even when driving a car, will take chances that the older man won't."

"Speaking of chances," another man said, one of the group that had gathered around DiMaggio, "did you see that guy on crutches in here last night?"

"Yeah, had his leg in a cast," a third said. "Skiing."

"I would never ski," DiMaggio said. "Men who ski must be doing it to impress a broad. You see these men, some of them 40, 50, getting onto skis. And later you see them all bandaged up, broken legs."

"But skiing's a very sexy sport, Joe. All the clothes, the tight pants, the fireplaces in the ski lodge, the bear rug — Christ, nobody goes to ski. They just go out there to get it cold so they can warm it up."

"Maybe you're right," DiMaggio said. "I might be persuaded."

"Want a belt, Clipper?" Reno asked.

DiMaggio thought for a second, then said, "All right — first belt tonight."

Now it was noon, a warm sunny day. DiMaggio's business meeting with the television retailers had gone well; he had made a strong appeal to George Shahood, president of Continental Television, Inc., which has eight retail outlets in Northern California, to put prices on color television sets and increase the sales volume, and Shahood had conceded it was worth a try. Then DiMaggio called Reno's bar to see if there were any messages, and now he was in Lefty O'Doul's car being driven along Fisherman's Wharf toward the Golden Gate Bridge en route to a golf course 30 miles upstate. Lefty O'Doul was one of the great hitters in the National League in the early thirties, and later he managed the San Francisco Seals when DiMaggio was the shining star. Though O'Doul is now 69, 18 years older than DiMaggio, he nevertheless possesses great energy and spirit, is a hard-drinking, boisterous man with a big belly and roving eye; and when DiMaggio, as they drove along the highway toward the golf club, noticed a lovely blonde at the wheel of a car nearby and exclaimed, "Look at *that* tomato!" O'Doul's head suddenly spun around, he took his eyes off the road, and yelled, "Where, *where?*" O'Doul's golf game is less than what it was — he used to have a two-handicap — but he still shoots in the 80s, as does DiMaggio.

DiMaggio's drives range between 250 and 280 yards when he doesn't sky them, and his putting is good, but he is distracted by a bad back that both pains him and hinders the fullness of his swing. On the first hole, waiting to tee off, DiMaggio sat back watching a foursome of college boys ahead swinging with such freedom. "Oh," he said with a sigh, "to have *their* backs."

DiMaggio and O'Doul were accompanied around the golf course by Ernie Nevers, the former football star, and two brothers who are in the hotel and movie-distribution business. They moved quickly up and down the green hills in electric golf carts, and DiMaggio's game was exceptionally good for the first nine holes. But then he seemed distracted, perhaps tired, perhaps even reacting to a conversation of a few minutes before. One of the movie men was praising the film *Boeing, Boeing,* starring Tony Curtis and Jerry Lewis, and the man asked DiMaggio if he had seen it.

"No," DiMaggio said. Then he added, swiftly, "I haven't seen a film in eight years."

DiMaggio hooked a few shots, was in the woods. He took a No. 9 iron and tried to chip out. But O'Doul interrupted DiMaggio's concentration to remind him to keep the face of the club closed. DiMaggio hit the ball. It caromed off the side of his club, went skipping like a rabbit through the high grass down toward a pond. DiMaggio rarely displays any emotion on a golf course, but now, without saying a word, he took his No. 9 iron and flung it into the air. The club landed in a tree and stayed up there.

"Well," O'Doul said casually, "there goes *that* set of clubs."

DiMaggio walked to the tree. Fortunately the club had slipped to the lower branch, and DiMaggio could stretch up on the cart and get it back.

"Every time I get advice," DiMaggio muttered to himself, shaking his head slowly and walking toward the pond, "I shank it."

Later, showered and dressed, DiMaggio and the others drove to a banquet about 10 miles from the golf course. Somebody had said it was going to be an elegant dinner, but when they arrived they could see it was more like a county fair; farmers were gathered outside a big barnlike building, a candidate for sheriff was distributing leaflets at the front door, and a chorus of homely ladies was inside singing "You Are My Sunshine."

"How did we get sucked into this?" DiMaggio asked, talking out of the side of his mouth, as they approached the building.

"O'Doul," one of the men said. "It's his fault. Damned O'Doul can't turn *anything* down."

"Go to hell," O'Doul said.

Soon DiMaggio and O'Doul and Ernie Nevers were surrounded by the crowd, and the woman who had been leading the chorus came rushing over and said, "Oh, Mr. DiMaggio, it certainly is a pleasure having you."

"It's a pleasure being here, ma'am," he said, forcing a smile.

"It's too bad you didn't arrive a moment sooner. You'd have heard our singing."

"Oh, I heard it," he said, "and I enjoyed it very much."

"Good, good," she said. "And how are your brothers, Dom and Vic?"

"Fine. Dom lives near Boston. Vince is in Pittsburgh."

"Why, *hello* there, Joe," interrupted a man with wine on his breath, patting DiMaggio on the back, feeling his arm. "Who's gonna take it this year, Joe?"

"Well, I have no idea," DiMaggio said.

"What about the Giants?"

"Your guess is as good as mine."

"Well, you can't count the Dodgers out," the man said.

"You sure can't," DiMaggio said.

"Not with all that pitching."

"Pitching is certainly important," DiMaggio said.

Everywhere he goes the question seems the same, as if he has some special vision into the future of new heroes, and everywhere he goes, too, older men grab his hand and feel his arm and predict that he could still go out there and hit one, and the smile on DiMaggio's face is genuine. He tries hard to remain as he was — he diets, he takes steambaths, he is careful; and flabby men in the locker rooms of golf clubs sometimes steal peeks at him when he steps out of the shower, observing the tight muscles across his chest, the flat stomach, the long sinewy legs. He has a young man's body, very pale and little hair; his face is dark and lined, however, parched by the sun of several seasons. Still he is always an impressive figure at banquets such as this — an "immortal" sports writers called him, and that is how they have written about him and others like him, rarely suggesting that such heroes might ever be prone to the ills of mortal men, carousing, drinking, scheming; to suggest this would destroy the myth, would disillusion small boys, would infuriate rich men who own ball clubs and to whom baseball is a business dedicated to profit and in pursuit of which they trade mediocre players' flesh as casually as boys trade players' pictures on bubble-gum cards. And so the baseball hero must always act the part, must preserve the myth, and none does it better than DiMaggio, none is more patient when drunken old men grab an arm and ask, "Who's gonna take it this year, Joe?"

Two hours later, dinner and the speeches over, DiMaggio was slumped in O'Doul's car headed back to San Francisco. He edged himself up, however, when O'Doul pulled into a gas station in which a pretty red-haired girl sat on a stool, legs crossed, filing her fingernails. She was about 22, wore a tight black skirt and tighter white blouse.

"Look at *that*," DiMaggio said.

"Yeah," O'Doul said.

O'Doul turned away when a young man approached, opened the gas tank, began wiping the windshield. The young man wore a greasy white uniform on the front of which was printed the name "Burt." DiMaggio kept looking at the girl, but she was not distracted from her fingernails. Then he looked at Burt, who did not recognize him. When the tank was full, O'Doul paid and drove off. Burt returned to his girl; DiMaggio slumped down in the front seat and did not open his eyes again until they arrived in San Francisco.

"Let's go see Reno," DiMaggio said.

"No, I gotta go see my old lady," O'Doul said. So he dropped DiMaggio off in front of the bar, and a moment later Reno's voice was announcing in the smoky room, "Hey, here's the Clipper!" The men waved and offered to buy him a drink. DiMaggio ordered a vodka and sat for an hour at the bar talking to a half-dozen men around him. Then a blonde girl who had been with friends at the other end of the bar came over, and somebody introduced her to DiMaggio. He bought her a drink, offered her a cigarette. Then he struck a match and held it. His hand was unsteady.

"Is that me that's shaking?" he asked.

"It must be," said the blonde. "I'm calm."

Two nights later, having collected his clothes out of Reno's back room, DiMaggio boarded a jet; he slept crossways on three seats, then came down the steps as the sun began to rise in Miami. He claimed his luggage and golf clubs, put them into the trunk of a waiting automobile, and less than an hour later he was being driven into Fort Lauderdale, past palm-lined streets, toward the Yankee Clipper Hotel.

"All my life it seems I've been on the road traveling," he said, squinting through the windshield into the sun. "I never get a sense of being in any one place."

Arriving at the Yankee Clipper Hotel, DiMaggio checked into the largest suite. People rushed through the lobby to shake hands with him, to ask for his autograph, to say, "Joe, you look great." And early the next morning, and for the next 30 mornings, DiMaggio arrived punctually at the baseball park and wore his uniform with the famous No. 5, and the tourists seated in the sunny grandstands clapped when he first appeared on the field each time, and then they watched with nostalgia as he picked up a bat and played "pepper" with the younger Yankees, some of whom were not even born when, 25 years ago this summer, he hit in 56 straight games and became the most celebrated man in America.

But the younger spectators in the Fort Lauderdale park, and the sports writers, too, were more interested in Mantle and Maris, and nearly every day there were news dispatches reporting how Mantle and Maris felt, what they did, what they said, even though they said and did very little except walk around the field frowning when photographers asked for another picture and when sports writers asked how they felt.

After seven days of this, the big day arrived — Mantle and Maris would swing a bat — and a dozen sports writers were gathered around the big batting cage that was situated beyond the left-field fence; it was completely enclosed in wire, meaning that no baseball could travel more than 30 or 40 feet before being trapped in rope; still Mantle and Maris would be swinging, and this, in spring, makes news.

Mantle stepped in first. He wore black gloves to help prevent blisters. He hit right-handed against the pitching of a coach named

Vern Benson, and soon Mantle was swinging hard, smashing line drives against the nets, going *ahhh ahhh* as he followed through with his mouth open.

Then Mantle, not wanting to overdo it on his first day, dropped his bat in the dirt and walked out of the batting cage. Roger Maris stepped in. He picked up Mantle's bat.

"This damn thing must be 38 ounces," Maris said. He threw the bat down into the dirt, left the cage, and walked toward the dugout on the other side of the field to get a lighter bat.

DiMaggio stood among the sports writers behind the cage, then turned when Vern Benson, inside the cage, yelled, "Joe, wanna hit some?"

"No chance," DiMaggio said.

"C'mon, Joe," Benson said.

The reporters waited silently. Then DiMaggio walked slowly into the cage and picked up Mantle's bat. He took his position at the plate but obviously it was not the classic DiMaggio stance; he was holding the bat about two inches from the knob, his feet were not so far apart, and when DiMaggio took a cut at Benson's first pitch, fouling it, there was none of that ferocious follow-through, the blurred bat did not come whipping all the way around, the No. 5 was not stretched full across his broad back.

DiMaggio fouled Benson's second pitch, then he connected solidly with the third, the fourth, the fifth. He was just meeting the ball easily, however, not smashing it, and Benson called out, "I didn't know you were a choke hitter, Joe."

"I am now," DiMaggio said, getting ready for another pitch.

He hit three more squarely enough, and then he swung again and there was a hollow sound.

"Ohhh," DiMaggio yelled, dropping his bat, his fingers stung. "I was waiting for that one." He left the batting cage, rubbing his hands together. The reporters watched him. Nobody said anything. Then DiMaggio said to one of them, not in anger or in sadness, but merely as a simply stated fact, "There was a time when you couldn't get me out of there."

Talese's portrait pulled the veil from DiMaggio, who had always bene-fited from a protective press corps that exchanged their objectivity for the cachet of his occasional company. Yet nothing we have subsequently learned about DiMaggio's off-field life has had much of an effect on how he is still perceived as a player. Nine world championships in thirteen seasons and the undying respect of his teammates remain the standard by which most fans judge his life.

Nevertheless, Talese's story was groundbreaking for its honesty and insight and has since influenced generations of sportswriters.

PART IV

THE DYNASTY

Casey Stengel and Mickey Mantle led the Yankees to their most dominant epoch, winning ten pennants and seven world championships in twelve seasons from 1949 through 1960, seasons often punctuated by Mantle's mammoth blasts and underscored by Stengel's inimitable commentary. Even as Stengel was forced into retirement after the 1960 season, the Yankees continued to dominate baseball like no other team in baseball ever has.

But it was not as easy as it looked. The Yankees were slow to embrace integration, and eventually that policy would prove costly to the franchise. Meanwhile, a new generation of sportswriters, best represented by the acid-tinged writing of the *Daily News*' Dick Young, took an increasingly critical view of the club's achievements. No longer in awe of the athletes, and trumped in daily reporting by television, this new generation of sportswriters looked for the story behind the story. They were also the first to realize that by the early 1960s, despite Roger Maris's record-setting 61 home runs in 1961, the Yankee dynasty would soon come to an end.

Areas that had previously been considered off limits for writers, such as the private lives of the players, were now pried open to scrutiny. Writers were less cozy with their subjects and less content with sticking to the game on the field. In New York, tabloid journalism and the resulting sensationalism fueled competition between the members of the sporting press, sparking creativity as the writers of the era took far more chances than their counterparts of an earlier era. It wasn't always enough anymore to write from the vantage point of the press box.

SCOUT'S HONOR

from *The Sporting News,* August 21, 1995

In October 1952, Yankees scout Tom Greenwade recalled how he signed Mantle in a letter to *TSN* publisher J. G. Taylor Spink:

Dear Taylor:

To the best of my knowledge and memory, the first person to talk to me about Mantle was his manager, Barney Barnett, in the Ban Johnson League. All the Midwestern scouts know Barney and drop by to see him.

This must have been in the early part of the 1948 season for I went to Alba, Mo., about August 1948 to see Mantle and other players that I had heard of on both clubs. Mantle, who at that time was referred to as "Little Mickey Mantle," was small and played shortstop. He pitched a couple of innings in this game. I wasn't overly impressed, but bear in mind he was only 16.

The following spring an umpire in the B.J. League, Kenny Magness, told me about a game the night before in which Mantle played, and he was very high on him. I caught the Baxter club at Parsons to see Mantle again. This was early in May, 1949. Mantle looked better and must have put on 20 pounds since the past August, and I became interested in a hurry for that was when I discovered he could really run, but wasn't hitting too much. So I inquired from other sources, probably Barney, when Mickey would graduate. It was to be the last Thursday in May, 1949, from the Commerce, Okla. H.S.

On Friday I drove to Commerce, and this is the first time the Mantles ever knew there was such a person as Tom Greenwade. I found out the graduation exercises had been postponed till that night for some reason. Since I had no desire to violate the H.S. tampering rule, I was careful not to mention contract or pro ball either, but had understood Mickey was to play in Coffeyville that night and I wanted to see him play and I didn't mention that I had seen him play before. Well, they talked things over with the coach and superintendent and decided to pass on the exercises since Mickey already had his diploma and go to Coffeyville instead.

Of course, I was there. Mickey looked better at bat, hitting left-handed. I still don't know he switches since the only pitching I have seen him against is right-handed. After the game Mr. Mantle tells me Mickey will play Sunday in Baxter Springs. I told him I would be at his house Sunday morning and go to the game with them. I was there about 11 A.M. I was scared to death for fear some scout had been there Saturday. I asked Mr. Mantle if anyone had been there. He said "no." I was relieved.

We all went to Baxter Springs, and for the first time I see Mickey hit right-handed. Mickey racked the pitcher for four "clothes lines," and I started looking all around for scouts, but none were there.

When the last out was made, Mr. Mantle, Mickey and I got in my car behind the grandstand and in 15 minutes the contract was signed. We agreed on $1500.00 for the remainder of the season and the contract (Independence of the K.O.M.) was drawn calling for a salary of $140.00 per month. Mickey reported to Harry Craft at Independence. He was slow to get started and as late as July 10th was hitting only .225, but finished the season over .300. The following year at Joplin he hit .383, I believe. You know the rest.

Best regards,
Tom Greenwade

The depth and breadth of the Yankee farm system, particularly in the decade after the war, allowed the dynasty to continue unabated. Mickey Mantle's discovery by scout Tom Greenwade is the perfect example of this often-ignored Yankee strength. Although the Yankees were correctly criticized for ignoring black prospects, they missed few others of talent and ability. Many prospects that other organizations either overlooked or never saw at all were signed by the Yankees for virtually nothing. Some, like Mantle, became the biggest stars in the game.

RED SMITH

··

OPENING DAY, YANKEE STADIUM

from *The New York Herald Tribune*, April 18, 1951

An hour and a half before the New Year dawned, Mickey Charles Mantle — he was christened Mickey, not Michael, after Mickey Cochrane, whose name is Gordon Stanley — was standing on the top step of the Yankees' dugout looking back into the stands where a kid in a bright windbreaker brandished a home-made sign fashioned from a big pasteboard carton. The sign bore a photograph of Phil Rizzuto, cut out of a program, and crude lettering read: "C'mon, Lil Phil. Let's go."

Sitting on the bench, Casey Stengel could see his newest outfielder only from the chest down. The manager grunted with surprise when he noticed that the sole of one baseball shoe had come loose and was flapping like a radio announcer's jaw. He got up and talked to the kid and came back shaking his head.

"He don't care much about the big leagues, does he," Casey said. "He's gonna play in them shoes."

"Who is he?" a visitor asked.

"Why, he's that kid of mine," said Mr. Stengel, to whom proper names are so repugnant he signs his checks with an X.

"That's Mantle?"

"Yeh. I asked him didn't he have any better shoes and he said he had a new pair, but they're a little too big."

"He's waiting for an important occasion to wear new ones," the visitor said.

Casey is not unaware of the volume of prose that was perpetrated about this nineteen-year-old during his prodigious spring training tour, when he batted .402, hit nine home runs and knocked in thirty-one runs.

"How about his first game in a big league park?" a kibitzer said.

"Saturday in Brooklyn, when he got only one single. What was wrong?"

"My writers," Mr. Stengel said, "had an off day."

Mr. Stengel told about Mantle asking him how to play the right-field wall in Ebbets Field.

"It was the first time the kid ever saw concrete," he said. "I explained how the ball hits the wall like this and bounces like this and how you take it as it comes off the wall. I told him, 'I played that wall for six years, you know.' He said, 'The hell you did!'"

"He probably thinks," Mr. Stengel said, "that I was born at the age of sixty and started managing right away."

A couple of newspaper men were talking to Bill Dickey. About Mantle, naturally.

"Gosh, I envy him," one of them said. "Nineteen years old, and starting out as a Yankee!"

"He's green," Bill said. "But he's got to be great. All that power, a switch hitter, and he runs like a striped ape. If he drags a bunt past the pitcher, he's on base. I think he's the fastest man I ever saw with the Yankees. But he's green in the outfield. He was a shortstop last year."

"Casey said that out in Phoenix he misjudged a fly and the ball stuck on his head."

"It hit him right here alongside the eye," Bill said. "He's green, and he'll be scared today."

"If anybody walks up to him now," a newspaper man said, "and asks him if he's nervous, Mantle should bust him in the eye. Golly, Bill, do you realize you were in the big league before he was born?"

"He was born in 1932," Dickey said, "and that was the year I played my first World Series."

"And I'd been covering baseball years and years," the guy said. "What's been happening to us?"

After that there was a half-hour relentless oratory at the plate, and then Whitey Ford, the Yankees' prize rookie of last year, walked out in his soldier suit to pitch the first ball, and then the season was open and it was New Year's Day.

Mantle made the first play of the season, fielding the single by Dom DiMaggio which opened the game for the Red Sox. He broke his bat on the first pitch thrown to him and was barely thrown out by Bobby Doerr. He popped up on his second turn at bat.

When he came up for the third time the Yankees were leading, 2 to 0, with none out and runners on first and third. Earlier, Joe DiMaggio had started a double play with an implausible catch of a pop fly behind second, as if to tell Mantle, "This is how it's done up here, son." Now Joe, awaiting his turn at bat, called the kid aside and spoke to him.

Mantle nodded, stepped back into the box and singled a run home. Dickey, coaching at third, slapped his stern approvingly. When the kid raced home from second with his first big-league run, the whole Yankee bench arose to clap hands and pat his torso. He was in the lodge.

Over the course of a career that spanned five decades, Red Smith may well have been the best sports columnist ever. After stints in St. Louis and Philadelphia he joined the Herald Tribune, *then moved on to the* Times, *for which he won a Pulitzer Prize in 1976. Like Ruth, Smith was made for New York, for it was in New York, where he was often writing about the Yankees, that his talent was best recognized and appreciated. He had a sixth sense about what was important enough to write about, and he always seemed to be the first to recognize the significance of a particular player or game. Yet at the same time he wrote with a wonderful sense of proportion, allowing personalities and events to speak for themselves.*

FAREWELL JOE, HELLO MICKEY

from *The New York Post*, October 11, 1951

OCT 11 — The sophisticates among us grumpily denounce the baseball devotees as frustrated children. They consider us to be deranged adults whose maturity is contaminated by a nonsensical exuberance that is only admirable in the very young. But the playoff between the Dodgers and the Giants and the World Series that the Yankees won yesterday by beating the Giants, 4–3, in the sixth game, was a prolonged metropolitan holiday.

The joyous hostility of sports brought the people of the big city closer together. Their animosity was a merry one. It was our series, but the people beyond the Hudson horned in. They watched our teams playing for the championship of New York on the television, like peeping Toms viewing a family argument in the flat across the courtyard. Did "South Pacific" set this town leaping? Did people stop work and throw things out windows because they saw a tragedy by Eugene O'Neill?

Well, the playoffs did. So did the World Series, although the fervor was slightly diminished. What the hell do the intellectuals mean by pegging baseball as a sport of the naive? Baseball is simpler, purer and truer than any other form of popular amusement in the United States.

It was a sweat opera without villains. Most of the town pulled for the Giants. Getting into the World Series was vindication for Leo Durocher, who has been roughed up constantly for his bellowing and nasty belligerence. But success seems to have reformed him. Durocher came into the series a placidly clever man, refined by the most exciting tournament ever promoted by the National League.

Durocher, who has made himself a reputation for snide violence, hustled his team into the sixth game of the series by treating them as equals. Usually, he hounds them with a profane bitterness. They didn't fold up even when Sal Maglie and Larry Jansen, their best pitchers, threw sloppily in the crisis.

Sal Yvars, an obscure catcher who is nothing more than a property man because he performs batting-practice chores, came up as a pinch-hitter with two on, two out and the score 4–3 in the ninth. It was a situation to make even an old-timer go clammy and develop the symptoms of a strep throat.

But Sal hit a furious line drive which, instead of sinking, hung. There was Hank Bauer falling forward on his buckled knees and catching it. If the ball had gotten past Bauer, it would have been a certain double despite Sal's slowness afoot.

The loser's end didn't seem enough compensation for the Giants. They behaved like winners all the way from August to the last out in the sixth game. Only the score exposed them.

It was the first pennant the Giants have strung up since '37. They have been trash in a city of baseball nobility. They bored their most passionate admirers who turned from them with regret and a mixture of shame. But they hung on and passed Brooklyn, tied them on the last day of the season and beat them in the playoff.

They lost the World Series because Eddie Lopat loused them up twice with his junk, and Allie Reynolds sailed it by them the second time out. It took Vic Raschi, Johnny Sain and Bob Kuzava to get them out of there yesterday. In the manager's office, Durocher was stamping his feet into custom-made shoes. The laces had tufted ends. They asked him who was most responsible for beating him.

"Phil Rizzuto," Durocher said. "He's a double pro."

Over in the Yankee dressing room, the most excited people in the joint were the hangers-on who swept past the doorman in a bragging tide. The players accepted congratulations as they dressed with weary haste. They had to work at forming a couple of cheers for the news reels.

Three times in three years Casey Stengel has won the World Championship. It is the team's 18th pennant and 14th championship since '21. It is Joe DiMaggio's 10th World Series. It started badly for DiMaggio as he went 0-for-12 but the afternoon he broke out the Yankees came out of it and took charge. It may be his last season

and Joe talked about that as the coat-holders gabbed up a loud commotion.

"If I told you yes or no and changed my mind we'd both look
bad," Joe said. "You for writing it . . . me for saying it. The truth is I
don't know what I'm going to do."

Music can turn my heart inside out and set me winging. So can
baseball. If I'm wrong, don't tell me.

*Jimmy Cannon was born to be a New York columnist. A native New
Yorker and son of a Tammany Hall politician who grew up on the
Lower East Side, Cannon was working in the newsroom by age sixteen.
Despite his lack of a formal education, he earned a doctorate in New
York.*

*Equally at home writing about sports, politics, or other matters,
Cannon was an inveterate DiMaggio fan and remains perhaps the
most eloquent chronicler of that era.*

MARTIN'S HIT IN 9TH WINS YANKS 5TH SERIES IN ROW

from *The New York Herald Tribune,* October 6, 1953

The morgue doors yawned yesterday, snapped shut, then swung open again, and as they carted the remains away a man in the press box gazed thoughtfully at the knot of Yankee baseball players at first base tossing Billy Martin aloft like a beanbag. "You wouldn't think," said Mike Lee, the man in the press box, "that they could — get so mercenary over a lousy $2,000."

The fiftieth World Series was over and this time the Dodgers really and truly was dead, beaten 4 to 3, in the sixth and final game after Carl Furillo had snatched them to temporary safety when they were only four strikes away from destruction.

In a florid finish that stretched dramatic license to the breaking point, Furillo saved the Dodgers from routine defeat by tying the score in the ninth inning with a two-run homer with one out and a count of three balls, two strikes on the scoreboard. Then Martin lowered the boom.

The gray and chilly day, suitable for funerals, had thickened in grayer, chillier twilight and some of the Yankee Stadium crowd of 62,370 had departed when Martin walked to the plate in the rusty glow of the floodlights. Hank Bauer was on second base, Mickey Mantle on first and Yogi Berra had been retired. Clem Labine, Brooklyn's best pitcher, threw one for a called strike.

He threw another and Martin slapped a ground single over second base into center field. Duke Snider fielded the ball but didn't trouble to throw as Bauer went ripping home with the winning run.

The Dodgers trudged to their dugout behind third base, looking over their shoulders toward first, where the Yankees were spanking Martin. It was a sight worth at least a backward glance. Never again, perhaps, will it be possible to look on a baseball team that has just won the championship of the world for a fifth consecutive year. It never was possible before, never in any age.

Martin's single was a mercenary stroke, worth something like $2,000 to each Yankee, this being the approximate difference between winners' and losers' shares. On the holy pages of the record books — and these are sacred writings to a ball player — it represents a good deal more, for the blow broke a noteworthy World Series record.

It was Martin's twelfth hit of the six games. Nobody ever made more, even in an eight-game series, and nobody ever made so many in six. Twelve hits had stood as a record since Washington's Sam Rice made that total in seven games in 1925, and the Cardinals' Pepper Martin did the same in 1931.

Those Martin guys. Pepper personally took the Athletics apart in 1931. Billy was a rookie star against the Dodgers last year and this time the brash, combative, fist-slinging little hellion tortured them as a child might pluck the wings from a fly. His namesake needn't be ashamed of yielding his share of the record to a ball player like this.

It is an extraordinary achievement which the Yankees have brought off and the manner of its completion was so outrageously melodramatic that witnesses were shrieking senselessly at the end. Even so, it was a Dodger crowd. Even in the Yankee fortress, the alien cries for Furillo were wilder than the cheers for Martin.

"How can you root for the Yankees?" an actor named Jimmy Little had asked a friend earlier in the series. "It's like rooting for United States Steel."

"Do not forsake us," the page-one bannerline of *The Brooklyn Eagle* had implored yesterday following the Dodgers' third defeat. They weren't forsaken in enemy territory. They were only defeated in splendid competition.

For a show with such a taut ending, the last act began limply. The Dodgers made three errors in the first three innings, and the Yankees three runs in the first two. Even the incomparable Billy Cox booted one, and he's the man who, Casey Stengel says, should be required in fairness to the opposition to play third base in chains.

Whitey Ford, who is really pinker than he is white, allowed the Dodgers only one run in seven innings, confirming Stengel's conviction that there's a future in this Ford. Carl Erskine, making his third start for Brooklyn, went out for a pinch-batter after four innings and might have departed earlier except for Ford's overdeveloped sense of sportsmanship.

In what should have been a big second inning, Ford was on third with the bases filled and one out when Berra hit a long fly to Snider. Ford tagged up, started home an instant before the catch. Twenty feet down the line his conscience overtook him. He started back, saw Joe Collins arriving from second base, turned toward the plate again, and was an easy half of a double play ending the inning.

This was light comedy. They came on with the corn in the eighth. First Allie Reynolds appeared unexpectedly, tramping in from the bullpen with purposeful stride, like a players' delegate come to make demands on the owners. He made demands, but chiefly on the Brooklyn hitters. Striking out Roy Campanella to close that inning, the Indian was really pouring that kickapoo joy-juice.

With two out and two on in the Yankee eighth, the crowd put in a pinch-batter. Joe Collins was up for his turn, but from everywhere came cries of "Mize! Mize!" Yielding to popular demand, Stengel sent John Mize up to howling applause for what John and the fans agreed would be his last time. He grounded out.

Silence fell, but not for long. It has only returned just now, as these last lines are written. Down in the clubhouse, Ford has had the last word.

"I felt bad when Casey took me out," he said. "Then I thought, 'Well, he hasn't been wrong in five years.'"

MILLION TO ONE SHOT COMES IN

from *The Washington Post,* October 9, 1956

The million-to-one shot came in. Hell froze over. A month of Sundays hit the calendar. Don Larsen today pitched a no-hit, no-run, no-man-reach-first game in a World Series.

On the mound at Yankee Stadium, the same guy who was knocked out in two innings by the Dodgers on Friday came up today with one for the record books, posting it there in solo grandeur as the only Perfect Game in World Series history.

With it, the Yankee right-hander shattered the Dodgers, 2–0, and beat Sal Maglie, while taking 64,519 suspense-limp fans into his act.

First there was a mild speculation, then there was hope, then breaths were held in slackened jaws in the late innings as the big mob wondered if the big Yankee right-hander could bring off for them the most fabulous of all World Series games.

He did it, and the Yanks took the Series lead three games to two, to leave the Dodgers as thunderstruck as Larsen himself appeared to be at the finish of his feat.

Larsen whizzed a third strike past pinch hitter Dale Mitchell in the ninth. That was all. It was over. Automatically, the massive 226-pounder from San Diego started walking from the mound toward the dugout, as pitchers are supposed to do at the finish.

But this time there was a woodenness in his steps and his stride was that of a man in a daze. The spell was broken for Larsen when Yogi Berra ran onto the infield to embrace him.

It was not Larsen jumping for joy. It was the more demonstrative Berra. His battery mate leaped full tilt at the big guy. In self-defense, Larsen caught Berra in mid-air as one would catch a frolicking child, and that's how they made their way toward the Yankee bench, Larsen carrying Berra.

There wasn't a Brooklyn partisan left among the 64,519, it seemed, at the finish. Loyalties to the Dodgers evaporated in sheer enthrallment at the show big Larsen was giving them, for this was a day when the fans could boast that they were there.

So at the finish, Larsen had brought it off, and erected for himself a special throne in baseball's Hall of Fame, with the first Perfect Game pitched in major-league baseball since Charlie Robertson of the White Sox against Detroit 34 years ago.

But this one was more special. This one was in a World Series. Three times, pitchers had almost come through with no-hitters, and there were three one-hitters in the World Series books, but never a no-man-reach-base classic.

The tragic victim of it all, sitting on the Dodger bench, was sad Sal Maglie, himself a five-hit pitcher today in his bid for a second Series victory over the Yankees. He was out of the game, technically, but he was staying to see it out and it must have been in disbelief that he saw himself beaten by another guy's World Series no-hitter.

Mickey Mantle hit the home run today in the fourth inning and that was all the impetus the Yankees needed, but no game-winning home run ever wound up with such emphatic second billing as Mantle's this afternoon.

It was an exciting wallop but in the fourth inning only, because after that Larsen was the story today, and the dumbfounded Dodgers could wonder how this same guy who couldn't last out two innings in the second game could master them so thoroughly today.

He did it with a tremendous assortment of pitches that seemed to have five forward speeds, including a slow one that ought to have been equipped with back-up lights.

Larsen had them in hand all day. He used only 97 pitches, not an abnormally low number because 11 pitches an inning is about normal for a good day's work. But he was the boss from the outset. Only against Peewee Reese in the first inning did he lapse to a three-ball count, and then he struck Reese out. No other Dodger was ever favored with more than two called balls by Umpire Babe Pinelli.

Behind him, his Yankee teammates made three spectacular fielding plays to put Larsen in the Hall of Fame. There was one in the second inning that calls for special description. In the fifth, Mickey Mantle ranged far back into left center to haul in Gil Hodges' long drive with a backhand shoetop grab that was a beaut. In the eighth,

the same Hodges made another bid to break it up, but third baseman Andy Carey speared his line drive.

Little did Larsen, the Yankees, the Dodgers or anybody among the
64,519 in the stands suspect that when Jackie Robinson was robbed
of a line-drive hit in the second inning, the stage was being set for a
Perfect Game.

Robinson murdered the ball so hard that third baseman Andy
Carey barely had time to fling his glove upward in a desperate at-
tempt to get the ball. He could only deflect it. But, luckily, shortstop
Gil McDougald was backing up, and able to grab the ball on one
bounce. By a half-step, McDougald got Robinson at first base, and
Larsen tonight can be grateful that it was not the younger, fleeter
Robinson of a few years back but a heavy-legged, 40-year-old Jackie.

As the game wore on, Larsen lost the edge that gave him five
strikeouts in the first four innings, and added only two in the last
five. He had opened up by slipping called third strikes past both
Gilliam and Reese in the first inning.

Came the sixth, and he got Furillo and Campanella on pops,
fanned Maglie. Gilliam, Reese and Snider were easy in the seventh.
Robinson tapped out, Hodges lined out and Amoros flied out in the
eighth. And now it was the ninth, and the big Scandinavian-Ameri-
can was going for the works with a calm that was exclusive with him.

Furillo gave him a bit of a battle, fouled off four pitches, then flied
mildly to Bauer. He got two quick strikes on Campanella, got him
on a slow roller to Martin.

Now it was the left-handed Dale Mitchell, pinch hitting for
Maglie.

Ball one came in high. Larsen got a called strike.

On the next pitch, Mitchell swung for strike two.

Then the last pitch of the game. Mitchell started to swing, but
didn't go through with it.

But it made no difference because Umpire Pinelli was calling it
Strike Number Three, and baseball history was being made.

Maglie himself was a magnificent figure out there all day, pitching
hitless ball and leaving the Yankees a perplexed gang, until suddenly
with two out in the fourth, Mickey Mantle, with two called strikes
against him, lashed the next pitch on a line into the right-field seats
to give the Yanks a 1–0 lead.

There was doubt about that Mantle homer because the ball was curving and would it stay fair? It did. In their own half of the inning, the Dodgers had no such luck. Duke Snider's drive into the same seats had curved foul by a few feet. The disgusted Snider eventually took a third strike.

The Dodgers were a luckless gang and Larsen a fortunate fellow in the fifth. Like Mantle, Sandy Amoros lined one into the seats in right, and that one was a near thing for the Yankees. By what seemed only inches, it curved foul, the umpires ruled.

Going into the sixth, Maglie was pitching a one-hitter — Mantle's homer — and being outpitched. The old guy lost some of his stuff in the sixth, though, and the Yankees came up with their other run.

Carey led off with a single to center, and Larsen sacrificed him to second on a daring third-strike bunt. Hank Bauer got the run in with a single to left. There might have been a close play at the plate had Amoros come up with the ball cleanly, but he didn't and Carey scored unmolested.

Now there were Yanks still on first and third with only one out, but they could get no more. Hodges made a scintillating pickup of Mantle's smash, stepped on first and threw to home for a double play on Bauer, who was trying to score. Bauer was trapped in a rundown and caught despite a low throw by Campanella that caused Robinson to fall into the dirt.

But the Yankees weren't needing any more runs for Larsen today. They didn't even need their second one, because they were getting a pitching job for the books this memorable day in baseball.

Povich covered baseball for the Washington Post *from 1923 to 1998. He saw it all, and his account of Don Larsen's perfect game is perhaps his best-known story.*

McDOUGALD, ONCE A QUIET YANKEE STAR, NOW LIVES IN QUIET WORLD

from *The New York Times*, July 10, 1994

SPRING LAKE, N.J.: It is a silent summer for Gil McDougald; they are all silent summers.

Once, summertime for Gil McDougald, a standout Yankee infielder in the 1950's, was full of the sweet sounds of baseball — balls being struck, the chatter and laughter of teammates, the roar of the crowd. He can no longer hear those sounds, although his wife, Lucille, says, "He can hear them internally."

Gil McDougald is deaf. He gradually lost his hearing during his playing days, after a freak accident in batting practice in which he was struck by a batted ball. Ironically, this occurred just two years before the famous incident in which he cracked a line drive off the right eye of Herb Score, a Cleveland Indians pitcher.

Until that moment against Cleveland, in the first inning of a game in Municipal Stadium on the night of May 7, 1957, Score appeared on the way to becoming one of baseball's best pitchers ever, and McDougald seemed to have a long career ahead of him.

"I heard the thud of the ball hitting his head and then saw him drop and lie there, bleeding, and I froze," McDougald recalled. "Someone hollered for me to run to first. When Score was taken off the field on a stretcher, I was sick to my stomach. I didn't want to play any more."

But Casey Stengel, his manager, insisted he continue. "He said, 'You're getting paid to play,' and while that seems harsh, it was right. It's like getting right back on a horse after you've been thrown.

"But I said that if Herb loses his eye, I'm quitting baseball."

McDougald remembers that Score's mother called and told him it wasn't his fault, that it was just an accident. He called Score in the hospital, to apologize, to offer his heartfelt best wishes, and kept in regular touch with him.

Score returned to action the next season, his eye healed. But in many ways, neither McDougald nor Score was ever the same again.

After the Score incident, fans in cities that the Yankees visited began to boo McDougald. "Some people would holler, 'Killer,'" he said. "Funny thing is, as bad as I felt, I went on a hitting spree. I can't explain it."

His Teams Honored, but He's Not There

Yesterday, Old-Timers Day at Yankee Stadium, McDougald, now 66 years old, chose not to attend, even though the theme involved his years as a Yankee. It was the 45th anniversary of the beginning in 1949 of the Casey Stengel era, and the first of Stengel's record five straight World Series championship teams, three of which McDougald was a member.

McDougald played superbly in those garlanded baseball days as a feared clutch hitter and a regular second baseman, third baseman and shortstop, wherever Stengel felt he needed him on a particular day. In McDougald's 53 games in eight World Series over his 10-year career, he started every game at one of those three positions.

"It is too frustrating and too exhausting for Gil to be around the other players and trying to understand all the banter and the reminiscences," said Lucille McDougald. "He was content to watch it on television at home."

It was during batting practice one afternoon that McDougald himself had been struck by a batted ball. He was standing behind a screen at second base talking with the Yankee coach, Frank Crosetti.

"I saw a ball lying on the ground nearby and reached to pick it up, my head going just beyond the screen," he said. "Just then Bob Cerv hit a ball that hit me in the ear. I collapsed and everyone came running over. They carried me off the field and I was out of action for a few games.

"The doctors told me I'd be all right. Well, I wasn't. The blow had broken a hearing tube. At first it just affected one ear, my left. One time I'm getting needled by some fan at third base and I turned to

Rizzuto at short and said, 'Too bad I didn't get hit in the right ear, then I wouldn't have to hear this guy.'"

But the hearing got progressively worse, although it had nothing to do with his leaving baseball after the 1960 season, at age 32.

"I just got tired of the travel, and the attitude of the baseball people," he said. "I started at $5,500 a year with the Yankees, and then was making $37,500 at the end. But they acted like they owned you and that they were giving you the moon and stars."

He had a family with four children at the time, and felt he needed more money to support it and saw a way to do it through a business of his own. He had already begun a dry cleaning business and it was doing nicely.

"Some of my teammates, and others asked, 'How can you quit baseball?' No one thought I'd follow through. But I found it was easy."

No Telephones, No Business Career

Because of his loss of hearing, McDougald says he hasn't answered a telephone in 10 years. Because of the handicap, he sold his share in the building maintenance company he owned, which employed 2,200 people on the East Coast, and he was forced into early retirement.

"When I couldn't use the phone, it became a real pain in the neck," he said. He keeps an interest in baseball, however, and while he watches some of it on television, he says he doesn't miss the voices of the announcers — except for his old teammates, Phil Rizzuto and Tony Kubek.

"The others just talk so much that it wears you out," said McDougald. "I'd just as soon watch the action and draw my own conclusions."

And what does he see? "I see a lot of guys making a million dollars," he said, and laughed. "There are some very good ballplayers, but some of the things they do are pretty funny. Like if a pitcher throws close to a batter, he faints. When he wakes up, he charges the mound."

McDougald sat at the kitchen table in his sprawling, 22-room Spanish colonial house where he lives with his wife and, depending on who happens to be staying or visiting, some or all of his seven children, seven grandchildren and one great-grandchild. He and Lu-cille adopted three of their children, of mixed races, later in life through Catholic Charities.

"We had four children to begin with, and then when they all grew up and left the house, Lucille and I started getting lonely," he said, "so when we were about 40 years old we set about to adopt the other kids."

In a white short-sleeve pullover and blue jeans and white sneak-ers, he appears as trim as in his playing days. Indeed, at 180 pounds, the 6-foot McDougald weighs about the same as when he was play-ing third base, shortstop and second base for the Yankees, from 1951, when he came up to the majors with Mickey Mantle, through 1960. He hit over .300 twice, and played an important role in the eight World Series the Yankees played in over his 10 years with them.

"He was a money player," said Saul Rogovin, who pitched for the White Sox in that era. "He would hurt you in the late innings."

Stengel the Book, Read by McDougald

Through the window behind McDougald is another large, white, columned house like his and, just beyond that, the ocean, sparkling in the morning sunlight, the waves hitting the beach with a sound of which McDougald is now unaware.

There remains an angularity to his ruddy face and body, and one is reminded of that odd, open, wide stance of his at the plate, head cocked to one side, like, well, like he was listening to a faraway sound.

"An awkward man, a wonderful man," Stengel said about him.

McDougald laughed now, recalling a move that Stengel used to make: "Casey always knew when a man was ready to pinch-hit or not. And I could read him like a book. He'd come by on the bench and stand and look you right in the eye. Like he'd stop in front of Bobby Brown, and he'd say something like, 'Bauer,' or 'Woodling, grab a bat.' Still looking at Brown. Casey was a hunch manager. No statistics for him. He'd look at a guy and get the feeling. It was funny."

There is no problem, to be sure, with McDougald's speech, and he responds when questions are written out for him, or, on occasion, when he reads lips, which is laborious for him: "You have to concentrate so hard that it begins to give you a headache," he said.

Sitting with Lucille at the kitchen table, McDougald recently tried to field a visitor's question. He knit his brow, trying to read the lips. "What did you say?" he said.

Lucille said, slowly, "He said, 'Did Stengel ever give you advice about hitting?'"

He recalled a moment in the fifth game in his first World Series, against the New York Giants in 1951. The bases were loaded and he was about to bat. Stengel called him back to the dugout.

"Casey said, 'Hit one out,'" McDougald said with a laugh. "And wouldn't you know, I went up to the plate and did. It was in the Polo Grounds. I hit a fly ball that carried about 260 feet down that short left-field line, just one of those Chinese homers, but it cleared the fence."

At the time, it was only the third bases-loaded home run in World Series history.

McDougald batted .306 during that regular season of 1951, the only Yankee batter to hit .300 or better, and was named the American League's rookie of the year, playing second base and third, ahead of either Jerry Coleman or Bobby Brown. He also hit 14 homers, one more than another rookie on the team, Mickey Mantle.

"I remember our first spring training together, and you couldn't believe the publicity for Mickey," he said. "He was in the newspapers and magazines more than the President. From that point forward, his life was never his own. That's what stardom does. It was like what I saw with Joe DiMaggio. Nineteen fifty-one was his last season as a ballplayer, and I don't think I saw him come down to eat in the hotel one time. He stayed in his room because he'd be so bothered by people.

"Mickey was a 19-year-old kid from Oklahoma. New York seemed like a huge place to him. I was different. I was from San Francisco, 22 years old, and had a year of college. He began hanging out with Billy Martin, and every night was a party. I roomed with Hank Bauer, and it wasn't the same for us.

"But Mickey had different pressures than me, being the star he was. I saw him on television recently and he talked about the drinking helping to relieve the pressure. It was very sad for me, knowing Mickey as I do, liking him, seeing what's happened."

He remembers the wild things some of his teammates did, including Ryne Duren, the pitcher. "Once I saw him drink two bottles of vodka out of both sides of his mouth," said McDougald. "I thought, 'He's crazy.'"

Duren is an alcoholic, who later rehabilitated, and now counsels others about their drinking problems. "I saw Ryne at a golf tournament a few years back," said McDougald, "and he looked beautiful."

Some Old Ties Are True Ties

McDougald shied away from other activities, such as dinners and banquets, because he found them frustrating, and somewhat embarrassing, because he was unable to hear. "I'd just sit there like a dummy," he said.

Over the years, he had grown more disturbed as the hearing began to wane. And when his family gets together, he still grows impatient with not being able to share in the conversations — "especially the jokes," he said — and so may retire upstairs where he can work on business interests he retains, or check the stock market, in which he remains active, or view television or read a book or magazine or newspaper, seeking to "keep up with the world." Or he may practice his putting on the small artificial green in his den.

McDougald still regularly plays tennis and golf. In a recent, genial dialogue with Ottilie Lucas, the blind wife of his nephew, they debated handicaps. She said she'd rather be blind than deaf because with loss of eyesight she is more sensitive to the world around her and so appreciates it more.

McDougald argued that he'd rather be deaf than blind. "If I was blind," he said, "I couldn't play golf."

At one point, McDougald considered getting a hearing implant but it wouldn't do much good, he was told, since he can occasionally hear sounds but the sounds are fragmented and he can make no sense out of them.

He remains in touch with some of his old teammates, like Rizzuto and Yogi Berra, and remembers his biggest thrill being his first game in Yankee Stadium.

"The ball park seemed so big to me," he said, "and the roar of the crowd was overwhelming."

He even occasionally gets a note from Herb Score. "He pitched again after I hit him but he was never the same again," said

McDougald. "I could see him recoiling after he threw, rather than following through as he had before. But he's done very well, as an announcer for the Indians, and I'm glad to see it."

McDougald had done well, too, succeeding in business and then, for seven years, coaching the Fordham University baseball team while still active in his business. He quit coaching baseball when he could no longer hear the crack of the bat.

"You know, there used to be a sportswriter for the *New York Times* named John Drebinger, who covered the Yankees," said McDougald. "He wore a hearing aid. We'd mock him all the time, and play tricks on him. He'd come over in the clubhouse and we'd be moving our lips, as if we were talking. He'd beat that squawk box in his ear, then he'd turn it up. And then we'd all start laughing. He'd say, 'Why you dirty so-and-so's.'" And McDougald laughed.

"And now it's happened to me," he said. "But you go on, you learn to live with it. You make your adjustments. There's still a lot to live for, and love."

Gil McDougald turned and looked out of the window, his face to the rays of sun that streamed in, silent and welcome, like the summertime.

This story has a happy ending, for shortly after Berkow's story first appeared, McDougald underwent an operation that restored his hearing. On a team of stars, McDougald rarely stood out, yet he was often the most valuable player on the team. Throughout the 1950s he filled in where needed, taking regular turns at third, shortstop, and second base without any dropoff in production or defense.

Berkow, who has written a biography of Red Smith and has edited collections of Smith's writing, was a worthy successor to his mentor with his erudite and eloquent reporting for the New York Times.

CASEY STENGEL and MICKEY MANTLE

TESTIMONY BEFORE THE
U.S. SENATE JUDICIARY COMMITTEE

from *The Congressional Record,* July 9, 1958

Senator Kefauver: Mr. Stengel, you are the manager of the New York Yankees. Will you give us very briefly your background and your views about this legislation?

Mr. Stengel: Well, I started in professional ball in 1910. I have been in professional ball, I would say, for forty-eight years. I have been employed by numerous ball clubs in the majors and in the minor leagues.

I started in the minor leagues with Kansas City. I played as low as Class D ball, which was at Shelbyville, Kentucky, and also Class C ball and Class A ball, and I have advanced in baseball as a ballplayer.

I had many years that I was not so successful as a ballplayer, as it is a game of skill. And then I was no doubt discharged by baseball in which I had to go back to the minor leagues as a manager, and after being in the minor leagues as a manager, I became a major-league manager in several cities and was discharged, we call it discharged because there was no question I had to leave.

And I returned to the minor leagues at Milwaukee, Kansas City and Oakland, California, and then returned to the major leagues.

In the last ten years, naturally, in major-league baseball with the New York Yankees; the New York Yankees have had tremendous success, and while I am not a ballplayer who does the work, I have no doubt worked for a ball club that is very capable in the office.

I have been up and down the ladder. I know there are some things in baseball thirty-five to fifty years ago that are better now than they were in those days. In those days, my goodness, you could not transfer a ball club in the minor leagues, Class D, Class C ball, Class A ball.

How could you transfer a ball club when you did not have a highway? How could you transfer a ball club when the railroad then would take you to a town, you got off and then you had to wait and sit up five hours to go to another ball club?

How could you run baseball then without night ball?

You had to have night ball to improve the proceeds, to pay larger salaries, and I went to work, the first year I received $135 a month.

I thought that was amazing. I had to put away enough money to go to dental college. I found out it was not better in dentistry. I stayed in baseball. Any other question you would like to ask me?

Senator Kefauver: Mr. Stengel, are you prepared to answer particularly why baseball wants this bill passed?

Mr. Stengel: Well, I would have to say at the present time, I think that baseball has advanced in this respect for the player help. That is an amazing statement for me to make, because you can retire with an annuity at fifty and what organization in America allows you to retire at fifty and receive money?

I want to further state that I am not a ballplayer, that is, put into that pension fund committee. At my age, and I have been in baseball, well, I will say I am possibly the oldest man who is working in baseball. I would say that when they start an annuity for the ballplayers to better their conditions, it should have been done, and I think it has been done.

I think it should be the way they have done it, which is a very good thing.

The reason they possibly did not take the managers in at that time was because radio and television or the income to ball clubs was not large enough that you could have put in a pension plan.

Now I am not a member of the pension plan. You have young men here who are, who represent the ball clubs.

They represent the players and since I am not a member and don't receive pension from a fund which you think, my goodness, he ought to be declared in that, too, but I would say that is a great thing for the ballplayers.

That is one thing I will say for the ballplayers, they have an advanced pension fund. I should think it was gained by radio and television or you could not have enough money to pay anything of that type.

Now the second thing about baseball that I think is very interesting to the public or to all of us that it is the owner's own fault if he does not improve his club, along with the officials in the ball club and the players.

Now what causes that?

If I am going to go on the road and we are a traveling ball club and you know the cost of transportation now — we travel sometimes with three Pullman coaches, the New York Yankees and remember I am just a salaried man, and do not own stock in the New York Yankees, I found out that in traveling with the New York Yankees on the road and all, that it is the best, and we have broken records in Washington this year, we have broken them in every city but New York and we have lost two clubs that have gone out of the city of New York.

Of course, we have had some bad weather, I would say that they are mad at us in Chicago, we fill the parks.

They have come out to see good material. I will say they are mad at us in Kansas City, but we broke their attendance record.

Now on the road we only get possibly 27 cents. I am not positive of these figures, as I am not an official.

If you go back fifteen years or so if I owned stock in the club, I would give them to you.

Senator Kefauver: Mr. Stengel, I am not sure that I made my question clear.

Mr. Stengel: Yes, sir. Well, that is all right. I am not sure I am going to answer yours perfectly, either.

Senator O'Mahoney: How many minor leagues were there in baseball when you began?

Mr. Stengel: Well, there were not so many at that time because of this fact: Anybody to go into baseball at that time with the educational schools that we had were small, while you were probably thoroughly educated at school, you had to be — we only had small cities that you could put a team in and they would go defunct.

Why, I remember the first year I was at Kankakee, Illinois, and a bank offered me $550 if I would let them have a little notice. I left there and took a uniform because they owed me two weeks' pay. But

I either had to quit but I did not have enough money to go to dental college so I had to go with the manager down to Kentucky.

What happened there was if you got by July, that was the big date. You did not play night ball and you did not play Sundays in half of the cities on account of a Sunday observance, so in those days when things were tough, and all of it was, I mean to say, why they just closed up July 4 and there you were sitting there in the depot.

You could go to work someplace else, but that was it.

So I got out of Kankakee, Illinois, and I just go there for the visit now.

Senator Carroll: The question Senator Kefauver asked you was what, in your honest opinion, with your forty-eight years of experience, is the need for this legislation in view of the fact that baseball has not been subject to antitrust laws?

Mr. Stengel: No.

Senator Langer: Mr. Chairman, my final question. This is the Antimonopoly Committee that is sitting here.

Mr. Stengel: Yes, sir.

Senator Langer: I want to know whether you intend to keep on monopolizing the world's championship in New York City.

Mr. Stengel: Well, I will tell you. I got a little concern yesterday in the first three innings when I saw the three players I had gotten rid of, and I said when I lost nine what am I going to do and when I had a couple of my players. I thought so great of that did not do so good up to the sixth inning. I was more confused but I finally had to go and call on a young man in Baltimore that we don't own and the Yankees don't own him, and he is doing pretty good, and I would actually have to tell you that I think we are more the Greta Garbo type now from success.

We are being hated, I mean, from the ownership and all, we are being hated. Every sport that gets too great or one individual — but if we made 27 cents and it pays to have a winner at home, why would not you have a good winner in your own park if you were an owner?

That is the result of baseball. An owner gets most of the money at home and it is up to him and his staff to do better or they ought to be discharged.

Senator Kefauver: Thank you very much, Mr. Stengel. We appre-

ciate your presence here. Mr. Mickey Mantle, will you come around?
. . . Mr. Mantle, do you have any observations with reference to the
applicability of the antitrust laws to baseball?

Mr. Mantle: My views are just about the same as Casey's.

Here is Stengel in full display, testifying before the U.S. Congress as it
considered the wisdom of baseball's antitrust exemption. Note that
while Stengel had very little to say about that, he had plenty to say
about everything else. Congress didn't mind.

But Stengel, despite his verbal high jinks, possessed a keen baseball
mind, as his record of seven world championships as Yankee manager
in only twelve seasons demonstrates.

SO LONG TO STENGELESE

from *The New York Post*, October 19, 1960

(*Post* reporter Leonard Shecter has been around Casey Stengel so long he's inclined, in moments of stress, to lapse into Stengelese. It last happened in 1959 when the Yankees dropped into last place. Now the firing of the Yankee manager has him all shook up.)

To tell you the truth I didn't think they'd back up the moving van for Stengel after he won 10 pennants in 12 years, look it up, and made all that money for his owners he got fired by more than one ball club, that is you could say he was fired because his services were no longer required but nothing like this has happened since he left Kankakee with a uniform because they owed him $500.

They made a big mistake about Stengel in Kankakee where they said he could hit, run and field and was a very good player from the shoulders down. He got smart pretty fast when he came to manage the Yankees and everybody started wondering how come he was so dumb so long.

But maybe the Yankees made the biggest mistake about him and what if he should get smart with another ball club now in this league or the other and win the pennant because age has nothing to do with managing, it's how you instill a ball club. Then you'll have to wonder who really got the vaseline pot because it'll be oops, how's it kid, with the Yankees in fourth place and what kind of place is that for the Yankees?

Had to Leave

You ask me the man who discharged Stengel which is Dan Topping, and you'd have to say he was discharged since there is no question he had to leave, couldn't be so smart just because he's rich. And you can put that in the paper. You want to know why? Because it's whiskey, beer and hop with Casey Stengel and the Yankees never flop.

He's got the spirit of seventy six and his players never could have done it without him. Maybe he got a little sarcastic on the field but all the players who worked for him made a living and he never thanked anybody except Jensen who was so great some place else and he retired.

If you ask me Stengel was smart before he got gray hair, maybe even when he was a WPA manager over in Brooklyn, or in Boston where they got the Charles River, that's the river that blows in from the outfield, so what's the use trying to hit it out of the park when you got to butcher boy it? When a man's done what he did you'd have to say he's a splendid manager in every way with excellent understanding of the game, a manager who never win it be defunct.

The Things He Said

What's the use of saying he wasn't good to his players when if they didn't get a World Series check the bills come in just the same? He knew it was no use asking a player to execute if he couldn't execute which is why some pitchers would hit away because they couldn't execute a bunt and get a base hit to right field.

You could look it up in a book for men to say the things he said and not find it. He said Bobby Richardson don't smoke and don't chew and don't stay out late and still can't hit .250 and admitted when he was wrong. And he said Jerry Lumpe looked like the greatest hitter in the world until you played him and what was wrong with that?

He had to handle players and you know how they are. They don't like to hit eighth but you can't skip eighth can you? The trouble with half the players is they're deceiving but they don't do it all the time. You manage 38 years with players like that and they got to build you a statue.

You'd have to say he got along with newspapermen too, which is not easy, even if he did say they write better on the petition asking him not to retire than they do in the paper. And I'll tell you something else. If you think we won't miss him, you're a Ned in the third reader.

Shecter, best remembered today as the ghostwriter of Jim Bouton's Ball Four, *was one of the new breed of baseball reporters whom Jimmy Cannon dubbed "the chipmunks," for their chatty, single-minded reporting. When Stengel was forced into retirement following the 1960 season, Shecter chose to eulogize the Yankees' manager with his own version of Stengelese, making use of Stengel's own trademark phraseology.*

DOUBLE M FOR MURDER

Maris and Mantle Are the Bludgeons That
May Bring the Pennant Back to New York.

from *Sports Illustrated,* July 4, 1960

Someday people may talk of the Great Yankee Slump, that brief period in the history of the American League when the mice whipped the cat. It began, they may remember, on August 9, 1958, when the New York Yankees, leading the league by 16½ games, lost a game to the Boston Red Sox, 9–6. It ended June 7, 1960, when the Yankees defeated the White Sox 5–2. They beat the White Sox again the next day and the next, then won two games from Cleveland, two from Kansas City and four more from Chicago. Last week they continued to win — two games from Detroit, two from Cleveland. The Yankees had won 15 out of 19 games and were in first place. The Great Slump was over, the cat was on the prowl, and the mice of the league were looking for a place to hide.

That period between August of 1958 and June of 1960 was one of almost continuous pain for the Yankees. They lost 25 of their last 44 games in 1958, and although they won the pennant, their fourth in a row, and the World Series, they were sick and they knew it. The spring of 1959 brought no improvement. The Yankees fell into last place in May and eventually finished a poor third with a record of 79 games won, 75 games lost. This season, the Yankees lost 20 of their first 41 games — making 120 losses in 239 games — and they floundered in fourth place. And then, without warning, they snapped out of it. There are many reasons for the Yankee resurgence. "Tell them we started winning when the old man got back," said one player sarcastically (a majority of the Yankee players dislike

Casey Stengel). Nonetheless, it is true that the team started winning the day Stengel returned after a week's illness.

A more concrete reason is the powerful and timely hitting of Mickey Mantle. "When he hits, we move," said pitcher Art Ditmar. Mantle, in the worst slump of his up and down career in April and May, cracked out of it in early June. During the three weeks of the Yankee rampage Mantle hit well over .400, with 18 runs batted in and eight home runs.

One Mantle home run in particular gave the Yankees a lift. Having just beaten the White Sox three times, the Yankees were playing the Indians at Yankee Stadium. At one point they led 3–1, but Cleveland fought back to make it 3–2 and then 3–3. Left-hander Dick Stigman, relieving for the Indians, was settling the Yankees down in order. ("He bothers us," says Stengel.) Mantle led off the eighth inning and took a strike. Then he swung foolishly and missed for strike two. He swung again at the third pitch and lined it into the left-field seats for a home run and, as it turned out, the victory.

Then there is Hector Lopez, who has been hitting well in the No. 2 spot, just in front of Mantle. His defensive play has improved, too, although he is still a liability in left field. In Detroit, he went back slowly for a line drive, jumped too soon and was nearly hit by the ball, which went for a double. Eventually the runner scored, and Detroit led 1–0. A few innings later Lopez hit a sharp single to left center, scoring a man from third and tying the score at 1–1. "You see," said Leonard Shecter of the New York Post, "Hector giveth and Hector taketh away."

But, good as Mantle and Lopez have been lately, it is extremely doubtful that the Yankees would be in first place were it not for their new right fielder, Roger Maris. As one New York writer said: "It is true that Mantle is mainly responsible for moving the team from fourth place to first. But if it weren't for Roger's strong hitting all season the Yankees might have been in sixth or seventh when Mantle got hot."

Maris opened the season against the Red Sox with two home runs, a double and a single, and he has not been below .320 since. Currently he leads the league with 22 home runs and 58 runs batted in. He has also fielded well. In Cleveland last week he made a leaping backhand catch of a ball just as it was falling over the fence for what would have been a grand-slam home run. It saved the game for the Yankees.

Roger Maris is 25 and powerfully built. He came to the Yankees from Kansas City last winter in a trade in which the Yankees gave away, among others, Hank Bauer, an old favorite at Yankee Stadium. "For the first few games I used to hear guys yelling for Bauer," Maris said recently, "but not much anymore."

This is Maris's fourth major league season. With both Cleveland and Kansas City he displayed flashes of promise, but misfortune — one year an appendectomy, another year some broken ribs — kept him from the big year. He gives some credit for his fast start this season to the good hitting Yankees who surround him in the batting order — Mantle before him, Skowron (before he was hurt), Berra, or Howard after him.

"I'm getting better pitches to hit than I did in Kansas City last year," Maris said last week in Detroit. "You hear people say it's easier to hit when you're on a bad ball club. Don't believe it. Pitchers throwing against second-division teams are generally loose. The ball is really moving. Once in a while in batting practice you'll see a pitcher with great stuff. That's because he knows he doesn't have to get anybody out, so he's relaxed. But any pitcher facing a team like the Yankees is likely to be in tight situations, which makes it tougher on him."

Batting directly after Mantle does present one problem, however. In Detroit, Mantle hit a home run off Frank Lary. When Maris got up, the first pitch was way inside, forcing him back from the plate. A few innings later Mantle hit another home run off Lary. This time the first pitch to Maris was directly over the top of his head. "I don't mind it," said Maris, "but I do think the umpire might have warned Lary after that second pitch." (Mantle, incidentally, is also frequently thrown at, but with him it is his legs. Knowing Mantle has a bad right knee, it is standard procedure with American League pitchers to make him skip rope periodically.)

On the base paths, Maris resembles a good college halfback. He is fast, especially when going from first to third, and he is rough. Shortstop Chico Fernandez of the Tigers, about to throw to first to complete a double play, was suddenly confronted with the vision of the 200-pound Maris bearing down on him. Fernandez was so anxious to evacuate the area, he threw wildly, allowing a Yankee runner to score.

Off the field, Maris presents, to the public at least, a quiet, serious, almost grim personality. He is polite, modest and friendly, but reveals little of himself or his feeling in a conversation. He is happy to be with the Yankees, but does not like New York City, which he considers too big. ("Don't ever let anybody tell you they don't like coming to a team like the Yankees," says Roger's roommate, Bob Cerv, who also came from Kansas City. "The Yankees are over the tracks and up the hill.") Roger's wife and two children are still living in Kansas City because she is pregnant. "Perhaps I'll bring them East next year," he said, and then added with a slight smile, "unless my wife's pregnant again, which she probably will be." In the meantime Roger is looking forward to this year's first All-Star Game, which will be played in Kansas City. He is a sure bet to make the team.

As Maris and Mantle have devastated the western teams with their hitting, the press began to link the two names in the tradition of Ruth and Gehrig. "The buzz-saw team," one Detroit writer called them. "Double M for Murder," said another. Mel Allen, reaching, called them "the gold dust twins" on one occasion and "those magic marvels, Mantle and Maris" on another. Casey Stengel provided the most succinct description. "The fella in right does the job if the other fella doesn't," Casey said.

Of course other Yankees have been doing the job too. Kent Hadley came off the bench, replacing the injured Moose Skowron, and hit home runs his first two times up. (The Yankees immediately started referring to Skowron as Wally Pipp, the Yankee first baseman who in 1925 let a fellow named Gehrig take over one day.) Tony Kubek also hit two home runs in a game to beat Cleveland, while Cletis Boyer and Bobby Richardson have been fielding excellently at third and second. Maris and Cerv credit the Yankee pitching for the hot streak.

Need That Pitching

"At Kansas City," said Cerv, "we had some good hitting teams, but no pitching. You need it to win. Ditmar and Coates have been good, and now Ford and Turley look like they're ready to win."

Ditmar, who after a slow start won four straight games, praises the hitting. "I'm pitching the same as I did earlier in the season, but now I'm getting runs."

A few hours later Ditmar was on the mound, trying to hold on to a 3–2 lead. He got out of the seventh inning, but he was tired and the Tigers were closing in. Then, leading off the Yankee eighth, Lopez tripled, Mantle doubled and Maris, on a 3–0 pitch, hit a towering home run. With three swings, the Yankees had wrapped up another game. It was just like old times, and the Yankees look like the Damn Yankees again.

RED SMITH

PILGRIMAGE

from *The New York Herald Tribune,* September 22, 1961

BALTIMORE: This is a city known for those architectural expedients called "row houses," block after block of identical brick fronts with identical white stoops at every door. Early every morning, housewives can be seen scrubbing the stoops, which are marble in the more expensive neighborhoods. The one at 216 Emory St., however, is cement dressed up with white paint which is now worn half away.

Emory is a narrow one-way street and the three-story row is short, with only four doors. The second door from the left is 216. Here Kate Schamberger Ruth, wife of a saloonkeeper and daughter of Pius Schamberger, the upholsterer whose home this was, bore a son on Feb. 6, 1895. He was named George Herman Ruth jr. and they called him Babe.

"The house used to be all three floors," said Mrs. Thomas Bell, a buxom, smiling Negro who occupies the ground floor with her husband, "but the company owns the building cut it up in apartments. There's another five-room apartment upstairs. Instead of going up from the street door there, the stairs used to be back here."

She led the way into a tiny, crowded, spotless living room heated by a stove. Lately when Roger Maris was closing in on Ruth's home-run record, Mrs. Bell said, a newspaper ran a photograph of the house — "They put our names in the article" — and since then a few strangers have been dropping around. She said her husband was an Oriole fan, but she couldn't care less whether the Babe's record fell or stood forever.

Shrine Number Two

A few blocks away, at 426 West Camden St., is Bludzuns' Tavern, a typical small neighborhood saloon. Ruth sr., had a bar here and the family lived upstairs in 1902 when Babe was sent to St. Mary's Industrial School where he lived — when he wasn't on the lam — until he joined the Orioles as a left-handed pitcher in 1914.

Vytante Bludzuns was behind the bar in front of a crudely lettered sign testifying to the tavern's membership in an Orioles' fan club. The proprietor is a small man, of Lithuanian extraction, he said, explaining his name.

"Bourbon and branch," a visitor said.

"No bourbon," Bludzuns said. "No call for it here. Rye or scotch."

"That's funny," the man said, "because they don't make Maryland rye any more. Anybody left in this neighborhood who knew the Ruths?"

"Unh-unh. How long's it been? Fifty years?"

"More, I guess. What happened to this place during Prohibition?"

"It stayed open. There were two breweries in town making near-beer, but they had to make good beer before they took the alcohol out."

"Do the customers argue about Ruth's record?"

"Sure. Some hoped that fella would do it, and some hoped he wouldn't. If it was our Jim Gentile going for it, now, everybody would be for him."

Lasting Memorial

Certainly Baltimore's three most famous sons were Babe Ruth, ballplayer; Henry L. Mencken, the sage; and Francis Scott Key, a lyric writer. Memorial Stadium, formerly called the Babe Ruth Stadium, stands on Babe Ruth Plaza, but neither the house on Emory St. nor the gin mill on Camden bears any sort of memorial to the mightiest figure baseball ever knew.

Perhaps that's all right, though. Perhaps the best possible place for a memorial is the place where it does appear — on page 22 of baseball's "Little Red Book." Under the heading "Most Home Runs — Season" a single line reads: "60 — George H. Ruth, New York A.L. (28 at home, 32 on road), 151 games, 1927."

That's going to stay right where it is for at least another year, because when the Yankees had won the pennant night before last in their 154th game of this season, Roger Maris had 59 home runs. No matter how many more he hits during the extended schedule of 162 games, the printed record will note the fact that he didn't exceed Ruth's total within the framework prescribed.

Now that the great ghost hunt is ended, the most striking aspect of it all seems, in retrospect, to be the way everybody got emotionally involved. While half the population was rooting passionately for Maris, the other half was buying do-it-yourself voodoo kits and memorizing incantations guaranteed to reduce the upstart to jelly.

The Levelest Head

Never in all of Ford Frick's administration had such controversy raged around the baseball commissioner, not even on that black day a decade ago when the players did feloniously and treasonably hire a lawyer. Militant moderns, scornful of tradition, abused the commissioner for his ukase that Ruth's record would not be considered broken unless somebody hit 61 inside 154 games. Idol-worshippers, jealously protective toward their chief deity, hailed Frick as a latter-day Solomon, if not a messiah.

Perhaps the individual who preserved a sense of proportion best of all was Maris himself. At the plate he heard obscene abuse from the creeps who think that a ticket to the game entitles them to horsewhip the entertainers. Off the field he was badgered ceaselessly by fans, the press, radio-TV, press agents, promoters. Only on rare occasions did this quiet, candid young man let his temper slip, and then it was due to some especially outrageous question or repeated references to "pressure," with the implication that he was choking up.

"But of course you were under pressure," a fellow said when it was over.

"Of course," he said simply.

WITH ROGER MARIS, VICTORY DINNER

from *The New York Post,* October 2, 1961

For 34 years we've been told about Babe Ruth's health-defying diet of hot dogs, pigs' knuckles, sour pickles and peanuts. This is what Roger Maris ate last night after becoming the first man in baseball history to hit 61 home runs in a major league season:

He had a shrimp cocktail, a steak medium, a mixed salad with French dressing, a baked potato, two glasses of wine, a sliver of cheese cake, two cups of coffee and three cigarets.

When he had finished his meal and sat back for a moment to enjoy a smoke, he said: "I really needed that. I was starved. That's the first thing I've had in my mouth today."

"Didn't you even have breakfast?" he was asked.

"No," he said. "Pat and I went to Mass at St. Patrick's this morning and then I went right up to the ball park."

"You had time to grab a bite."

"I couldn't eat," Roger said, "I just couldn't."

Five of us were around a table for what, if you're so romantically or historically inclined, could be called a celebration. There were Roger and Pat, his wife; Julie and Selma Isaacson, the Marises' two closest friends in New York, and me. It was no celebration, except for a toast Isaacson proposed with the first glass of wine. "To many more healthy and successful happy years like this one," Julie said.

We all drank, Roger thanked his friend, but then he said: "This was the greatest experience of my life. It had to be, but I wouldn't want to go through it again for anything."

"It's over now, Rog," he was told. "Relax if you can."

"Relax?" Maris said. "I haven't unwound yet. I'm just beginning to unwind. A lot of it is still a little hazy."

He seemed thoroughly at ease and yet he wasn't because his name is the most celebrated in the world at the moment. Say Kennedy, say Khrushchev, say Maris and you've said it all. His face is the mirror of fame. He can no longer hide as a faceless athlete from Hibbing, Minn., Fargo, N.D., or Kansas City.

All over the restaurant last night people were observing every move made by the man who beat Babe Ruth. They watched each bite of food he put into his mouth more than what was on their own plates. Commissioner Ford Frick can have his asterisk, but Roger will never be anonymous again. He knows it will get worse before it gets better.

Between courses, he sat there trim, but still tense in his dark blue suit. He wore a light blue silk broadcloth shirt with a tastefully monogrammed RM on the left breast in still lighter blue. A dark blue tie seemed to help set off the sharpness of his features and the emotional drain in his face that the past few weeks of racing against Ruth's ghost have put there.

"As it got closer and closer," Roger said, "I'd find myself unable to think clearly or straight. I'd be thinking something and all of a sudden my mind would be on something else and I wouldn't be able to remember at all what I'd been thinking about. It was like everything else was being crowded out."

It isn't difficult to understand how this could be so. Earlier in the day, Roger was in the dressing room when Darrell Johnson, the former Yankee catcher who is now with the Reds, visited briefly with him.

Maris joshed Johnson, who had been a coach with the Cardinals this season, then a catcher with the Phillies and finally was picked up by Cincinnati.

"You've had a long year," Maris said.

"You must have had a long one yourself," Johnson said.

"I was thinking about just one thing, after we knew we were going to clinch the pennant. It was the only thing on my mind."

Later, Roger said, as though the desire within him was so compelling that on this last day of the season he had to tell it, "Today I should be on the target. Friday, after the two days rest, I was under the ball; yesterday I was over it. Today I should be right on it. I just feel it."

Still later, as he stepped out of the batting cage, there was a look of dissatisfaction on his face. "I hope it improves in the game," he said, "because this bat doesn't feel like it's got it."

Yet it was this same 35-inch, 33-ounce bat with which he had hit his 60th, and he believes he used for his 59th, that he crashed his history-making home run off Tracy Stallard of the Red Sox. It came on the third pitch in the fourth inning on a fast ball that Roger knew was epochal as soon as he contacted it.

He rounded the bases, a man of history, happiness within himself, but with not a solid thought in his mind.

"Do you believe a guy's mind could go blank at a time like that?" Roger asked. "Mine was."

Then Maris' lips curled into that twisted, little-boy's grin that is so much a part of his 27-year-old's personality. He stopped his fork with the piece of steak on it midway to his mouth and gestured with it and there was a touch of anger in his voice.

"A radio guy called me in the dressing room afterward," he said, "and asked me to do an interview with him to be taped over the phone. I'm talking to him, when all of a sudden he asks, 'As you were running around the bases, were you thinking about Mickey Mantle?' Wasn't that the damndest question to ask? What are they trying to make between Mickey and me?"

"I'll tell you about Mickey," said Roger, who shared an apartment with Mantle and Bob Cerv this summer. "Last winter I was home and kidding with my daughter Susan. She's only a little girl. She wasn't four then. I asked her, who's the best baseball player in the world? 'Mickey Mantle,' she says."

But we were finishing dinner at Joe Marsh's Spindletop and Roger was saying that he wanted to hurry to Lenox Hill Hospital to visit Cerv and Mantle when a teen-aged girl came to the table and asked for his autograph.

"Would you put the date on it, too, please?" the girl said. "The date?" Roger said. "What is today's date?"

"The date," said Isaacson, "is the one you did what nobody else ever did."

While many reporters went overboard with their criticism of Maris as he chased Babe Ruth's home run record in 1961, the reporting of Mil-

ton Gross stands out for its sympathy and respect. While many writers whined that Maris wasn't half the player Ruth was, Gross chose to focus on the impact of the home run chase on Maris as a man, capturing both his fatigue during this pressure-packed time and his determination and stoicism during a time of intense scrutiny.

TAVERNS IN THE TOWN

from *The New Yorker,* October 26, 1963

Already, two weeks after the event, it is difficult to remember that there was a World Series played this year. It is like trying to recall an economy display of back-yard fireworks. Four small, perfect showers of light in the sky, accompanied by faint plops, and it was over. The spectators, who had happily expected a protracted patriotic bombardment culminating in a grand crescendo of salutes, fire-balls, flowerpots, and stomach-jarring explosions, stood almost silent, cricking their necks and staring into the night sky with the image of the last brief rocket burst still pressed on their eyes, and then, realizing at last that there was to be no more, went slowly home, hushing the children who asked, "Is that *all?*" The feeling of letdown, of puzzled astonishment, persists, particularly in this neighborhood, where we have come to expect a more lavish and satisfactory autumnal show from our hosts, the Yankees, the rich family up on the hill. There has been a good deal of unpleasant chatter ("I always knew they were really cheap," "What else can you expect from such stuckups?") about the affair ever since, thus proving again that prolonged success does not beget loyalty.

By choice, I witnessed the Los Angeles Dodgers' four-game sweep at a remove — over the television in four different bars here in the city. This notion came to me last year, during the Series games played in Yankee Stadium against the San Francisco Giants, when it became evident to me that my neighbors in the lower grandstand were not, for the most part, the same noisy, casually dressed, partisan, and knowing baseball fans who come to the park during the regular season. As I subsequently reported, a large proportion of the ticket-holders appeared to be well-to-do out-of-towners who came to the games only because they could afford the tickets, who seemed to have only a slipshod knowledge of baseball, and who frequently departed around the sixth or seventh inning, although all of last year's games were close and immensely exciting. This year, then, I decided to seek out the true Yankee fan in his October retreat — what the baseball beer commercials refer to as "your neighborhood tavern." I was especially happy about this plan after the Dodgers clinched the National League pennant, for I well remembered the exciting autumns here in the late forties and the mid-fifties, when the Dodgers and the Yanks, both home-town teams then, met in six different Series in what seemed to be a brilliant and unending war, and the sounds of baseball fell from every window and doorway in town. Those Series were a fever in the city. Secretaries typed only between innings, with their ears cocked to the office radio down the hall, and if business drew you reluctantly into the street (fingering your pool slip, designating your half-inning, in your pocket), you followed the ribbon of news via elevator men's rumors, snatches of broadcasts from passing taxi radios, and the portable clutched to a delivery boy's ear, until a sudden burst of shouting and laughter sucked you into a bar you were passing, where you learned that Campy or Duke had parked one, or that Vic Raschi had struck out Furillo with two on.

Even before Stan Musial had thrown out the honorary first ball to open the first game this year, I discovered that there would be no such attendant melodrama in the city. Just before game time, I walked west in the mid-forties and turned up Eighth Avenue, searching for the properly athletic saloon in which I could, in Jimmy Durante's words, "mix wit' de *hoi pollew*" who had not felt inclined to plunk down thirty-two dollars for a block of four home-game tickets at the Stadium. I stuck my nose in three or four likely-looking bars, only to find no more than a handful of fans who had staked out bar stools and were watching Whitey Ford and Sandy Koufax complete their warmups. Finally, exactly at game time, I walked into O'Leary's Bar, on the northwest corner of Fifty-third Street and Eighth Avenue, and found an audience of sufficient size and expectancy to convince me that it was not about to watch an afternoon quiz program. There wasn't a woman in the place, and the bar stools and nearly all the standing slots along the bar were taken. It was mostly a young crowd — men in their twenties, in sports shirts and with carefully combed hair. There were some off-duty postmen in uniform up front, with their empty canvas mailbags under their feet. I ordered a beer and took up a stand beside the shuffle alley, near the front door, from where I could see the television screen just above the head of the bar. It was a color set, and I was appalled to discover that Whitey Ford had turned blue since I last saw him; he and all the other ballplayers were haloed in rabbit's-eye pink, like deities in early Biblical color films. There was a black-and-white set at the back of the bar, and from time to time during the afternoon I turned around and watched that, just to reassure myself that Victor Mature was not kneeling in the on-deck circle.

It was a Yankee crowd at O'Leary's. There were winks and happy nudges when Whitey struck out Maury Wills, the lead-off man, and silence when Koufax fanned the side in the first. Frank Howard's double off the centerfield screen in the next inning won an astonished "Oooh!" and a moment later, when Skowron and then Tracewski singled, a man to my left shook his head and said, "Whitey ain't got it today." I wasn't sure yet, but I had to agree when Roseboro homered into the right-field stands, to make the score 4–0; left-handed hitters do not hit homers off Ford when he is pitching low and to the corners. Koufax stepped up to the plate, and several watchers suggested to Ford that he would do well to hit him in the pitching arm.

It was sound advice, though ignored. For a time, Koufax simply got better and better. He struck out Mantle and Maris in the second, and Pepitone in the third. With his long legs, his loose hips, his ropelike motion, and his lean, intelligent face, he looked his part elegantly — a magnificent young pitcher at an early and absolute peak of confidence, knowledge, and ability. In the fourth, facing the top of the order again, he struck out Kubek swinging, with a dipping curve that seemed to bounce on the ground in front of Roseboro, and got Richardson out on another big changeup curve; when he fanned Tresh, also for the second time, for his ninth strikeout, the men around me cried *"Wow!"* in unison. They had been converted; now they were pulling for Koufax. They knew their baseball — in the third, there had been expert admiring comment on a throw of Maris's that almost nailed Willie Davis at third base — and they knew they were watching something remarkable. What they had in mind, of course, was Carl Erskine's Series strikeout record of fourteen batters, which had been set exactly ten years before. Koufax, straining a bit now, struck out Mantle in the fifth, and then yielded three singles in a row before fanning Lopez, a pinch-hitter, for No. 11. In the sixth, he temporarily lost his poise; in spite of his 5–0 lead, he seemed edgy and his motion had grown stiff and elbowish. He walked Richardson and Tresh in succession. There was a stirring under the TV set, a brief resurgence of Yankee hopes, but Koufax took a few deep breaths on the mound, went back to his fast ball, and got Mantle and Maris to pop up, ending the inning.

Two innings later, the strikeouts stood at thirteen, and there was much less interest in Kubek's single and Tresh's two-run homer than in Richardson's strikeout, which tied the old record. O'Leary's was jammed now; no one had left, and those who had wandered in stayed to watch Koufax. A middle-aged man came in and asked one of the men near the bar to order him a Fleischmann's whisky and a beer chaser. "I won't get in your way," he said apologetically. "I'm gonna *drink* it and then go right out." But he stayed, too.

Elston Howard led off the bottom of the ninth with a liner to Tracewski. Pepitone singled, and Boyer flied out to Willie Davis. Koufax's last chance — a pinch-hitter named Harry Bright — came up to the plate. The count went to two and two, and there was a mass expulsion of held breath when Bright hit a bouncer that went foul. Then Koufax stretched and threw, Bright swung and missed, and the young men in O'Leary's burst into sustained applause, like an audience at Lincoln Center. Up on the pink-and-blue stage, Koufax was being mobbed by his accompanists. The sporting crowd left O'Leary's, blinking in the pale, unreal late-afternoon sunshine on Eighth Avenue and chattering about what it had seen. Not one of them, I was certain, was worried about what had happened to his team.

Oblivion descended on the Yankees after ten minutes of the second game. Maury Wills, leading off, singled, and was instantly trapped off first by Al Downing, the Yankees' young left-hander. But Pepitone's throw to second was a hair wide, and Wills skidded safely in on his belly. Gilliam singled to right, Willie Davis lined to right, and Roger Maris fell while going for the ball (or so Vin Scully, the announcer, told us — the camera missed the play), and the Yankees were down, 2–0. These rapid events were received with overpowering ennui in my second observation post, a spacious restaurant-bar called the Charles Café, just west of Vanderbilt Avenue on Forty-third Street. I had chosen the spot as a likely sporting headquarters because of the dozens of jumbo-size baseball and boxing photographs that hang above the mirrors on its walls, but the customers had nothing in common with the décor. These were youngish men too, but they were wearing dark suits and subdued neckties, and most of them were giving more attention to their hot-pastrami sandwiches and their business gossip than they were to the events on the television screens at either end of the long, shiny bar. One junior executive next to me at the bar ordered a Beefeater dry martini on the rocks — a drink that has perhaps never been served in O'Leary's. The only certifiable Yankee fan near me was a man who banged his palm on the bar when Maris tapped to the box in the second. His fealty was financially oriented. "Oh, God," he said. "For that they pay him seventy thousand a year." Subsequently, another railbird was unable to detect the considerable difference in appearance and batting style between two Yankee veterans. "Here's the man who took the catching job away from Yogi Berra," he said to me when Hector Lopez, an outfielder, came up in the fourth.

By the middle innings, shortly after two o'clock, these zealots were all back at their desks, the Yankees were down, 3–0, and I was lonely as a cloud in the Charles. Johnny Podres, the veteran Dodger lefty, was, unbelievably, pitching even better than Koufax had. He was less flashy but more efficient, working on the premise that it takes five or six pitches to strike a batter out but only two or three to get him to pop up or ground one to an infielder. This had become a nice, dull pitchers' Series. The TV announcers, Scully and then Mel Allen, tried to disguise the fact that the fall classic was laying an egg by supplying me with a steady stream of boiler-plate news. A dandruff of exclamation points fell on my shoulders as I learned that Dick Tracewski and an umpire named Joe Paparella came from *the same home town,* that Tommy Davis was the youngest batter to win the National League batting championship *two years running,* that Al Downing had been *twelve years old* when Jim Gilliam played in his first World Series, and that the Dodgers' Ron Perranoski and the Red Sox' Dick Radatz had *both attended Michigan State!* There was still another non-news flash from Mel Allen, but his peroration — "something that means nothing but is nonetheless interesting" —

was so arrestingly metaphysical that I didn't catch the rest of the message.

Languishing, I studied the pictures on the wall — shots of Ketchel fighting Billy Papke, Dempsey knocking out Jess Willard — and wished I were at ringside. Then I found a framed motto and studied *that:*

> Life is like a journey taken on a train
> With a pair of travelers at each window pane,
> I may sit beside you all the journey through,
> Or I may sit elsewhere never knowing you.
> But if fate should mark me to sit by your side
> Let's be pleasant travelers, it's so short a ride.
>
> — A Thought

I straightened my tie and looked about for someone to be pleasant to, but the nearest fellow-traveler was fourteen feet down the bar and totally occupied in making rings on the mahogany with his beer glass. I had to finish this particular part of life's journey, a longish one, alone with Mel Allen. Eventually, Podres ("The Witherbee, New York, Wonder!") won, 4–1, with a little help in the ninth from Peranoski, and the Series ("America's *greatest sporting spectacle!*") removed itself to California.

I was understandably anxious for company during the next game, and I found it at the Cameo, a Yorkville snuggery at Eighty-seventh Street and Lexington Avenue. The U-shaped bar, which enclosed two bartenders, two islands of bottles, and the TV set, was almost full when I came in, and everyone there seemed to know everyone else. It was a good big-city gumbo — men and women, Irishmen and Negroes and Jews and Germans, most of them older than the spectators I had encountered downtown. This was a Saturday afternoon, and the game, being played in Los Angeles, began at four o'clock, which is drinking time on Yorkville weekends. Boilermakers were the favorite, but there were interesting deviations, including one belt I had never seen before — a shot glass of gin with lemon juice squeezed into it. Everybody kept his drinking money out on the bar in front of him. With their club down two games, Yankee fans had grown reticent, but there was one brave holdout, a woman in her late forties named Millie, who was relying on voodoo. She had fashioned a tiny Dodger image out of rolled and folded paper napkins held together with elastic bands, and throughout the game she kept jabbing it viciously and hopefully with toothpicks. When Jim Gilliam came up in the bottom of the first, she stuck a toothpick in each of the doll's arms. "He's a switch-hitter," she explained, "so I gotta get him both ways."

The arrows failed to reach Los Angeles in time, though. Gilliam walked and then took second when Jim Bouton, the Yankees' sophomore fast-baller, threw a bullet all the way to the foul screen behind home plate. Tommy Davis hit a ball that bounced off the pitcher's mound and then off Bobby Richardson's shin, and Gilliam scored. The Yankees were again behind in the very first inning (as it turned out, they never led in a single game of the Series), and the Dodger glee club in the Cameo was in full voice. "None of that sweet sugar for the Yanks *this* year!" one man exclaimed.

In the next few innings, I evolved the theory that the Dodger pitching staff had made a large pre-Series bet on their comparative abilities, because Don Drysdale, the handsome home-team pitcher, was easily surpassing both Koufax and Podres. His fast ball and his astonishing curves, pitched three-quarters overhand from the apparent vicinity of third base, had the Yankee batters bobbing and swaying like Little Leaguers. Even so, it was an exciting, lively afternoon, because Bouton, although in a lather of nerves, kept pitching his way out of one jam after another, and the game, if not the entire Series, now almost surely hung on that one run. In the seventh, the Dodgers seemed certain to widen the gap when they put Roseboro on third and Tracewski on second, with none out. The combination of tension and boilermakers proved too much for one fan at this juncture. "This Roseboro's gonna blast one," he announced loudly. "Just watch and see."

"What's the matter with you?" his companion said, embarrassed. "Roseboro's standing on third. What are you — bagged or something?"

"That's what I *said*," the other insisted. "He's gonna hit a homer. Roseboro's gonna hit a homer."

What did happen was almost as unlikely. Drysdale hit a sharp grounder between second and first, which Richardson ran down with his back to the plate and pegged to Pepitone for the out at first. Pepitone then jogged happily across the infield, having found both Roseboro and Tracewski hopefully toeing third base. Roseboro had held up, Tracewski had run, and it was a double play. The man on the bar stool just to my right, who had told me that he once played semi-pro ball, was disgusted. "What's the *matter* with that Roseboro?" he said in disbelief. "No outs and the ball's hit hard to right, you got to run. You don't even look — you just *go!* That's baseball. Everybody knows that."

As it turned out, the insurance run was unnecessary. With two out in the top of the ninth, Pepitone hit a high smash that seemed to be headed for the bleachers. The Cameo's Yankee fans gave their only yell of the afternoon, but Ron Fairly, with his back almost against the right-field wall, put up his hands and made the catch that ended the game. Millie shook her head slowly and then crumpled her doll into a wet ball on the bar.

The next afternoon, I witnessed the obsequies in the bar of the Croydon, a genteel residential hotel on Eighty-sixth Street just off Madison Avenue. Surrounded almost entirely by women, but joined from time to time by bellboys and doormen and waiters who dropped into the bar to catch the action, I saw Frank Howard, the Dodger monster, apparently swing with one hand as he hit a hyperbolic home run into the second tier in left field — a blow that Mickey Mantle almost matched with his tying poke in the seventh. Whitey Ford pitched perhaps the best of all his twenty-one World Series games, giving the Dodgers only two hits, but he was up against Koufax again, and the Yankee hitters remained hopelessly polite. In the seventh, Clete Boyer's throw to Pepitone went through the Yankee first baseman as if he had been made of ectoplasm, and Gilliam steamed all the way around to third on the error, immediately scoring on Willie Davis's fly. At this juncture, the talk in the bar, which had been pro-Dodger (when it was not concerned with *haute couture*, Madame Nhu, Elizabeth Taylor, and lower-abdominal surgery), took a sharp, shocked swerve toward disbelief and sadness. Even a lifelong Dodger fan who had come with me to the Croydon was affected. "I never thought the Yankees would go out like this, without winning one damned game," he said, shaking his head. He sounded like a tormented foretopman who had just learned that Captain Bligh was dying of seasickness. The demise came quickly. Richardson singled, but Tresh and then Mantle took third strikes with their bats resting comfortably on their shoulders. There was an error by Tracewski, but Lopez dribbled to Wills for the last out, and the Dodger squad galloped out and tried to tear souvenir chunks off their baby, Koufax.

As drama, the 1963 World Series was wanting in structure and development. This lack of catharsis was sensed, I am sure, even by Dodger supporters. The disappointment, the small, persistent resentment, about the outcome of the Series which is felt (or so I believe) by Yankee fans is at least partly a result of the fact that they had to wait through a long summer of vapid American League baseball, in which the Yankees walked over such feeble and acquiescent challengers as the Chicago White Sox, the Minnesota Twins, and the Baltimore Orioles. The only crucial series for the Yanks in 1963 was the last one, and they muffed it shockingly.

Those millions of us who saw the Series on television were left with the emptiest balloon of all. There is a small paradox here, because these were pitchers' games, and the television camera, hovering over the home-plate umpire's shoulder and peering down the back of the pitcher's neck, gives a far better view of each ball and strike than any spectator can get from the stands. But baseball is not just pitching. A low-scoring series of games is stirring only if one can sense the almost unbearable pressure it puts on base-running and defense, and this cannot be conveyed even by highly skilled cameramen. This World Series was lost by a handful of Yankee mistakes, most of which were either not visible or not really understandable to television-watchers. The cameras were on the hitter when Maris fell in the second game. The grounder that bounced off Richardson in the third game and Pepitone's astonishing fluff in the final game caused everyone near me to ask, "What *happened?*" On the same two-dimensional screen, it looked as if the throw to Pepitone had hit the dirt, instead of skidding off his wrist, as it did. It is the lack of the third dimension on TV that makes baseball seem less than half the game it is, that actually deprives it of its essential beauty, clarity, and excitement.

Yankee fans grew increasingly invisible as the Series progressed, and now they must nurse their winter puzzlement and disappointment with whatever grudging grace they can muster; to do otherwise would seem ungrateful in the face of their team's nine world championships and thirteen American League pennants in the past fifteen years. But it must be clear to them now that this Yankee team is not the brilliant, almost incomparable squad that many baseball writers claimed it was. No team can be judged entirely on one series, and the Yankees were not disgraced, for all the games were close; this was nothing like the dreary one-sided pasting that the Yankees gave the Cincinnati Reds in five games in 1961. And the Dodgers' pitching, opportunism, and nerve were magnificent. But fine pitching inevitably means bad batting; the terms are synonymous. Hard luck and injuries notwithstanding, the Yankees' best and most publicized athletes have not been of much help to them in recent Octobers. Mickey Mantle has batted .167, .120, and .133 in his last three Series; Roger Maris has hit .105, .174, and .000 in the same span. Whitey Ford has failed to win one of the last four Series games he has pitched. There is something wrong here — too little day-to-day opposition, perhaps a tiny lack of pride, perhaps a trace of moneyed smugness. Whatever it is, it probably explains this year's collapse and makes it certain that this Yankee team cannot be compared to the Ruffing-Gehrig-Dickey teams of the nineteen-thirties or the DiMaggio-Henrich-Rizzuto Yanks of the nineteen-forties and -fifties. What made those Yankee teams so fearsome, so admirable, so hated was typified by the death-ray scowl that Allie Reynolds, their ace right-handed pitcher a decade ago, used to aim at an enemy slugger stepping into the box in a crucial game. I can think of no member of the current team capable of such emotion, such combative pride. I suspect that local Yankee fans sensed the absence of this ingredient almost unconsciously, even before the Series began. That would explain, most of all, why the deepest passions and noisiest pleasures of baseball were so conspicuously absent in the bars and streets and offices of the city this autumn.

For nearly five decades Roger Angell's baseball reporting for The New Yorker *has been required reading for any baseball fan. This acute portrait of the city and the team during the 1963 World Series captures the waning days of the Yankee dynasty. Angell seems to sense that the end of an era is approaching, something the Yankee brass and most other reporters never saw coming.*

DICK YOUNG

YOUNG IDEAS

from *The New York Daily News,* October 16, 1964

ST. LOUIS, OCT. 15 — It is the eighth inning of the seventh game of the World Series, and the Cardinals have men on second and third with one down and the Yankee infield comes in tight, because when you're behind, 7–3, you can't afford to concede another run.

The batter is Hoot Gibson, World Series hero, en route to a strike-out record of 31 men, not counting the three times he struck out himself. This time, Gibson hit a bouncer to Clete Boyer, and in the next moment you get a pretty good picture of why the Yankees are losing World Series these years.

Boyer fires the ball home to Ellie Howard, heading off the runner, Timmy McCarver, second-place finisher to Gibson in the run for the Corvette. McCarver retreats toward third, with Ellie hot after him. Howard waits a little too long to give the ball back, and when he does, McCarver is sliding back into third, and the ball hits him on the side and slithers off toward short.

They Never Used to Laugh at the Yankees

Boyer chases the ball down, and whirls to see McCarver back on his feet and homeward-bound once more, whereupon Clete throws home again, and the Yanks go through this thing again. Having re-hearsed it once, they are much better at it, and this time McCarver is tagged out.

Clete Boyer is known as a magical fielder, and he must be to start two rundowns on one play, but the Cardinal fans laughed at the commotion, and that's the crux of the story. Nobody ever laughed at the old Yankees in the field.

These Yankees don't make the play. These Yankees made nine Series errors and a few other goofs that escape the boxscore, like the trial rundown on McCarver. People used to talk about the power of the invincible Yankees, and how the homers won the pennants and the World Series, but that was only partially the truth.

The whole truth is that the old Yankees knew how to stop the other guy from scoring, too, and these Yankees don't.

More Like the Mets Than Mets Themselves

In the fourth frame today, when the bottom began to fall out of their world, the Yankees looked more like the Mets than the Mets. Linz made a bad play. Howard made a bad play. Richardson made a bad play. Mantle made a bad throw, and in went three ragged runs for St. Louis, and the Yanks were never again in the ballgame.

They run on Mantle now, because they know the arm has gone along with the legs, so they take liberties they wouldn't have dared a few years ago, when Mantle was a whole ballplayer, and great. Now, only his strength is left, and it is still awesome, this fasces of biceps and back muscle which powered three homers in the Series.

When the defense of these Yankees fell apart, and St. Louis was 3–0 ahead, Mel Stottlemyre had to come out for a pinch-swinger in the next stanza, and on came Al Downing to be bombed. That is the other part of the story — the pitching Yogi Berra had available to fire at the enemy. He had, in truth, Mel Stottlemyre, Jim Bouton and Al Downing. Stottlemyre had pitched in 13 big league games, Downing in 67, and Bouton was a craggy veteran. He had pitched in 114.

Berra also had, in half truth, Whitey Ford, whose left arm is so dead it has no pulse, and it is cold to the touch. They tried to conceal the true nature of Whitey's ailment by saying his heel was troubling him, and that's why he was bombed out within six innings of the first game and never came back again.

But Nobody Could Do Anything for Berra

Then, the truth leaked out. Ford had a sore arm, and it's not simply sore the way a pitcher's muscles become strained, or their ligaments inflamed. This one has a vascular block, similar to what Jack Sanford had earlier this year. Sanford was on the operating table for nine hours one day this summer, having circulatory transplants done, and maybe he will pitch again and maybe he won't, which is what Whitey Ford must now worry about.

The point is that Whitey Ford, who made Stengel look great in so many World Series, and Ralph Houk, too, could do nothing for Yogi Berra, and that is why Yogi lost in seven; that and the boots.

The last Yankee manager to lose a World Series in seven got fired. He was 70 years old, they said, but they don't have that excuse this time. Yogi Berra is only 39, like Jack Benny, and just as precious. There were times he may have felt 70, because never was a Yankee manager given so little, and asked to win.

Today, Yogi and Dan Topping rendezvous at a secret meeting place, and Berra will be told if he is to be retained. The club's share of the World Series was announced as $302,547.40. How do you fire a man who makes that much dough for the company in one week?

HALL OF FAME INDUCTION SPEECH

August 12, 1974

Thank you very much, Commissioner. I would really like to thank you for leaving out those strikeouts. He gave all those records, but he didn't say anything about all those strikeouts. I was the world champion in striking out and everything, I'm sure. I don't know for sure, but I'm almost positive I must have had that record in the World Series, too. I broke Babe Ruth's record for all-time strikeouts. He only had, like, 1,500 I think. I ended up with 1,710. So that's one that no one will ever break probably, because, if you strike out that much, you don't get to play very long. I just lucked out.

One of the reasons I'm in the Hall of Fame right now is not because of my speaking, so everybody be patient here. I know it's hot and I'll try to get through with what I gotta say real fast here. I was named after a Hall of Famer. I think this is the first time it's ever happened that a guy's ever come into the Hall of Fame that was named after one. Before I was born, my father lived and died for baseball and he named me after a Hall of Famer: Mickey Cochrane. I'm not sure if my dad knew it or not, but his real name was Gordon. I hope there's no Gordons here today, but I'm glad that he didn't name me Gordon.

He had the foresight to realize that someday in baseball that left-handed hitters were going to hit against right-handed pitchers and right-handed hitters were going to hit against left-handed pitchers; and he taught me, he and his father, to switch-hit at a real young age, when I first started to learn how to play ball. And my dad always told me if I could hit both ways when I got ready to go to the major leagues, that I would have a better chance of playing. And believe it or not, the year that I came to the Yankees is when Casey started platooning everybody. So he did realize that that was going to happen someday, and it did. So I was lucky that they taught me how to switch-hit when I was young.

We lived in a little town called Commerce, Oklahoma, and my mother, who is here today — I'd like to introduce her right now . . . Mom. We didn't have a lot of money or anything. She used to make my uniforms and we would buy the cleats or get 'em off of somebody else's shoes or somethin' and then we would take 'em and have 'em put onto a pair of my street shoes that were getting old. So that's how we started out. We lived in Commerce till I can remember I was about in high school, then we moved out to a farm. We had a 160-acre farm out in White Bird, Oklahoma, I remember. I had three brothers, but one of them was too little. My mom used to have to make the twins come out and play ball with me. We dozed a little ballpark out in the pasture and I think that I probably burnt my twins out on baseball. I think by the time the twins got old enough to play ball they were tired of it, because I used to make 'em shag flies for me and play all day, which I'm sorry of because they could have been great ballplayers.

My dad really is probably the most influential thing that ever happened to me in my life. He loved baseball, I loved it and, like I say, he named me after a baseball player. He worked in the mines, and when he came home at night, why, he would come out and, after we milked the cows, we would go ahead and play ball till dark. I don't know how he kept doing it.

I think the first real baseball uniform — and I'm sure it is — the most proud I ever was was when I went to Baxter Springs in Kansas and I played on the Baxter Springs Whiz Kids. We had — that was the first time — I'll never forget the guy, his name was Barney Burnett, gave me a uniform and it had a BW on the cap there and it said Whiz Kids on the back. I really thought I was somethin' when I got that uniform. It was the first one my mom hadn't made for me. It was really somethin'.

There is a man and a woman here that were really nice to me all through the years, Mr. and Mrs. Harold Youngman. I don't know if all of you have ever heard about any of my business endeavors or not, but some of 'em weren't too good. Probably the worst thing I ever did was movin' away from Mr. Youngman. We went and moved to Dallas, Texas, in 1957, but Mr. Youngman built a Holiday Inn in Joplin, Missouri, and called it Mickey Mantle's Holiday Inn. And we were doin' pretty good there, and Mr. Youngman said, "You know, you're half of this thing, so why don't you do something for it." So we had real good chicken there and I made up a slogan. Merlyn doesn't want me to tell this, but I'm going to tell it anyway. I made up the slogan for our chicken and I said, "To get a better piece of chicken, you'd have to be a rooster." And I don't know if that's what closed up our Holiday Inn or not, but we didn't do too good after that. No, actually, it was really a good deal.

Also, in Baxter Springs, the ballpark is right by the highway, and Tom Greenwade, the Yankee scout, was coming by there one day. He saw this ball game goin' on and I was playing in it and he stopped to watch the game. I'm making this kind of fast; it's gettin' a little hot. And I hit three home runs that day and Greenwade, the Yankee scout, stopped and talked to me. He was actually on his way to Broken Arrow, Oklahoma, to sign another shortstop. I was playing shortstop at that time, and I hit three home runs that day. A couple of them went in the river — one right-handed and one left-handed — and he stopped and he said, "You're not out of high school yet, so I really can't talk to you yet, but I'll be back when you get out of high school."

In 1949, Tom Greenwade came back to Commerce the night that I was supposed to go to my commencement exercises. He asked the principal of the school if I could go play ball. The Whiz Kids had a game that night. He took me. I hit another home run or two that night, so he signed me and I went to Independence, Kansas, Class D League, and started playing for the Yankees. I was very fortunate to play for Harry Craft. He had a great ball club there. We have one man here in the audience today who I played with in the minors, Carl Lombardi. He was on those teams, so he knows we had two of the greatest teams in minor league baseball at that time, or any time probably, and I was very fortunate to have played with those two teams.

I was lucky when I got out. I played at Joplin. The next year, I came to the Yankees. And I was lucky to play with Whitey Ford, Yogi Berra, Joe DiMaggio, Phil Rizzuto — who came up with me — and I appreciate it. He's been a great friend all the way through for me.

Lots of times I've teased Whitey about how I could have played five more years if it hadn't been for him, but, believe me, when Ralph Houk used to say that I was the leader of the Yankees, he was just kiddin' everybody. Our real leader was Whitey Ford all the time. I'm sure that everybody will tell you that.

Casey Stengel's here in the Hall of Fame already and, outside of my dad, I would say that probably Casey is the man who is most responsible for me standing right here today. The first thing he did was to take me off of shortstop and get me out in the outfield where I wouldn't have to handle so many balls.

At this time I'd like to introduce my family. I introduced my mother. Merlyn, my wife, we've been married 22 years. That's a record where I come from. Mickey, my oldest boy, David, Billy and Danny. That's my family that I've been with for so long.

I listened to Mr. Terry make a talk last night just for the Hall of Famers, and he said that he hoped we would come back, and I just hope that Whitey and I can live up to the expectation and what these here guys stand for. I'm sure we're going to try to. I just would — before I leave — would like to thank everybody for coming up here. It's been a great day for all of us and I appreciate it very much.

PART V

YANKEE ELEGIES

The successes enjoyed by the Yankees on the field have not come without a cost, and the story of the team is not one of uninterrupted triumph. For tragedy has also stalked the club. A series of Yankee stars and major figures have been lost before their time.

While the tragedies that have befallen the franchise are not unique, in a place like New York private tragedy rapidly becomes public. Each event takes on a larger sense of importance and somehow seems symbolic. As such, these tragedies have provided a challenge for writers, for it is the writer's responsibility to make sense of what seems senseless.

Lou Gehrig's farewell speech in 1939 provided the only necessary words in regard to his tragedy, but how does one summarize in words the passing of a figure like Babe Ruth, or communicate the loss felt by all of New York in 1979 after Thurman Munson's death in a plane crash? These are times when writers are put into perhaps the most difficult position imaginable. They must report both the facts of an event and its genuine emotional impact, a task often made even more difficult by the long-standing relationship the writer has to the subject.

The result has been some of the more poignant and memorable writing in baseball history.

FAREWELL SPEECH

July 4, 1939

Fans, for the past two weeks you have been reading about a bad break I got. Yet today I consider myself the luckiest man on the face of the earth. I have been in ballparks for 17 years and have never received anything but kindness and encouragement from you fans. Look at these grand men. Which of you wouldn't consider it the highlight of his career just to associate with them for even one day?

Sure, I'm lucky. Who wouldn't consider it an honor to have known Jacob Ruppert; also the builder of baseball's greatest empire, Ed Barrow; to have spent six years with that wonderful little fellow, Miller Huggins; then to have spent the next nine years with that outstanding leader, that smart student of psychology — the best manager in baseball today, Joe McCarthy? Who wouldn't feel honored to have roomed with such a grand guy as Bill Dickey?

Sure, I'm lucky. When the New York Giants, a team you would give your right arm to beat, and vice versa, sends you a gift — that's something. When everybody down to the groundskeepers and those boys in white coats remember you with trophies — that's something.

When you have a wonderful mother-in-law who takes sides with you in squabbles against her own daughter — that's something. When you have a father and mother who work all their lives so that you can have an education and build your body — it's a blessing. When you have a wife who has been a tower of strength and shown more courage than you dreamed existed — that's the finest I know.

So I close in saying that I might have been given a bad break, but I have an awful lot to live for. Thank you.

*   *   *

Few people in the stands knew that Gehrig was dying when he delivered his unforgettable farewell speech. Fewer still knew that Gehrig's speech was an extemporaneous homily spoken from the heart. At first he was too moved to speak at all, but as the crowd at Yankee Stadium roared and chanted his name, Gehrig recovered his composure and stilled the crowd with these heartfelt words.

DOWN MEMORY LANE WITH THE BABE

from *The New York Sun,* June 14, 1948

The old Yankees, going back twenty-five years, were dressing in what used to be the visiting clubhouse in the Yankee Stadium, some of them thin, some of them stout, almost all of them showing the years. Whitey Witt was asking for a pair of size 9 shoes. Mike McNally, bending over and going through the piles of uniforms stacked on the floor, was looking for a pair of pants with a waist.

"Here he is now," somebody added but when he said it he hardly raised his voice.

The Babe was the last to come in. He had on a dark suit and a cap oyster white. He walked slowly with a friend on either side of him. He paused for a moment and then he recognized some one and smiled and stuck out his hand.

They did not crowd him. When some one pointed to a locker he walked to it and it was quiet around him. When a few who knew him well walked up to him they did it quietly, smiling, holding out their hands.

The Babe started to undress. His friends helped him. They hung up his clothes and helped him into the parts of his uniform. When he had them on he sat down again to put on his spiked shoes, and when he did this the photographers who had followed him moved in. They took pictures of him in uniform putting on his shoes, for this would be the last time.

He posed willingly, brushing a forelock off his forehead. When they were finished he stood up slowly. There was a man there with a small boy, and the man pushed the small boy through the old Yankees and the photographers around Ruth.

Youngster Meets Babe

"There he is," the man said, bending down and whispering to the boy. "That's Babe Ruth."

The small boy seemed confused. He was right next to the Babe and the Babe bent down and took the small boy's hand almost at the same time as he looked away to drop the hand.

"There," the man said, pulling the small boy back. "Now you met Babe Ruth."

The small boy's eyes were wide, but his face seemed to show fear. They led the Babe over to pose him in the middle of the rest of the 1923 Yankees. Then they led him into the old Yankee clubhouse — now the visiting clubhouse — to pose in front of his old locker, on which is painted in white letters, "Babe Ruth, No. 3."

When they led him back the rest of the members of the two teams of old Yankees had left to go to the dugouts. They put the Babe's gabardine topcoat over his shoulders, the sleeves hanging loose, and they led him — some in front of him and some in back in the manner in which they lead a fighter down to a ring — down the stairs and into the dark runway.

They sat the Babe down then on one of the concrete abutments in the semi-darkness. He sat there for about two minutes.

"I think you had better wait inside," some one said. "It's too damp here."

Returns to Clubhouse

They led him back to the clubhouse. He sat down and they brought him a box of a dozen baseballs and a pen. He autographed the balls that will join what must be thousands of others on mantels, or under glass in bureau drawers or in attics in many places in the world.

He sat then, stooped, looking ahead, saying nothing. They halted an attendant from sweeping the floor because dust was rising.

"I hope it lets up," the Babe said, his voice hoarse.

"All right," somebody said. "They're ready now."

They led him out again slowly, the topcoat over his shoulders. There were two cops and one told the other to walk in front. In the third base dugout there was a crowd of Indians and 1923 Yankees and they found a place on the bench and the Babe sat down behind the crowd.

"A glove?" he said.

"A left-handed glove," some one said.

They found a glove on one of the hooks. It was one of the type that has come into baseball since the Babe left — bigger than the old gloves with a mesh of rawhide between the thumb and first finger — and the Babe took it and looked at it and put it on.

"With one of these," he said, "you could catch a basketball."

They laughed and the Babe held the mesh up before his face like a catcher's mask and they laughed again. Mel Allen, at the public address microphone, was introducing the other old Yankees. You could hear the cheering and the Babe saw Mel Harder, the former Cleveland pitcher, now a coach.

"You remember," he said, after he had poked Harder, "when I got five for five off you and they booed me?"

Harder Didn't Forget

"Yes," Harder said, smiling, "You mean in Cleveland."

The Babe made a series of flat motions with his left hand.

"Like that," the Babe said. "All into left field and they still booed the stuff out of me."

The Babe handed the glove to some one and some one else handed him a bat. He turned it over to see Bob Feller's name on it and he hefted it.

"It's got good balance," he said.

"And now —" Allen's voice said, coming off the field.

They were coming to boo Babe now. In front of him the Indians moved back and when they did the Babe looked up to see a wall of two-dozen photographers focused on him. He stood up and the topcoat slid off his shoulders onto the bench.

" — George Herman," Allen's voice said, "Babe Ruth!"

The Babe took a step and started slowly up the steps. He walked out into the flashing of flash bulbs, into the cauldron of sound he must know better than any other man.

In the opinion of his peers, W. C. "Bill" Heinz may well have been the greatest sports writer of them all. He felt confined as a columnist and left the Sun *in 1950 to concentrate on magazine profiles and books. His signature portraits for* True, Life, *and other magazines still read as fresh and original today as they did when he first wrote them. They appear in the recent collection* What a Time It Was.

GAME CALLED

from The North American News Alliance, August 19, 1948

Game called by darkness — let the curtain fall,
No more remembered thunder sweeps the field.
No more the ancient echoes hear the call
To one who wore so well both sword and shield.
The Big Guy's left us with the night to face,
And there is no one who can take his place.
Game called — and silence settles on the plain.
Where is the crash of ash against the sphere?
Where is the mighty music, the refrain
That once brought joy to every waiting ear?
The Big Guy's left us, lonely in the dark,
Forever waiting for the flaming spark.
Game called — what more is there for one to say?
How dull and drab the field looks to the eye.
For one who rules it in a golden day
Has waved his cap to bid us all good-bye.
The Big Guy's gone — by land or sky or foam
May the Great Umpire call him "safe at home."

The greatest figure the world of sport has ever known has passed from the field. Game called on account of darkness. Babe Ruth is dead.

There have been mighty champions in their day and time from John L. Sullivan to Jack Dempsey — such stars as Bobby Jones, Ty Cobb, Walter Johnson, on and on, who walked along the pathway of fame.

But there has been only one Babe Ruth — one Bambino, who

caught and held the love and admiration of countless millions around the world.

From the time he appeared on the big league scene with the Boston Red Sox in 1914, to the day his playing career ended more than 20 years later, Ruth was the greatest all-around ballplayer in the history of the game. He was a brilliant left-handed pitcher — the top power hitter of all time — a star defensive outfielder who could be rated with the best.

He was the one ballplayer who was a master of offense and defense — the nonpareil in both.

But Ruth was something more than a great ballplayer. He was an emblem, a symbol. No other athlete ever approached his color, not even the colorful Jack Dempsey, who had more than his share.

Babe Ruth's appeal to the kids of this nation was something beyond belief. He loved them and the kids knew it. There was nothing phony about his act. The kids knew the Babe was the greatest home run hitter of all time — that he was one of the greatest pitchers of all time — that he was an able place-hitter — that he could do more with a bat and a baseball than any player that ever lived. And the Babe could. But they also knew he was their pal.

I was present when he drove 60 miles one night before a world series game in Chicago to see a sick boy. "And if you write anything about it," he said, "I'll knock your brains out." He meant it that way.

Oddly enough, the Babe and Walter Johnson, the two stars on offense and defense, the mighty hitter and the whirlwind pitcher, died from the same cause — a tumor attached to the brain.

And once again, oddly enough, it was Babe Ruth who was Johnson's nemesis in the box and at the bat. He told me once that he had beaten Johnson six times by the score of 1 to 0. And even the great Johnson was none too keen about facing him from the firing hill.

I've been a close friend of Babe Ruth since 1919, nearly 30 years ago when the Red Sox and Giants traveled north from spring training together.

The true story of Babe's life will never be written — the story of wrecked cars he left along the highway — the story of the night he came near dropping Miller Huggins off a train — the story of the $100,000 or more he lost in Cuba one racing winter. (The Babe told me it was $200,000.)

The story of the ribald, carefree Babe who ignored all traffic signals. I was riding home with Ruth one night after a game of golf. The Babe was late. He ignored red lights and everything else in a big car. I begged Babe to let me get out and take a taxi. The Babe only laughed.

"These cops are my pals," he said. "A funny thing happened yesterday. Maybe I'd had a shot or so too much. Anyway, my car stalled. A big cop came up and asked what the matter was.

"'It won't run,' I said.

"'You're drunk,' the cop said.

"I hit him in the nose.

"'Now I know you're drunk, you so-and-so,' the cop said.

"He shoved me out of the way and drove me home."

One day the Babe was going the wrong way on a road to some golf club.

"Hey, this is a one-way street," some traffic cop hollered.

"I'm only driving one way, you dumb ———," the Babe said.

The cop, enraged, came rushing up, "Oh, hello Babe," he said. "I didn't know it was you. Drive any way you want to."

I sat one day with Babe at St. Albans, his golf club. The Babe took out a .22 rifle, and he and a pal began shooting away the door knob at a $1 a shot. The Babe missed some guy who had just opened the door by two inches. "He should have knocked," the Babe said.

Just one day with the Babe was a big adventure. There was the time he planted a small explosive bomb in some pal's car and almost blew up the place, including the Babe and myself. "I didn't know it was that strong," was all he said.

He was a rough, rowdy, swaggering figure, more profane than anyone I ever hope to meet again, with a strong sense of decency and justice and fair play. He was a sportsman, if I ever saw one. He wanted no advantage at any start.

There was the day Miller Huggins was going to fine Ruth $5,000. He had been absent two days. The fine was to be plastered after the game. All baseball writers were notified. The Babe appeared before the game, red-eyed and dazed looking. He was in terrible shape. He hit two home runs and a triple. Huggins forgot the fine.

These are among the true stories of Babe Ruth, who had no regard for the conventions of the common or normal man, whether this included action or words. But, beyond all this, he was open-hearted, friendly, always cheerful, a great guy to be with.

I can still hear the roar of voices wherever he was. There was nothing quiet and sedate about the Babe.

He could recall few names. "I caught back of him for 10 years," Mickey Cochrane once told me. "But he never knew my name. It was 'Hello, kid.'"

Driving around, Babe always responded to those who called out, "Hey, Babe." His reply was "Hello, Mom," or "Hello, Pop."

"They can't forget my funny-looking pan," he said once. They won't forget his funny-looking pan soon. His records were terrific, but they meant little when compared to the man who was so far above all the records he ever set. I've never seen him turn a mean trick.

No game will ever see his like, his equal again. He was one in many, many lifetimes. One all alone.

Every sports reporter in the country was called to eulogize Ruth following his death from throat cancer in 1948. Grantland Rice demonstrated that he still had his fastball and penned perhaps the most memorable of these accounts.

DAVE ANDERSON

FACE ON THE SCOREBOARD

from *The New York Times*, August 4, 1979

Out on the Yankee Stadium scoreboard, Thurman Munson's face looked down from the huge screen, his walrus mustache dominating his familiar glower. Nearby, the American flag hung limply at half-staff. And for eight minutes, the 51,151 spectators applauded reverently, their ovation slightly louder each time the face reappeared between flashes of the message that George Steinbrenner, the Yankees' principal owner, had composed for the occasion: "Our captain and leader has not left us — today, tomorrow, this year, next. Our endeavors will reflect our love and admiration for him." When the Yankees took the field to hear Terence Cardinal Cooke intone a prayer and Robert Merrill sing "America the Beautiful" before last night's game with the Baltimore Orioles, the Yankee catcher, Jerry Narron, remained near the dugout, staying there until the game was about to begin. But earlier, two switchboards kept beeping in the Yankee reception area outside George Steinbrenner's office.

"World champion Yankees," one of the switchboard operators was saying now. "The game is at 8 o'clock."

Some people wondered if the Yankees should have played last night, if they should have asked the Orioles for permission to postpone the game in honor of Thurman Munson's memory. But according to George Steinbrenner, that's not the way Thurman Munson would have wanted it. Bobby Murcer, the longtime buddy of the Yankee captain who was killed in the crash of his twin-engined jet Thursday near the Akron-Canton, Ohio, airport, had consoled Diane Munson that night.

"Bobby told us," George Steinbrenner was saying now, "that Diane said Thurman would have wanted the team to play all their games. That's what he would want the team to do and that's what we're going to do."

There Were Warnings

In his plush glass-walled office that overlooked the grassy field, George Steinbrenner sat at the big round wooden table where Thurman Munson often had visited with him, asking business advice.

"I don't think most people knew how close we were," Steinbrenner said. "Nobody knew how much time we spent together. He used to come up here and talk with me, sometimes before the games or sometimes even after batting practice. He would be wearing his uniform pants and a T-shirt and sandals and he'd put his feet up on the desk and have a glass of orange juice and we'd talk. He liked to talk to me about business because he had all those deals going in Canton, where his home was.

"I remember telling him not long ago to get liquid, that we were going into a recession, and to get fixed-interest rates for his money rather than floating on prime. As a businessman, he was the same way he was as a player — a hard-working, smart guy."

But now George Steinbrenner was shaking his head and staring through the glass at the message board with Thurman Munson's face.

"Can you imagine Dock Ellis saying that I'm responsible for Thurman Munson's death because I let him fly that plane," he continued, referring to a quote from the former Yankee pitcher published yesterday. "I didn't want him to fly that plane. Back in spring training, he told me he had ordered that Cessna Citation and I told him, 'You don't need it, don't get it.'

"Later on he told me he could lease it to somebody for $100,000 and I told him to do it because flying a jet is not like flying a prop plane. I told him that he was jumping too fast from a prop plane to a jet, that a Cessna Citation is harder to fly than a Lear, that flying a jet is a fulltime job. And his wife was dead against it, too. But you know Thurman.

"I think he got the jet just before the All-Star break. I think he was only checked out in it for 10 days but he had nothing but problems with it. Somebody over at Teterboro told me he had problems with it and then Thurman told me he had to return it to Wichita to check out the problems. And he had problems when he flew it back from the Coast a couple of weeks ago. He had all sorts of problems with it."

Trade Talk with Gabe Paul

But at around that time Thurman Munson was having problems with his knees, too. His days as a catcher appeared to be over. His knees no longer could stand the constant bending. He talked about moving to the outfield or to first base next season. But, it is whispered now in the Yankee offices, he also talked about retiring after this season ended. He even mentioned that to George Steinbrenner shortly before the Yankees went on their recent road trip, Thurman Munson's last road trip.

"Would it make any difference to you if we traded you to Cleveland like you always wanted?" George Steinbrenner asked him.

"It might," Thurman Munson said. "If you got a deal for me with the Indians, maybe I'd consider playing a couple more years."

With that in mind, George Steinbrenner phoned Gabe Paul, the Indians' president, and they agreed to pursue a deal when the season ended. But as it turned out, Thurman Munson remained a Yankee throughout his career. And when his teammates gathered before last night's game, his pinstriped uniform shirt was hanging in his empty locker near the trainer's room, the "NY" facing out. Pete Sheehy, the venerable Yankee clubhouse man who goes back to Babe Ruth, did it that way.

"I just thought that was the way to do it," Pete Sheehy said. "I've never had this happen before."

Pete Sheehy remembered when Thurman Munson arrived at Yankee Stadium a decade ago as a member of the Binghamton farm team that was playing a game there.

"I had to find a pair of pants to fit him," Pete Sheehy said. "His rear end was too big. I always kidded him about that. He was grumpy but he didn't mean it."

And in the Stadium catacombs, Frank Messer, the broadcaster, stopped and recalled a conversation with Thurman Munson.

"I sat down in Chicago with him Tuesday night," Frank Messer said. "Thinking back on it now, it was almost as if he was giving his own eulogy. Near the end of the conversation, he looked at me and said, 'I just want the fans to remember me the way I was — stretching a single into a double.'"

Dave Anderson succeeded Red Smith as author of the notable "Sports of the Times" column, for which he won a Pulitzer Prize in 1981 for his commentary on sports.

MICHAEL PATERNITI

THE HOUSE THAT THURMAN MUNSON BUILT

from *Esquire*, September 1999

I give you Thurman Munson in the eighth inning of a meaningless baseball game, in a half-empty stadium in a bad Yankee year during a fourteen-season Yankee drought, and Thurman Munson is running, arms pumping, busting his way from second to third like he's taking Omaha Beach, sliding down in a cloud of luminous, Saharan dust, then up on two feet, clapping his hands, turtling his head once around, spitting diamonds of saliva: Safe.

I give you Thurman Munson getting beaned in the head by a Nolan Ryan fastball and then beaned in the head by a Dick Drago fastball — and then spiked for good measure at home plate by a 250-pound colossus named George Scott, as he's been spiked before, blood spurting everywhere, and the mustachioed catcher they call Squatty Body/Jelly Belly/Bulldog/Pigpen refusing to leave the game, hunching in the runway to the dugout at Yankee Stadium in full battle gear, being stitched up and then hauling himself back on the field again.

I give you Thurman Munson in the hostile cities of America — in Detroit and Oakland, Chicago and Kansas City, Boston and Baltimore — on the radio, on television, in the newspapers, in person, his body scarred and pale, bones broken and healed, arms and legs flickering with bruises that come and go like purple lights under his skin, a man crouched behind home plate or swinging on-deck, jabbering incessantly, playing a game.

I give you a man and a boy, a father and a son, twenty years earlier, on the green expanse of a 1950s Canton, Ohio, lawn, in front of a stone house, playing ball. The father is a long-distance truck driver, disappears for weeks at a time, heading west over the plains, into the desert, to the Pacific Ocean, and then magically reappears with his hardfisted rules, his maniacal demand for perfection, and a photographic memory for the poetry he recites. . . . "No fate / can circumvent or hinder or control / the firm resolve of a determined soul."

Now the father is slapping grounders at the son and the boy fields the balls. It is the end of the day and sunlight fizzes through the trees like sparklers. As the boy makes each play, the balls come harder. Again and again, until finally it's not a game anymore. Even when a ball takes a bad hop and catches the boy's nose and he's bleeding, the truck driver won't stop. It's already a thing between this father and son. To see who will break first. They go on until dusk, the bat smashing the ball, the ball crashing into the glove, the glove hiding the palm, which is red and raw, until the blood has dried in the boy's nose.

I give you the same bloody-nosed boy, Thurman Munson, in a batting cage now before his rookie year, taking his waggles, and a lithe future Hall of Famer named Roberto Clemente looking on. Clemente squints in the orange sun, analyzing the kid's swing, amazed by his hand speed, by the way he seems to beat each pitch into a line drive. If you ever bat .280 in the big leagues, he says to Thurman Munson by way of a compliment, consider it a bad year.

When the Yankees bring Thurman Munson to New York after only ninety-nine games in the minors — after playing in Binghamton and Syracuse — he just says to anyone who will listen: What took them so long? He's not mouthing off. He means it, is truly perplexed. What took them so goddamn long? Time is short, and the Yankees need a player, a real honest-to-God player who wants to win as much as blood needs oxygen or a wave needs water. It's that elemental.

And wham, Thurman Munson becomes that player. He wins the Rookie of the Year award in 1970. He takes the starting job from Jake Gibbs as if the guy's handing it to him and plays catcher for the next decade, the whole of the seventies. He's named the Yankees' first captain since Lou Gehrig forty years earlier and shows up at a press conference in a hunting vest. He wins the Most Valuable Player award in 1976, and he still wears bad clothes: big, pointy-collared shirts and dizzying plaid sport coats. Not even disco explains his wardrobe. He helps lead the Yankees from a season in which the team ends up twenty-one games out of first place to the 1976 World Series, where they fall in four straight to the Cincinnati Reds despite the fact that Thurman Munson bats over .500. Then he helps take the Yankees back to the Series in 1977 and 1978 — two thrilling, heaven-hurled, city-rocking, ticker-tape-inducing wins!

And shoot if those seventies teams weren't a circus. The Bronx Zoo. Manager Billy Martin dogging superstar Reggie Jackson, superstar Reggie Jackson dogging pit bull Thurman Munson, pit bull Thurman Munson dogging everyone, and then George — you know, Steinbrenner — the ringmaster and demiurge, the agitator and Bismarckian force who wants to win as badly as Thurman Munson. Birds of a feather. And alongside, a hard-nosed gaggle of characters — Catfish Hunter, Graig Nettles, Ron Guidry, Lou Piniella, Sparky Lyle, Mickey Rivers, Goose Gossage, Bucky Dent, Willie Randolph — who are fourteen and a half games behind the Boston Red Sox in late July 1978 and come screaming back to beat them in a one-game playoff to win the division, then trounce the Royals to win the pennant and thump the Dodgers to win the World Series. One of the greatest comebacks of all time.

And since this is New York, the press has an opinion or two. They call Thurman Munson grouchy, brutish, stupid, petty, greedy, oversensitive. It becomes a soap opera: Thurman Munson pours a plate of spaghetti on one reporter's head and nearly kicks another's ass. But the fans — all they see is this walrus-looking guy who plays like he's a possessed walrus. During a game against Oakland, when he commits an error that scores Don Baylor and then he subsequently strikes out at the plate, they heap all kinds of abuse on him, and, heading back to the dugout, he just ups and gives them the finger. Hoists the finger to everyone at Yankee Stadium. That's not family entertainment! The next day when he comes to bat, when his name is announced and Thurman Munson steels himself for a rain of boos, the same fans begin to applaud, then give him a tremendous ovation.

See why? Bastard or not, the man cares. Thurman Munson cares. Never backed down from anyone in his life — not his father, not another man, not another team, let alone fifty thousand fans calling for his head. And they love him for it. See part of themselves in him.

To this day they hang photographs of him in barbershops and delis and restaurants all over the five boroughs — all over the country. A Thurman Munson cult. Tens of thousands of people who bawled the day he died.

Including me.

So, I give you a boy — me — and a pack of boys: Bobby Stanley and Jeff DeMaio, Chris Norton and Tommy Gatto, Keith Nelson and John D'Aquila. All kids from my neighborhood, playing ball in the 1970s. All of us — each of us — pretending to be someone else: Catfish Hunter pitching to George Brett or Ron Guidry pitching to Carl Yastrzemski or Reggie Jackson or Lou Piniella or Graig Nettles batting against Luis Tiant in the ninth inning of a hot summer eve in suburban Connecticut as blue shadows fall over the freshly mowed backyards.

In our town's baseball league, I play catcher. I suit up in oversized pads and move as if I'm carrying a pack of rocks on my back. When a pitcher starts out shaky — maybe walks the bases loaded and then walks in a couple of runs to boot — I call time and trot out to the mound, kick some dirt around, chew gum. Keep throwing like that, I say, but can you try to throw strikes?

And, naturally, my man is Thurman Munson. Or not so naturally. I mean, why would a skinny, hairless nine- or ten- or eleven-year-old twerp identify with a gruff, ungraceful grown man who's known to throw bats at cameramen? What shred of sameness could exist between a do-gooding altar boy and a foulmouthed truck driver's son? But then, just playing Thurman Munson's position bestows some of his magic on me. Each wild pitch taken to the body, each bruise and jammed finger, is in honor of the ones taken by Thurman Munson. Each foul tip to the head becomes a migraine shared with Thurman Munson, and each hobbled knee brings a boy closer to the ecstatic revelations of a war-tested veteran, pain connecting two human beings on a level that goes beneath intellect and experience and age. Goes to a feeling. Writ on the body. We are the same dog.

At night during these muggy summers, my brothers and I watch the Yankees on television. When Munson takes the field and crouches behind home plate, or when he comes to bat, spitting into either glove and turtling his head once around, we watch. We watch him hoofing in the batter's box like an angry bull, excavating the earth, twinkle-toeing a pile of it in circles like a ballerina, and then digging in. For some reason, his presence is mesmerizing. He bears a striking resemblance to the butcher at our local supermarket: the same weak chin, the same fleshy cheeks. He has a number of little tics and twitches — cocks his head, messes with his sleeves — as if being harassed by horseflies. Yet somewhere deep in those brown eyes, he is as calm as a northern pond waiting for ducks to land. In that place he is seeing things reflected before they actually happen, and then he makes them happen.

And there is one magnificent night — October 6, 1978 — when Thurman Munson drives a Doug Bird fastball as deep as you can take a pitcher to left-center field at Yankee Stadium for a playoff home run that seals the deal: Yankees beat the Kansas City Royals 6–5 despite George Brett's own three home runs and then beat them once more for the pennant and it's nothing but bedlam. At the Stadium, the dam explodes; in this Connecticut suburb where the leaves are turning in the fingers of an autumn chill, four boys pump their fists, hooting and hollering and then rioting themselves — pig-piling, whacking one another with pillows, hyperventilating with happiness. A free-for-all!

So I give you a boy and a neighborhood of boys and a town of boys. I give you a suburbia of boys, and I give you five boroughs of boys, a city following a team that is a circus. A stitched-together bunch of brawlers and hustlers, cussers and bullies, led by their captain, who, as Ron Guidry puts it, can make you laugh and then just as soon turn around and put a bullet through your chest.

I'm not sure how the news about Thurman Munson gets out — maybe someone's older brother hears it on the radio or maybe someone's mother sees it on television. A friend dons a Yankee uniform and disappears inside his house, watching the news behind drawn curtains with his father and brother. Another friend hears about it in the backseat on the way to football practice and puts on his helmet to blubber privately, behind his face mask. Another simply won't come out of his bedroom.

For me, August 2, 1979, has been like other summer days: swim-team practice, some baseball, lawn mowing, then down to the

Sound with my buddy Mark Zengo to swim again. And that's where I hear that Thurman Munson is dead. I'm dripping salt water, and someone's brother says that Thurman Munson was burned alive.

When I get home, the downstairs is empty. Somewhere I can hear running water — my mom pouring a bath for my youngest brother. Something is cooking and I turn on the television. An anchorman and then the wrecked Cessna Citation, a charred carapace emblazoned with NY15, and flashing lights everywhere like some strange Mardi Gras.

It was an off day for the Yankees, and Thurman Munson was practicing takeoffs and landings, touch-and-gos. He'd had less than forty hours of experience with his new jet, and he accidentally put it into a stall. The Cessna dipped precipitously before the runway. It scraped trees, tumbled down toward a cornfield, hit the ground at about 108 miles per hour, spun, and had its wings shorn off. It crashed a thousand feet short of the runway and sailed to a stop some five hundred feet later, on Greensburg Road. The two other passengers — a friend and a flight instructor — survived, and they tried to drag Thurman Munson from the wreckage. He was conscious, probably paralyzed, calling for help. And all of a sudden jet fuel leaked, pooling near Thurman Munson, and the Cessna exploded.

Afterward, he was identified by dental records. Nearly 80 percent of his body was badly burned. The muscles of his left arm were wasted. He had a busted jaw and a broken rib, and the corneas of his eyes were made opaque by flame. He had a bruised heart and a bloody nose.

"The body is that of a well developed, well nourished, white male," read the autopsy, "who has been subjected to considerable heat and fire, which has resulted in his body assuming the pugilistic attitude."

The truth is I've had only one hero in my life. And his death coincided with a million little deaths — of boyhood, the seventies, a great Yankee team, an era in baseball, some blind faith. I didn't go Goth after Thurman Munson's death, I just changed a little without knowing it, in full resistance to change. And to this day, I don't understand: What happens when your hero suddenly stands up from behind home plate, crosses some fold in time, and vanishes into thin air?

One answer: You go after him. You enter your own early thirties and, as a man, you cross the same fold and try to bring him back, if only for a moment. You go to Canton, Ohio, on a hot day not unlike the day Thurman Munson died, to the house that Thurman Munson built, a fourteen-room colonial set on a knoll, a house with pillars out front like some smaller, white-brick, suburban version of Tara, and meet Thurman Munson's family — his wife, Diana, and the three kids: Tracy, who has three kids of her own now; Kelly, who just got married; and Michael, who was four when his father died and who himself played catcher in the Yankees' farm system.

Their father has been gone twenty years and they still don't exactly know who he is. Or, he is something different for each of them, and then different in each moment. An ideal, an epiphany, a hero, a betrayal. People didn't know Thurman, says Catfish Hunter today, they just loved the way he played. And sometimes his wife didn't know the real Thurman, either. He might visit some kids in a hospital, and later, when Diana learned about it, she'd get angry and say, Why didn't you tell me, your own wife?

'Cause you'd go tell the press, said Thurman Munson.

Maybe I would, she said. And why not? They think you're a spoiled ball-player.

And Thurman Munson said, That's why. That's exactly why.

Show the world that he was a goof-ball? A sap? A romantic? The man was a koan even to himself — he couldn't be figured or unraveled. He'd help lead the Yankees to a World Series victory — one of the proudest, sweetest moments of his life, he told Diana — then, based on some perceived locker-room slight, refuse to go to the ticker-tape parade.

There were five, six, seven Thurman Munsons, not counting his soul, and the one who mattered most was the private one, the one who came walking down a long hall like the one at the beginning of *Get Smart*, with doors and walls closing behind him. When he walked over the threshold after a long road trip, he'd hug his wife and say I love you in German. Ich liebe dich. He wrote poetry to her. He scribbled philosophical aphorisms. He loved Neil Diamond — "Cracklin' Rosie," "I Am . . . I Said" — played the guy's music nonstop, incessantly, ad infinitum, ad nauseam, carried it with him on a big boom box. Thurman Munson, the grim captain, identifying with picaresque songs about being on the road, lost and alone against the world, having something to prove, falling in love.

And the kids went bananas every time he came home, hanging off him like he was some kind of jungle gym. Two doe-eyed girls and a young, red-headed son who was afraid of the dark. Thurman Munson would sit at the kitchen table and eat an entire pack of marshmallow cookies with them. He'd take barrettes and elastic bands and disappear and do up his hair and then leap out of nowhere, Hi-yahing! from around a corner, wielding a baseball bat like a sword, doing his version of John Belushi's samurai. After the girls took a bath, Thurman Munson did the blow-drying. Then he combed out their hair. He never hurt us, remembers Kelly, the second daughter. I mean, our mom would kill us with that stupid blow-dryer and brush, and he said, I don't want to hurt you. And he took so much time and our hair would be so smooth and he'd take the brush and make it go under and then comb it out.

When Michael, the youngest, couldn't sleep, his father went to him. As a kid, Thurman Munson was afraid of the dark, too, but in his father's world, Thurman Munson would lie there alone; you were humiliated for your fear, and you learned to be humiliated — often. On the day Yankee general manager Lee MacPhail came to Canton to sign Thurman Munson, the boy's father, Darrell, the truck driver, lay in his underwear on the couch, never once got up, never came into the kitchen to introduce himself. At one point, he just yelled, I sure do hope you know what you're doing! He ain't too good on the pop-ups!

But Thurman Munson would sit with his own boy in the wee hours — at two, three, four, five A.M. Often he couldn't sleep himself, lying heavily next to Diana, his body half black and blue, his swollen knees and inflamed shoulders and staph infections hounding him awake. So he'd just go down the hall and be with Michael awhile. Just stretch out in the boy's bed. It's all right, he'd say. There's nothing to be afraid of.

And maybe, too, he was talking to himself, his body having aged three years for every one he played. So that at thirty-two, after a decade behind the plate, his body was old. In the very last game he played, he started at first but left after the third inning with an aggravated knee, just told the manager, Billy Martin, Nope, I don't have it. Went up the runway and was gone. But it was his body that was making money, realizing a life that far exceeded the life that had been given to him — or that he'd dreamed for himself. Including the perks: a Mercedes 450SL convertible, real estate, a $1.2 million Cessna Citation.

It's a life that Diana remembers wistfully when we go driving. We visit the cemetery. We talk about the current Yankees, and she confesses that she's just started following the team closely again, wonders if Thurman Munson means anything to today's players, is more than just some ghost from the past. Like with her young grandkids, who know him as a photograph or an action figure.

Diana takes me to the crash site, too. Maybe takes me there to prove that she can do it, has done it, will do it again. Did it six months after the crash when the psychiatrist said that maybe Diana and the kids were always late for counseling because Diana was afraid to pass the airport. Maybe Diana is always late, thought Diana, because she has three little kids and no husband. And, right then and there, she put them in the car and drove to Greensburg Road, to the very place where Thurman Munson's plane left black char marks on the pavement. To prove to them — and herself — that Thurman Munson doesn't reside in this spot, five hundred feet away and forty feet below the embankment to runway 19 at Akron-Canton Regional Airport. The distance of one extremely long home run. No, she says to me now, he may live somewhere else, but he doesn't live here.

So I go to see Ron Guidry and Lou Piniella, Willie Randolph and Reggie Jackson, Bobby Murcer and Catfish Hunter. At Fenway, I talk to Bucky Dent. I talk to Goose Gossage and Graig Nettles. I go to Tampa and sit with the Force himself, George Steinbrenner. The old Bronx Zoo, minus a conspicuous few. There are stories about Thurman Munson, a thousand, it seems. Funny and sad and inspiring. And these men — they are men now — they, too, are by turns funny and sad and inspiring.

When I visit Ron Guidry at his home in Lafayette, Louisiana, he's working alone in the barn, chewing tobacco. He's about to turn forty-nine, the same number he used to wear when he was pitching, when he was known as Gator and Louisiana Lightning. He looks as if he just stepped off the mound — all sinew and explosion. He works part-time as a pitching coach for the local minor league team, the Bayou Bullfrogs, and shows up for several weeks each year at the Yankees' spring-training facility in Tampa. Mostly, he hunts duck.

He remembers his first start as a Yankee. He came in from the bull pen, nervous and wired, and Thurman Munson walked up to him and said: Trust me. That's it. Trust me. Then walked away. As Guidry remembers it, everything after that was easy. Like playing catch with Thurman Munson. Thurman calls a fastball on the outside corner. Okay, fastball outside corner. He calls a slider. Okay, slider. Eighteen strikeouts in a game. A 25–3 record. The World Series. Just trusting Thurman Munson. Can't even remember the opposing teams, Guidry says, just remember looking for Thurman's mitt. Remembers that very first start: Thurman Munson came galumphing out to the mound, told him to throw a fastball right down the middle of the plate. Okay, no problem.

But I'm gonna tell the guy you're throwing a fastball right down the middle, says Thurman Munson.

Guidry says, Now, Thurman, why'n the hell would you do that?

Trust me, says Thurman Munson. Harumphs back to the plate. Guidry can see him chatting to the batter, telling him the pitch, then he calls for a fastball right down the middle of the plate. Damn crazy fool. Guidry throws the fastball anyway, batter misses. Next pitch, Thurman Munson is talking to the batter again, calls a fastball on the outside corner, Guidry throws, batter swings and misses. Talking to batter again, calls a slider, misses again. Strikeout. Thurman Munson telling most every batter just what Gator is going to throw and Gator throwing it right by them. After a while Thurman Munson doesn't say anything to the batters, and Gator, he's free and clear. Believes in himself. Which was the point, wasn't it?

I find Reggie Jackson at a Beanie Baby convention in Philadelphia, sitting at a booth. He's thicker around the waist and slighter of hair, but he's the same Reggie, by turns gives off an air of intimacy, then of distance. He's here to sign autographs and hawk his own version of a Beanie Baby, Mr. Octobear, after his nom de guerre, Mr.

October — a name sarcastically coined by Thurman Munson after Reggie went two for sixteen against the Royals in the 1977 play-offs, before he redeemed himself with everyone, including Thurman Munson, when he hit three consecutive World Series dingers on three pitches to solidify his legend. Manufactured by a California company, the Octobear line includes a Mickey Mantle bear and a Lou Gehrig bear — and a Thurman Munson bear, too.

I don't like doing media, says Reggie. You can't win, and there's nothing for me to say. And then he starts. Says Thurman Munson was the one who told George Steinbrenner to sign Reggie Jackson. Says he never meant for there to be a rift between Reggie Jackson and Thurman Munson, that he mishandled it, and when that magazine article came out at the beginning of the 1977 season — when Reggie was quoted as saying that he was the straw that stirred the drink and Thurman Munson didn't enter into it at all, could only stir it bad — that's when Reggie Jackson was sunk.

I would take it back, says Reggie. I was having a pina colada at a place called the Banana Boat, and I was stirring it and I had a cherry in it, some pineapples, and I said it's kind of like everything's there and I'm the straw, the last little thing you need. That killed my relationship with Thurman, me apparently getting on a pedestal, saying I was the man and then disparaging him.

Near the end in 1979, says Reggie, we were getting along really well, and I was really happy about it, because feelings were rough there for a long time. You know, I wanted his friendship, and he wanted to make things easier.

The day of the crash, Reggie had business in Connecticut. I'll never forget that day, he says. I had on a white short-sleeved and a pair of jeans and penny shoes and I was driving a silver-and-blue Rolls-Royce with a blue top. Heard it over the radio: A great Yankee superstar was killed today. And at first, I thought it was me. I wanted to touch myself. I went like that. . . . Reggie grabs his forearm, a forearm still the size of a ham hock, squeezes the muscle, tendon, and bone. He seems moved, or just spooked by the memory of how he imagined his own death being reported on the radio. He's driving his Rolls-Royce, and he's here at a Beanie Baby convention. He's hitting a home run at Yankee Stadium, and he's here, twenty years later, going down a line of autograph seekers, shaking with both hands, as if greeting his teammates one last time at the top of the dugout steps.

Of course, everyone else remembers that day, too. Bucky Dent was told by a parking-lot attendant after a dinner at the World Trade Center and nearly fainted. Catfish got a call from George Steinbrenner and went across the street and told Graig Nettles, who was already talking to George himself, and both of them thought it was a joke at first, that someone was putting them on. Goose Gossage and his wife were in the bedroom, dressing to go see a Waylon Jennings concert. It was just, God damn, says Goose. We all felt bulletproof, and then you see such a strong man, a man's man, die. . . . Then it's like we're not shit on this earth, we're just little bitty matter.

Lou Piniella remembers arguing past midnight with Thurman Munson at Bobby Murcer's apartment in Chicago a couple nights before the crash — the Yankees were in town playing the White Sox; Murcer had just been traded from the Cubs back to the Yankees — arguing about hitting until Murcer couldn't stand it anymore, took himself to bed at about 2:00 A.M. Piniella was poolside at his house when George called. I was mad, says Piniella, now the manager of the Seattle Mariners, sitting before an ashtray of stubbed cigarettes in the visitor's clubhouse at Fenway before a game against the Red Sox. He doodles on a piece of paper, drawing stanzas without notes. Over and over. I was mad, he repeats. I'm still mad.

Bobby Murcer, the last player to see Thurman Munson alive, remembers standing at the end of a runway with his wife and kids at a suburban airport north of Chicago where Thurman Munson was keeping his jet, declining his invitation to come to Canton, watching Thurman Munson barrel down the runway in this most powerful machine, then disappearing in the dark. Remembers him up there in all that night, afraid for the man.

And George Steinbrenner remembers it today in his Tampa office, surrounded by the curios of a sixty-nine-year life, some signed footballs, some framed photographs. He dyes his hair to hide the gray, but seems immortal. The living embodiment of the Yankees past and present. He has the longest desk I've ever seen.

He remembers clearly when Thurman came to his office at Yankee Stadium, flat-out refused to be captain, said he didn't want to be a flunky for George, and George finally talked him into it, said it was about mettle, not management. He remembers flying out to Canton at Thurman's request to see Thurman's real estate, eating breakfast with the family. And, of course, he remembers the day. He got a call from a friend at the Akron-Canton Regional Airport, and at first he didn't put two and two together, not until the man said, George, I've got some bad news. Then it hit him.

I just sat there, says George Steinbrenner now, folding his hands on his lap. Sat paralyzed. Everything about Thurman came flooding back to me — his little mannerisms and the way he played. When George could move his arms again, he picked up the phone and started calling his players. I don't think the Yankees recovered for a long time afterward, he says. I'm not sure we have yet.

It's 1999 at Yankee Stadium. A papery light and the good sound of hard things hitting. And yet again, there are new faces, new names: Derek Jeter, Bernie Williams, David Cone, Paul O'Neill, Roger Clemens. Luis Sojo jabbering in Spanish, cracking up the Spanish-speaking contingent, Joe Girardi chewing someone out for slacking through warm-ups ("Keep smiling, rook," he says, "keep smiling all the way back to Tampa"), Hideki Irabu in midstretch, a big man from Japan, messing with a blade of grass, lost in some reverie, like a stunned angel fallen from the heavens, contemplating his next move.

It's a team that last year came as near to perfection as any team in history, with a 125–50 record. If the 1977 Yankees, with their itinerant stars, were the first truly modern baseball club, then the 1998 Yankees were the first modern team to play like a ball club of yore, with no great standout, no uncontainable ego. A devouring organism, they just won.

The problem with a year like 1998 is a year like 1999: a great team playing great sometimes and looking anemic at other times. But always haunted: Paul O'Neill haunted by the 1998 Paul O'Neill; Jorge Posada haunted by the 1998 Jorge Posada. And then every Yankee haunted by every Yankee who's ever come before. Ruth, DiMaggio, Mantle. To this day, even though the clubhouse is a packed place — Bernie Williams is jammed in one corner with his Gibson guitar and crates of fan mail; big Roger Clemens is jammed next to O'Neill, no small man himself — Thurman Munson's locker

remains empty. It stands near Derek Jeter's, on the far left side of the
blue-carpeted clubhouse, near the training room, a tiny number 15
stenciled above it.

When I ask Jeter if he remembers anything about Thurman Munson, he smiles, looks over his shoulder at the empty locker, and says,
Not really. He was a bit before my time. Jeter is twenty-five, which
would make him a Winfield-era Yankee fan. But when I ask Jeter if
anyone ever uses it, even just to stow a pair of cleats or some extra
bats or something, he looks at me quizzically and says, Uh, no, it's
like his locker, man. It still belongs to him.

In Jorge Posada's locker, among knickknacks that include a cruci-
fix and a San Miguel pendant, he's got a picture of Thurman Munson, in full armor, accompanied by a quote from a 1975 newspaper
article: Look, I like hitting fourth and I like the good batting average, says Thurman Munson. But what I do every day behind the
plate is a lot more important because it touches so many more people and so many more aspects of the game.

It's a sentiment that the twenty-seven-year-old Posada takes to
heart. And it's not just Posada. Sandy Alomar Jr., the catcher for the
Cleveland Indians, wears number 15 on his uniform in memory of
the man he calls his favorite player, a connection he was proud to ac-
knowledge even when the Indians met the Yankees for the American
League pennant last year. He says it brings him luck.

I try to imagine guys like Derek Jeter and Jorge Posada five, ten,
fifteen years from now. Even as they've really just begun to play, they
will stare down the ends of their careers, on their way to the Hall of
Fame or a sad Miller Lite commercial or restaurant ownership. You
play hard, hoard your memories, and then suddenly you can't see
the ball or you get thrown out at second on what used to be a stand-
up double, you separate a shoulder that won't heal or just miss your
wife and children, and then you go home to Kalamazoo or Wichita
or Canton, Ohio. And then who are you, anyway? Just another stiff
who played ball.

Except you get the second half of your life. You get to try to be
a man.

The house that Thurman Munson built first appears in a vision.
One day Thurman Munson and his wife are driving around the sub-
urbs of New Jersey when they turn a corner. Thurman Munson hits

his brakes and says, Whoa, I have to live in that house! I'm serious, Diana, that's my dream house! It speaks to some ideal, something orderly, regal, and Germanic in him, a life beyond baseball, an after-life, and he sheepishly rings the doorbell and does something he never does. I play catcher for the New York Yankees, he says, and I have to live in this house. I mean, not now. . . . I just want the plans. I promise you I won't build this house in New Jersey. This will be the only one of its kind in New Jersey. I'd build it in Canton, Ohio. This house. In Canton.

The woman eyes him suspiciously, takes his name and number, says her husband will call him. He figures that's the end of that. But the husband calls. Invites the Munsons for dinner. By then Thurman Munson has composed himself, and the man eventually gives him the plans. And then it really begins — years of Sisyphean work. First they have to find the perfect piece of land, which takes forever. Then, instead of hiring a contractor, Thurman Munson subs out the job, picks everything right down to the light fixtures himself. He gets stone for the fireplace from New Jersey; stone for the rec room from Alaska; stone for the living room from Arizona. He wants crown moldings in all the rooms. He wants a lot of oak and high-gloss and hand-carved cabinets. In the rec room, a big walk-down bar . . . then, no, wait a minute, not a big bar, a small bar, and more room to play with the kids. Pillows on the floor to listen to Neil Diamond on the headphones.

He flies in on off days during the season to check how things are going. But they're never going well enough. Thurman Munson rages and bellyaches. He throws tantrums. He has walls torn down and rebuilt. He chews the workers out like Billy Martin all over an ump. Like his own father all over him. The guys start to hide when they know he's coming. Sure, you want your house to look nice, but this guy's a maniac. He's dangerous. He's Lear. He's Kurtz. He's a dick.

And the stone keeps coming. From Hawaii, Georgia, Colorado . . .

Then finally it's done. It's 1978. Thurman Munson's father, the truck driver, has abandoned his mother, moved to the desert, is working in a parking lot in Arizona, a dark shadow in a shack some-where, and Thurman Munson moves his own family into the house that Thurman Munson built.

Something lifts off his shoulders then — after all the tumult, after the two World Series victories, after his body has begun to fail, after the constant rippings in the press. And yet, he's also become more inward and circumspect. He doesn't hang out with Goose and Nettles and Catfish for a few pops after games anymore. No, many nights, nights in the middle of a home stand, even, he goes straight to Teterboro Airport, where he keeps his plane, and flies back to Diana and the kids, follows the lights of the Pennsylvania Turnpike, the towns of Lancaster and Altoona and Clarion flashing below and the stars flashing above, until Canton appears like a bunch of candles. Sometimes he's home by midnight.

And here's the odd thing now: There's always someone in the house when he comes through the door. There's Thurman Munson and Thurman Munson's wife and Thurman Munson's kids, but there is someone else, too. A part of himself in this house. A presence, a feeling around the edge of who he is that waits for a moment to penetrate, to prick his consciousness, to change him once, forever.

Until it does: one summer evening on a day with no game when Thurman Munson has had three home-cooked meals and the family has finished dinner and the kids are playing. Diana is in the kitchen tidying, washing dishes. Thurman Munson is wearing a blue-and-white-checked shirt and gray slacks. He rolls up his sleeves, lights a cigar, goes out back, and lounges in a lawn chair, feet up on the brick wall. He's never one to relax, always has a yellow legal pad nearby, running numbers for some real estate deal. But it's that quiet time of evening, a few birds softly chirping in the maples, blue shadows falling over the backyard, the sweet scent of tobacco. Thurman Munson just gazes intently at the sparklers of lights in the trees, a wraith of smoke around him.

Diana glances out the kitchen window and sees his big, blue-and-white-checked back, sees Thurman Munson shaking his head. A little while later she looks out the window and again he's shaking his head. And then again, until she can't stand it any longer, and she barges out there and says, What are you looking at? Why are you shaking your head? Thurman Munson doesn't seem to know what to say, but when he looks at her, his eyes are all lit up and he's crying. It's one of the only times she's ever seen him cry.

I just never thought any of this would be possible, he says. And that's it. For one brief moment, the man he is and the man he wants to be meet on that back lawn, become one thing, and then it just overwhelms him.

After the crash, the psychiatrist told Diana to get rid of her husband's clothes quickly or it would just get harder and harder. So that's what she did, she got rid of Thurman Munson's clothes, the hunting vest and bell-bottom pants, the bad hats and suits and coats. It took an afternoon, going through his entire wardrobe. Sometimes it made her laugh — to imagine him again. Sometimes it was harder than that. And she got rid of almost everything.

But that blue-and-white-checked shirt — she kept that.

I go to Catfish Hunter's farm in Hertford, North Carolina, not far from the Outer Banks, on a swampy summer night. He owns more than a thousand acres, grows cotton, peanuts, corn, and beans, and after retiring at the age of thirty-three, this is where he came. Always knew he was going to come back here after baseball, just thought his daddy would be here, too. But he died a week before Thurman Munson. The darkest weeks of Catfish's life. Out in the fields, living with the ghost of his father, sometimes something would pop into his mind and he would remember Thurman.

He could make a $500 suit look like $150, says Catfish now, then he smiles. In the past year, the fifty-three-year-old former pitcher has been diagnosed with amyotrophic lateral sclerosis, or Lou Gehrig's disease. Started as a tingle in his right hand when he was signing autographs down at Woodard's Pharmacy for the Lions Club in the spring, then he had to use two hands to turn the ignition on his pickup when he went dove hunting, by Halloween knew something was seriously wrong, and now his arms hang limply at his sides. Seems farcical and cruel. The same arm that won 224 games, that helped win five World Series rings, that put him in the Hall of Fame, lies dead next to him. Wife and kids and brothers and buddies help feed him, take him to the pee pot. And then no telling what the disease will do next.

If Thurman had played five more years, he'd own half the Yankees, says Catfish. Everybody liked the guy. The whites, the blacks, the Hispanics. We sit on a swing by the side of the house, the fields stretching behind us, family and friends out on the front lawn watching Taylor, the four-year-old grandchild, bash plastic baseballs with a plastic bat. A fly buzzes Catfish, but he can't lift his arms to wave it away. Even if he could, I'm not sure he would now. Remembering Thurman Munson keeps bringing Catfish back to his father, the proximity of their deaths, a double blow with which he still hasn't really come to terms. And his own condition — a thing suddenly hurtling him nearer to the end.

Every time I came home from playing ball, says Catfish, the first thing I always did was go over and see my dad. He lived seeing distance from here. My wife said, You think more of your daddy than you do of me. And every day that we went hunting, my wife would fix us bologna-and-cheese or ham-and-cheese sandwiches and every day I ate two and he ate one. When Thurman died, his uniform was still hanging in his locker. I just thought he was going to come back. Every time I walked in the clubhouse, I thought he was coming back.

His eyes well with tears, he seems to look out over the road, reaching for his daddy again or Thurman Munson, then shakes his head once. Remembers a story: pitching to Dave Kingman in the All-Star Game, the same Dave Kingman who hit a Catfish change-up in a spring-training game for a home run the length of two fields, and here he is again, and here is Thurman Munson calling for a change-up again. Catfish shakes it off and Thurman Munson trundles to the mound, says, Gotta be shitting me, won't throw the change-up. Millions of people watching tonight that'd love to see him hit that long ball. Oh, let him hit it as long as he can! Munson goes back, flashes the change-up, Catfish throws a fastball and pops him up. When he goes to the dugout, Thurman Munson shakes his head. Gotta be shitting me, he says, won't throw the change-up, then walks away.

Yes, Thurman Munson might put you on like that, but Catfish says he only saw him truly angry once. Saw the napalm Thurman Munson, the one that sought to undo the other Thurman Munsons. Some corporate sponsor gives Munson and Catfish a white Cadillac to drive around for the summer, and the two cruise everywhere in it. One night after a game, they walk out and see the front windshield is smashed, all these glass spiderwebs running helter-skelter. Catfish isn't happy, but Thurman Munson starts cussing and ranting and raving. He says, I'm gonna kill whatever sons of bitches did this! He goes berserk. Stalks toward the Caddy, opens the trunk, and suddenly pulls out a .44 Magnum revolver.

Catfish is standing in front of the Caddy, and when he sees Thurman Munson with that .44, his eyes nearly pop out of his head. He goes, Holy shit, Thurman, you got a gun!

I'm going to kill them, says Thurman Munson.

Kill who? says Catfish.

Kill whoever it is I see on the other side of that fence.

Don't load that gun, says Catfish.

Yes, I am, says Thurman Munson. And he does — then raises it, points it at shadows moving behind the fence, and fires. Crack!

Shit! yells Catfish.

Thurman Munson fires at the shadows again, and again — Crack! Crack! Without thinking, Catfish rushes him, gets his own powerful paws on the Magnum, and wrestles it away. Please, God, don't let someone be hit, prays Catfish out loud, because now my fingerprints are all over that damn thing.

I didn't hit anybody, says Thurman Munson. But I'm gonna run them over.

And that's what he tries to do. He gets in the car and barrels through the parking lot, people leaping out of the way.

God damn, you're crazy, says Catfish. Even today, Catfish can't figure it out. Could have ended up killing someone, thrown in prison. The man he says he loves actually shot at those shadows.

It's getting on toward evening now. When it's time for dinner, Catfish's wife comes and fetches us. Without my knowing it, I have been invited to stay. Because of Thurman Munson. And so I stand with Catfish Hunter and his family before a table full of food — lobster, a pan of warm corn bread, mashed potatoes, and slaw — on a June night in North Carolina, cicadas droning, heat releasing from the earth. Twenty of us gathered in a circle — fathers and sons, mothers and daughters — and everyone joins hands. Even Catfish, though he can't raise his at all. His wife takes his right hand and, following her lead, I take his left. A heavy, bearlike thing, warm and leathery and still callused from farming. The hand of a man. I bow my head with all of them. And we pray.

I give you a boy and a man, a son and a father — and then the father's father. Together for the first time, at Thurman Munson's funeral. The son wears a miniature version of the Yankee uniform that his father wore. The father lies in a coffin. And his father, the truck driver, has magically appeared from Arizona, sporting a straw sombrero. For a thin, hard man, he has a large nose.

It's the biggest funeral Canton has seen since the death of President McKinley, thousands gathering at the orange-brick civic center, hundreds more lining the route as the hearse drives to the cemetery. Thurman Munson's old golf buddy, a pro, waits on a knoll at the local course and doffs his cap when Thurman Munson passes. All the Yankees are there. Bobby Murcer and Lou Piniella deliver the eulogy. And that night Murcer, who's not penciled into the starting line-up, asks to play, knocks in five runs, including a two-run single to win the game, and limps from the field held up by Lou Piniella, then gives his bat to Diana Munson. A bat kept today somewhere in the house that Thurman Munson built.

When the hearse arrives, Thurman Munson is wheeled into a mausoleum, followed by his family: Diana, the kids, Diana's mother, Pauline, and Diana's father, Tote, who over the years had become Thurman Munson's best friend. The old man, the truck driver, stands apart. When he's asked by a stranger how long it's been since he last saw his son, he says, Quite a while, quite a while. Thurman never found himself, he says.

Then he does something disturbing. The truck driver holds an impromptu press conference, not more than fifty feet from Thurman Munson's coffin, telling a group of reporters that his boy was never a great ballplayer, that it was really him, Darrell Munson, who was the talent, just didn't get the break. Later, he approaches the coffin and, according to Diana, addresses his son one last time, says something like: You always thought you were too big for this world. Well, look who's still standing, you son of a bitch.

That's when Tote can't stand it anymore. He rises from his seat, meaning to tear him limb from limb. The police jump in and the old man, Darrell, is escorted from the cemetery, vanishes again, back to the desert, a shadow in a shack somewhere.

And what happens to the son? Michael Munson is graced and doomed by his own name. He grows up and wants to play baseball, builds a batting cage in the backyard. As a sophomore in high school, he can't hit breaking balls or sliders, but he busts his ass until he can. He wills himself to hit. And then he does. He goes to Kent State, his father's alma mater, and stars as an outfielder. In 1995, the Yankees sign him to their rookie league, switch him to catcher. Must think it's in the genes.

He goes over to the Giants and then winds up in Arizona, in the desert. He wakes at dawn, gets to the ballpark an hour and a half before everyone else. He's pale-skinned and freckled, has bright, clear eyes, the body of his father. He puts on his uniform and lifts, then runs and stretches. His arms bear bruises, his knees feel like grapefruits, the back of his neck is sun-scorched.

And every day he plays in the shadow of his father. He won't let himself be outhustled, outplayed, outthought, if he can help it. Because now when he goes back and watches those old Yankee games, he can see what his dad was thinking, how he called a game, how his quick release came from throwing right where he caught the ball, how he had as many as ten different throwing motions depending on the ailment of the day, how he did a hundred little things to win. He can see his dad jabbering incessantly and smacking his mitt on Guidry's shoulder after a win. He can see how his teammates looked up to him. And it's something like love. He sits and watches his dad crouch behind the plate, in a tight situation, maybe bases loaded and the Yankees up by a run, maybe Goose on the mound, the season on the line, and Thurman Munson, the heart and soul of those seventies teams, doesn't even give a signal. Just waves like, Bring it on, sucker. Trust me.

So I give you a boy — me — and a pack of boys and neighborhoods of boys who have grown into men. We are now stockbrokers and real estate agents, computer consultants and a steel guitarist for a country-western band. Some of the best of us are gone, buried in our home-town cemetery, and the others are fathers or fathers to be or have dreams of kids. My brothers are all lawyers, and I live in a house that I own with a woman who is going to be my wife.

I did cry the day Thurman Munson died. I'm glad to admit it. And I cried the night I left Catfish Hunter in North Carolina, driving straight into a huge orange moon. I hadn't cried like that in years, but I was thinking about them — and myself, too — and I just did.

What happens when your hero suddenly stands up from behind home plate, crosses some fold in time, and vanishes into thin air?

You go after him.

So I give you Thurman Munson, rounding third in the half-light of the ninth inning and gently combing out the hair of his daughters. I give you Thurman Munson, flying over America, looking down on the same roads his father drives, and returning home to his wife, speaking the words Ich liebe dich. I give you Thurman Munson shooting at shadows and leaping into the arms of his teammates. I give you Thurman Munson beaned in the head and sleeping next to his son again.

I give you the man on his own two feet.

Few Yankee fans — and few of his teammates — were ambivalent about Thurman Munson. More than twenty years after his death, Michael Paterniti, the author of Driving Mr. Albert: A Trip Across America with Einstein's Brain, *revisits the death of the Yankee captain.*

A CAREER THAT TOUCHED US ALL IN A BIG WAY

from *The Sporting News*, August 21, 1995

He was a Yankees fan out of the past. He sat behind the left-field line in the shade and looked out at the green outfield grass of Yankee Stadium, looked into the bright sunlight that tried to make everyone young. And Jim Kearney saw things the way they were, for Mickey Mantle and the Yankees and even himself. This was an afternoon when he had been told that Mantle might be dying in a Texas hospital, far from the 1950s and '60s and far from New York.

"I used to sit directly across from here in right, by the foul pole," said Kearney, who, at 77, saw all of Mantle's career. "Even when he was in the outfield, out there on that grass, you couldn't take your eyes off him. When he was young, you never saw anything that fast on a baseball field."

Kearney came to watch the Yankees play the Orioles with his wife. He goes back to Babe Ruth and grew up a Yankees fan, but said he is not a Yankees fan now. He came to root for Cal Ripken, who got one day closer to Lou Gehrig on a day when the medical reports on Mantle seemed so final. Across the field was the right-field foul pole, with "314" written right next to it. To his left was Monument Park, which honors Yankees immortals, living and dead. "I remember when the monuments were part of the playing field," Kearney said. "I remember when they were in center, right behind Mickey."

Darryl Strawberry came to the plate as Kearney was talking, and there was all the noise, mostly good, that follows Strawberry these days. There is even this romantic idea going around now that Strawberry was once a beloved baseball star around here. He was not, even when he was young. Strawberry could hit the ball over the sky, the way Mantle could when he was young. But he was never Mantle, or even close.

This has nothing to do with drinking or drugs, the mistakes either one of them made. This is about the way Mantle was framed by this place, and by Jim Kearney's memory, and the memory of everybody who ever saw him on this grass.

Strawberry struck out. Kearney wasn't watching. He stared into the outfield, where the monuments and Mantle once were.

"You must understand something about him," Kearney said. "We were a little resentful of him at the start. We were always protective of our legends here, protective of the past. So we wanted to know who this Mantle kid was who was going to replace Ruth and Gehrig. How dare anybody think that somebody could replace Joe DiMaggio in center field at Yankee Stadium.

"But then we saw him play, and it was as if all questions were answered."

It was not so far from Kearney's seat to Monument Park and plaques for Jacob Ruppert and Ruth and DiMaggio and Gehrig. And Mantle.

It was not the plaques that mattered so much, on a glorious day for baseball, in what still is the best baseball place, whatever they say about other ballparks, in other cities. It was the view. Yankee Stadium has changed in the years since Mantle retired. You still could stand there in the sun and look at the people in the stands and see it all as Mantle saw it once. Jim Kearney had a wonderful view from the seats in lower right field, when he was young and Mantle was younger. Mantle's view, from the great lawn, was better.

He was the fastest thing they had seen on a ballfield and came here with more power than anyone since Ruth. They always have called this The House That Ruth Built. But there were years, glory years, when it was built around Mickey Mantle.

There were people like Jim Kearney in the stands who remembered. Nick Priore, the clubhouse man, can tell you Mantle stories all day long, the same way he can tell you about the man he always calls "Joe D." Frankie Albone, who worked on the grounds crew when Mantle played, who worked on that grass, had a million Mantle stories, but Frankie Albone passed on in the spring.

This was down the hall from the Yankees clubhouse. The game had moved into the late innings. In those hallways you mostly heard questions being asked about Mickey Mantle by some of the security people in grey sports jackets and others on the maintenance staff of Yankee Stadium.

Bill Burbridge was one of the staff guys in the hall. He said he began work as a vendor at the old Yankee Stadium July 4, 1949. So he was around when Mantle played his first game in 1951. "People will always talk about the power, but I remember the speed," Burbridge said. "I never had seen blazing speed like that in my life. When he was young, he could do anything."

Burbridge leaned against a wall, and closed his eyes, and smiled. "This place was made for history," Burbridge said in a quiet voice. "And Mickey Mantle was made for this place."

Mantle's death caused a generation to look back and lament. Lupica, a best-selling author and award-winning columnist for the Daily News, *wisely chose not to write about how he felt about Mantle, but to allow another, more genuine observer to speak for him.*

PART VI

THE BRONX ZOO

After a decade at the bottom, the Yankees slowly rebuilt in the early 1970s as the surprising Mets captured the affections of New York. The signing of free agent pitcher Catfish Hunter before the 1975 season signaled the beginning of a new era, one best symbolized by the Sturm und Drang between manager Billy Martin, slugger Reggie Jackson, and new owner George Steinbrenner. Not even New York City was big enough to allow those three egos to coexist for long. And in news-savvy New York, scorekeeping in the media was often as important as the game on the field.

The result was what third baseman Graig Nettles dubbed "The Bronx Zoo." The Yankees fought it on the field and on the back pages of the New York tabloids. A new generation of writers schooled in the 1960s to break all the rules didn't bother trying to protect the players or the franchise anymore. Instead, they looked at the Yankees for what they were — an ongoing soap opera.

And at the same time, New York was coming apart at the seams. The city was bankrupt, crime was on the rise, and the rest of America looked upon New York with something approaching horror. The Yankees, flush with cash, dove into the free agent market with gusto and caused much of baseball to view them with a similar set of emotions. Yet somehow, in spite of it all, the Yankees won. In a strange way they became emblematic of the city's indomitable spirit, refusing to fall prostrate before the many challenges they faced and somehow thriving amid chaos.

It was a time in which there were always stories within stories. The press struggled to keep the varying plot lines coherent, to communicate the disarray and still make sense of it all. For even in the midst of such disorder, the Yankees, improbably and somewhat impossibly, were the Yankees again as players like Chris Chambliss and Reggie Jackson managed to provide transcendent moments that, for a time, seemed to make the rest of it, however briefly, not matter at all.

CHAMBLISS HR ENDS 12-YEAR DROUGHT

Rivers Bangs 4 Hits; Brett, Mayberry HR

from *The New York Daily News*, October 15, 1976

A home run as dramatic as the one Bobby Thomson hit 25 years ago this month touched off a victory demonstration last night reminiscent of Shea Stadium of 1969 and gave the Yankees a sudden death 7–6 victory over the Royals and their first American League championship in 12 years.

Chambliss connected on the first pitch of the last of the ninth inning and drove it over the blue fence in rightfield and, as the ball disappeared, the Yankees had won their 30th AL pennant.

Chambliss remained at home plate, watching the ball head for the fence. When it was gone, he threw his arms in the air in celebration and danced around the bases. His teammates were on the field and, before Chambliss could reach second base, thousands of young fans were swarming on the field, trying to get at Chambliss. He pushed and bulled his way through the crowd, but he never touched third and he still hasn't touched home.

Chambliss tried, but by the time he reached home plate there was no home plate. It had been carried off as a souvenir by some urchin and is probably in a Bronx apartment this morning. If necessary, Chris will make a house call.

Brett Connects in 8th

The blast by Chambliss came against Mark Littell and broke up a game that the Yankees seemed to have had under wraps until George Brett crashed a three-run homer in the eighth to tie it at 6–6 and set up Chambliss' dramatic shot.

The clock in rightfield said 11:43 and the centerfield scoreboard flashed the news: "Yankees, 1976 American League champions."

Thousands of fans who have waited so long for a return to the glory days celebrated wildly, even destructively. They climbed on the screen behind home plate, bouncing on it and dangling from it perilously. They shouted and screamed for more than 15 minutes. And they covered every inch of the field, picking up everything that didn't move for souvenirs of this exciting and historic moment in baseball history.

They were delirious. They were ecstatic. Their beloved Yankees were going to the World Series again, scheduled to meet the Reds in Cincinnati in the first game tomorrow.

Almost an hour passed before the field was cleared. All four bases were gone. So were the New York and KC emblems that served as the on-deck circles. And there were pieces of sod missing on the field that made it look like craters on the moon.

There was some talk, inane talk, that Chambliss' homer might not count because he failed to touch the plate. Thurman Munson put an end to that talk.

"I saw about 50,000 people touch home plate," the catcher said. "He could have been one of them. I want to see them take it back."

They won't take it back. The Yankees are champions and there isn't any doubt they earned it against a Kansas City team that had class and character that never quit.

The Royals came out fighting last night. They put it right to the Yankees, as Brett doubled and John Mayberry homered in the first, his first four-bagger since Aug. 14, and the Royals had a 2–0 lead against Ed Figueroa.

Right back came the Yankees. A triple by Mickey Rivers, his first of four hits, an infield single by Roy White, a single by Munson and a sac fly by Chambliss and it was tied.

The Royals jumped out in the lead with a run in the second and then the Yankees scored two in the third (Chambliss drove in one of those runs) and two in the sixth that seemed to wrap the game and the pennant in a nice neat bundle.

But something kept telling you that it couldn't end this way, so easily, so undramatically; something kept telling you there were fireworks left, and thrills and heroics.

Jackson Replaces Figueroa

Sure enough, the Royals came back courageously in the eighth. Al Cowens ripped a single to start it and Billy Martin decided Figueroa had gone far enough. He chose Grant Jackson to put the loose ends together.

But Jim Wohlford pinch hit a single and that brought up Brett, who had 215 hits during the regular season and seven in the playoffs, but only eight homers all year.

"The idea was to keep the ball in the ballpark," said Munson. "That's why we brought in the lefthander. But just what we didn't want to happen, happened."

You could hear a pennant fall as Brett's towering shot disappeared into the rightfield seats.

But the Yankees survived the eighth and Dick Tidrow came in to pitch the ninth. He got the first two outs, then gave a single to Buck Martinez and walked Cowens. Wohlford was the batter and that man, Brett, was on deck when Tidrow got Wohlford on a close force play at second.

In the Royals' tenth, if there had been a Royals' tenth, the hitters would be Brett, Mayberry, McRae. It would be wise to avoid a tenth inning.

Chambliss waited off to the side as an announcement was made about fans throwing debris on the field. Littell took extra warmup pitches, probably thinking about how he would pitch Chambliss. And Chambliss was thinking about how Littell would pitch him.

As he stepped to the plate, Chambliss already had tied championship series records for most hits (10) and most RBI (7). He had singled in a big run in the Yankees' third-game victory and they asked him if that was the biggest hit of his career.

He said it wasn't. He should have said: "Not yet."

One to Tell Their Sons

Now he stepped in the box and wound up as if he knew what was coming. He uncoiled out of his swing and when the sound of bat meeting ball reverberated throughout the Stadium, you knew the ball was gone, the game was over, the pennant was won. Chris Chambliss knew it. Mark Littell knew it. And 25 Yankees and 25

Royals and 56,821 fans knew it and especially the young ones. They knew it, too.

For years they had heard their dads tell about Bobby Thomson and Ralph Branca and the miracle of Coogans Bluff.

And some remembered the year the Mets won — the then Amazing Mets — the NL flag the first time. Now they will have something to tell their kids. They will tell them about Chris Chambliss and Mark Littell and that marvelous October night in Yankee Stadium.

The back page dubbed it "The Shot Heard Round the Bronx," for not since Bobby Thomson's pennant-winning blast in 1951 had New York celebrated a home run like this. And as Phil Pepe's account notes, in fact they had never quite celebrated like this before, as Chambliss was forced to run through a gauntlet of fans on his way home. Forced to run for his life before reaching home plate, umpires escorted him back onto the field after the mayhem had expired to watch him touch home plate — or where it had once been — and make the result official. Pepe is the author and co-author of a number of Yankee books, most recently Few and Chosen *with Whitey Ford.*

ROBERT WARD

REGGIE JACKSON IN NO-MAN'S-LAND

from *Sport*, June 1977

Oh golden, yellow light shimmering on Reggie Jackson's chest! Yes, that's he, the latest member of the American League Champion New York Yankees, and he is standing by his locker, barechested, million-dollar sweat dripping from his brow, golden pendants dangling from his neck. God, he looks like some big baseball Othello as he smiles at the gaggle of reporters who rush toward him, their microphones thrust out, their little 98-cent pens poised, ready to take down his every word. But somehow, it's hard to ask the man questions . . . certainly not such standard ballplayer questions as "How's the arm?" or "Toe hurt?" . . . for not all ballplayers are Reggie Jackson, whose golden pendants catch the sunlight filtering through the steamy Fort Lauderdale clubhouse windows and reflect dazzlingly into your eyes. What are these priceless reflectors? Well, first, there is a small golden bar with the word "Inseparable" on it, a gift from Reggie's Norwegian girlfriend, and gyrating next to that memento is a dog tag — the inscrutable Zen koan (though slightly reminiscent of the Kiwanis Club), "Good Luck Is When Hard Work Meets Opportunity." And, finally, there is the most important bauble of all, an Italian horn which Reggie tells a reporter is supposed to keep the evil spirits away!

Evil spirits? Egads. What evil spirits can be following Reggie Jackson? The man has been on three World Series Championship teams (Oakland A's 1972–1974), has led the league in RBIs (1973: 117), home runs (1973: 32, 1975: 36) and was the American League's MVP in 1973. Since then he has topped his on-the-field-feats by playing out his option under Charles O. Finley, and refusing to sign with his new club, the Baltimore Orioles, until they gave him a gigantic raise. Finally, came the *coup de grace:* Signing with the New York Yankees for three million big ones. Reggie is expected to be the biggest thing to hit New York since King Kong. So where are the evil spirits?

"No evil spirits actually," Reg says, answering a newsman's question. "Just in case, you know? Hey, could you move that mike out of the way? Shoving it up my nose like that is *sooooo* uncomfortable. . . ."

The little man yanks his mike back.

"I am not merely a baseball player," Reggie says to another reporter, who nods gravely. "I am a black man who has done what he wants, gotten what he wanted and will continue to get it.

"Now what I want to do," he adds, "is develop my intellect. You see, on the field I am a surgeon. I put on my glove and this hat. . . ."

He picks up the New York Yankee baseball hat. Itself a legend. Legendary hat meet legendary head!

"And I put on these shoes. . . ." Reggie points down to his shoes. "And I go out on the field, and I cut up the other team . . . I am a surgeon. No one can quite do it the way I do. But off the field . . . I try to forget all about it. You know, you can get very narrow being a superstar."

Reggie removes his cap. "I mean, being a superstar . . . can make life very difficult. Difficult to grow. So I like to visit with my friends, listen to some *fine* music, drink some *good* wine, perhaps take a ride in the country in a *fine* car, or . . . just walk along the beach. Nature is extremely important to me. Which may be just about the only trouble I'll have in New York. I'll miss the trees!"

Then, in his quiet, throaty voice, Reg politely says he must be off to the training room.

"Terrific," a jaunty reporter says as Reggie leaves. "He's so terrific. He's the kinda guy you don't want to talk to every day . . . because he gives you so much. It's like a torrent of material. He overwhelms you!"

"Yes," I say. "But how do the other guys on the Yankees feel about having a tornado in their presence? I heard Thurman Munson and some of the others gave him a chilly reception."

"No problem," says the reporter. "All that stuff about problems on the team is just something somebody wrote to sell papers. Hell,

Reggie hasn't even been here for a week. There hasn't been time for resentment yet!"

The next day after practice, Reggie Jackson is once again standing by his locker, once again surrounded by reporters, who ask him to reveal his "personal philosophy of life."

I look down the seats before lockers and see last year's Yankee stars sitting like dukes around the king. Next to Jackson is Chris Chambliss. Remember him? He hit the home run that won the pennant for the Yanks. But no one seems much interested in this instant (though brief) hero's developing intellect or his reflections on recombinant DNA, which happens to be the subject Chambliss is discussing with Willie Randolph. And down the line a little farther is old gruff and grumble himself, Thurman Munson. Today he rubs his moustache, and stares at the floor, looking like Bert Lahr in *The Wizard of Oz.* Folks aren't rushing to ask him about the philosophical questions that are addressed to Jackson, yet Munson is the acknowledged "team leader."

And across the room is Catfish Hunter, the wise old Cat, and businesslike Ken Holtzman. Their combined salaries are enough to send up a space shot to Pluto, but no one is asking them if they like to recite Kahlil Gibran. It's strange, a little dreamlike. Here is the Superteam, but if this first week is any example, Reggie Jackson has taken over so totally that it's almost as if the other players were rookies who had yet to prove themselves to the press.

Now, Jackson says goodbye to the reporters, and tells me he is going outside to sign a few late-afternoon autographs. Would I like to come? Certainly.

And so we stand out by the first baseline while the fans crowd around, pushing and shoving and holding up their cameras.

"Smile, Reggie," says a woman with a scarf on her head, tied up so she looks like she has two green rabbit ears.

Reggie produces a semi-smile.

"You have such white teeth," she says.

Jackson turns to me and raises his eyebrows, then moves along signing scraps of paper and baseballs, when a man on crutches is pushed precariously close to the edge of the stands. Jackson stops signing and demands that the other fans help the crippled man. The fans do what he says.

Finally, after Reggie has signed endless signatures, a young boy says, "Thank you, Mr. Jackson."

Reggie stops, looks up at me and says: "You sign a million before anyone ever says thank you."

On that perfect exit line, Reggie does a perfect exit. He picks up a loose ball and flips it to the crowd, who cheer and applaud.

Waiting for Jackson to get his rubdown, I ask Sparky Lyle, who is seated in front of his locker: "How's it going?"

"Great," says Lyle. "I may be leaving tomorrow. We are only about $250,000 away from one another."

Perhaps not the best time to ask him about the new three-million-dollar superstar. But duty must be done.

"I don't think we need him," Lyle says. "Not to take anything away from his talents, but what we really needed was a good righthanded hitter. A righthanded superstar."

Jackson comes strutting into the room. Not a self-conscious strut. Just his natural superstar strut. He can't help it if he is bigger than all indoors.

Lou Piniella strides across the room and says, "Hey, Reg. How you doing?"

"How you doing, hoss?" Reggie says affably.

"I'm not the horse, Reg," Piniella says, with a good deal of uncertainty in his voice. "You're the hoss. . . . I'm just the cart."

Jackson smiles, trying to pass the remark off as a joke.

Jackson and I enter the Banana Boat Bar, and he undoes his windbreaker just enough to reveal the huge yellow star on his blue T-shirt. Around the star are the silver letters which spell out SUPER-STAR! At the bar, he discards the jacket. All around us people start staring and the waitresses start twitching in their green Tinkerbelle costumes.

We order Lite beers, and Reggie gives me a pregnant stare and says, "If I seem a little distant, it's because I got burned once by *Sport* magazine. They wrote a piece which said I caused trouble on the team. That I have a huge ego. That I only hit for a .258 average. That I wasn't a complete ballplayer. They only say that kind of stuff about black men. If a white man happens to be colorful, then it's fine. If he's black, then they say he's a troublemaker."

I tell him that I have no intention of showing him as a troublemaker. Which I don't. As far as I'm concerned the league could use 50 more Reggies, and 50 fewer baseball players who sound like shoe salesmen.

But almost before I'm finished, Reggie has forgotten his fears.

"You see," he says, "I've got problems other guys don't have. I've got this big image that comes before me, and I've got to adjust to it. Or what it has been projected to be. That's not 'me' really, but I've got to deal with it. Also, I used to just be known as a black athlete, now I'm respected as a tremendous intellect."

"A tremendous intellect?" I say.

"What?" says Jackson waving to someone.

"You were talking about your tremendous intellect."

"Oh, was I?" Jackson says. "No, I meant . . . that now people talk to me as if I were a person of substance. That's important to me."

I mention Jackson's reportage on the Royals-Yankees pennant playoffs last year for ABC, saying that most of my friends felt that Reggie had done a much better job of analyzing the motivation of the players than Howard Cosell. What's more, he did it in the most hostile atmosphere imaginable, with Cosell constantly hassling him and chiding him for defending Royals' centerfielder Al Cowens on a controversial call.

"Well, that is part of my problem," says Reggie. "I do everything as honestly as I can. I give all I have to give. But I don't let people get in my way. Cosell was insecure. He thought I was trying to put him down, make him look bad by correcting him. He made quite a stink about me to the big people at ABC, but they took up for me. I really wasn't trying to compete with him. I was just being myself. And it got me in trouble."

Jackson smiles, sits back and folds his arms over his SUPERSTAR chest. A second later we are joined by Jim Wynn, who at 35 is trying to make a comeback with the Yankees. Once a tremendous long-ball hitter known as "The Toy Cannon," Wynn has been faltering, and certainly he can't have more than a year or so left. He orders a drink, and then Reggie and he begin to talk about hitting in Boston's Fenway Park.

"You are gonna love that left-field fence," Reggie says.

"I know I will," Wynn says. "If they play me, you know I'll hit some out."

But he doesn't sound convinced.

There is a lull in the conversation and then Wynn looks over at Reggie and says, "You know, Reggie, I hope my son grows up to be like you. Not like me. Like you."

Wynn smiles in awe at Jackson, and I realize that for all their professionalism, the Yankees are just as subject to the mythology of the press as any fan. Just by showing up, Jackson has changed the ambiance of the locker room. And no one yet knows if it's for good or ill.

As I ponder, two of the original mythmakers appear at the Banana Boat — Mickey Mantle, now a spring batting coach, and his old cronie, manager Billy Martin. Soon they are settled into drinking and playing backgammon, and when they are joined by Whitey Ford, Jackson hails a waitress and sends them complimentary drinks. The waitress comes back to Reggie and says, "Whitey Ford appreciates your offer of a drink, but says he would rather have your superstar T-shirt."

Jackson breaks into a huge smile, peels off his shirt, and runs barechested across the room. He hands the shirt to Ford, and then Ford, in great hilarity, takes off his pink cashmere sweater and gives it to Jackson. A few minutes later Reggie is back at the bar, the sweater folded in his lap.

"That's really something, isn't it!" Jackson says. "Whitey Ford giving me his sweater. A Hall-of-Famer. I'm keeping this."

He smiles, looking down lovingly at the sweater.

On the Yankees the old-timers still retain their magic, even to the younger stars like Jackson. In a way it is easier for him to relate to them than his own teammates. For they were mythic, legends, as he is. . . . In fact, their legends are still stronger than Reggie's, coming as they did back when ugly salary disputes didn't tarnish both players and managers.

This becomes even more apparent when Jackson moves to the backgammon table to join the crowd watching Mantle and Martin play one of the most ludicrously bad, but hilarious games in recent history. Both of them beginners and slightly loaded, the two men resort to several rather questionable devices. The object of the game is to get your men, or chips, around the board, and into your opponent's home, then "bear them off the board." The man who gets all his men out first wins. (You throw a pair of dice to decide how many spaces you can move.) Martin rolls a seven and quickly moves nine spaces. Jackson and Ford laugh hysterically. Mantle rolls his dice, moves the properly allotted amount, and then simply slips three of his men off the board and into his pants pocket. Martin, busy ordering drinks and taking advice from Reggie, misses Mantle's burglary, which gives Mickey a tremendous advantage in the game. Martin's next roll lands him on two of Mantle's men and sends them back to the center bar. Mantle rolls the dice, orders another round of drinks and, while Martin chats with the waiter, takes four more of his chips off the table and puts them under his chair. Mantle chuckles as Martin, unaware of what has happened, rolls the dice. Reggie tries to control his laughter — unsuccessfully — the mirth bursting out of him. And now everyone is laughing, Mantle so hard that tears are streaming down his face. Martin suddenly notices that Mantle, despite weaker rolls of the dice, already has fewer men on the board.

"You bastard!" Martin shouts. "Where are all your chips?"

Mantle protests his innocence with great vigor but Martin reaches down and pulls out the evidence from under Mantle's chair. Mantle screams in mock surprise, and then throws up his hands. "Hell, Billy," he says, "you were beating me even though I was cheating."

"You bum," says Martin, "you bum. I'm just too good. I'm a winner."

"Nobody can beat Billy," Mantle says as he beams at his old buddy.

Reggie is still laughing, shaking his head, and I can't help but feel that he has missed something. Mantle, Ford and Martin have a kind of loyalty and street-gang friendship that today's transient players don't have time to develop. Soon Mantle and Martin are involved in another humorous game, and Reggie goes back to the bar. Alone.

Minutes later I join him and try to gauge his mood. What did he feel watching Mantle and Martin? In a second I have my answer, for Reggie starts talking and now he is less the showman. He seems to be talking directly from his bones:

"You know," he says, "this team . . . it all flows from me. I've got to keep it all going. I'm the straw that stirs the drink. It all comes back to me. Maybe I should say me and Munson . . . but really he doesn't enter into it. He's being so damned insecure about the whole thing. I've overheard him talking about me."

"You mean he talks loud to make sure you hear him?"

"Yeah. Like that. I'll hear him telling some other writer that he wants it to be known that he's the captain of the team, that he knows what's best. Stuff like that. And when anybody knocks me, he'll laugh real loud so I can hear it. . . ."

Reggie looks down at Ford's sweater. Perhaps he is wishing the present Yankees could have something like Ford and Martin and Mantle had. Community. Brotherhood. Real friendship.

"Maybe you ought to just go to Munson," I suggest. "Talk it out right up front."

But Reggie shakes his head.

"No," he says. "He's not ready for it yet. He doesn't even know he feels like he does. He isn't aware of it yet."

"You mean if you went and tried to be open and honest about it, he'd deny it?"

Jackson nods his head:

"Yeah. He'd say, 'What? I'm not jealous. There aren't any problems.' He'd try to cover up, but he ought to know he can't cover up anything from me. Man, there is no way. . . . I can read these guys. No, I'll wait, and eventually he'll be whipped. There will come that moment when he really knows I've won . . . and he'll want to hear everything is all right . . . and *then* I'll go to him, and we will get it right."

Reggie makes a fist and clutches Ford's sweater: "You see, that is the way I am. I'm a leader, and I can't lie down . . . but 'leader' isn't the right word . . . it's a matter of PRESENCE. . . . Let me put it this way: No team I am on will ever be humiliated the way the Yankees were by the Reds in the World Series! That's why Munson can't intimidate me. Nobody can. You can't psyche me. You take me one-on-one in the pit, and I'll whip you. . . . It's an attitude, really. . . . It's the way the manager looks at you when you come into the room. . . . It's the way the coaches and the batboy look at you. . . . The way your name trickles through the crowd when you wait in the batter's box. . . . It's all that. . . . The way the Yankees were humiliated by the Reds? You think that doesn't bother Billy Martin. He's no fool. He's smart. Very smart. And he's a winner. Munson's tough, too. He *is* a winner, but there is just nobody who can do for a club what I can do. . . . There is nobody who can put meat in the seats [fans in the stands] the way I can. That's just the way it is. . . . Munson thinks he can be the straw that stirs the drink, but he can only stir it bad."

"You were doing it just a few minutes ago over there with Martin, weren't you?" I say. "Stirring a little."

"Sure," says Jackson, "but he has presence, too. He's no dummy. I can feel him letting me do what I want, then roping me in whenever he needs to . . . but I'll make it easy for him. He won't have to be 'bad' Billy Martin fighting people anymore. He can move up a notch 'cause I'll open the road. I'll open the road, and I'll let the others come thundering down the path!"

Jackson sits back, staring fiercely at the bar. A man in love with words, with power, a man engaged in a battle. Jim Wynn resumes his seat next to Reggie and watches him with respect. An ally. But, I wonder — are there any others?

Billy Martin is sitting in his office at Yankee Stadium South. He is half dressed and his hair is messed, but for all that he still has what Jackson called PRESENCE. Now he runs his hand through his hair and laughs: "I couldn't lose to Mantle could I?" he says.

"You had him psyched."

Martin laughs again and nods: "And he was trying to act like he wasn't mad. . . ."

Mantle comes in the door sipping coffee and looking about two years older than the night before. "You know," he says, "I woke up this morning, and I had me a whole pocket full of them white things!"

After we finish laughing, I ask Martin if he thinks there will be any problems having Reggie Jackson on the team.

Martin, who as Reggie himself said is "no dummy," smiles and asks, "What kind?"

"Like team-leader problems?"

Martin shakes his head: "Not a chance. We already have a team leader. Thurman Munson."

I walk into the locker room and sit with Catfish Hunter in front of his locker and talk about Reggie. Catfish shoots a stream of tobacco juice on the floor, and shakes his head slowly, philosophically. "Reggie is a team leader," he says. "The thing you have to understand about Reggie is he wants everyone to love him."

For a second I think Cat is going to elaborate on this theme, but he holds back, chooses a new path — a safer one. "I mean," he says, "he can get hot with his bat and carry a team for three weeks. He's always ready to go all the time."

Hunter squints at me as if to say, "That's all, my friend. I'm staying out of this one."

Chris Chambliss' locker is right next door to Reggie Jackson's. The men literally rub elbows when they dress. Yet when I ask Chambliss how he feels about Reggie, he says, "I haven't had a chance to talk to him yet. I think he'll help the ball club. Most of the rumors you have heard are untrue. Still, we do have a lot of personalities on this team . . . things could happen. I doubt it. But they could."

I catch Thurman Munson as he comes in to practice. An hour late. I wonder if he isn't having some kind of psych battle with Jackson. Which star arrives on the field the latest? Gruffly, he declines to talk to me until after practice, and then he declines again for some 30 minutes. Finally, he nods me over and I ask him about Jackson.

"What are you asking me for?" he says. "Why does everybody ask me?"

"I'm not singling you out," I say. "I've asked quite a few others. But there has been talk that you two will have problems competing as team leader."

Munson shakes his head, makes a face. "No. No way. And what difference does it make if I'm not team leader? There are a lot of leaders on this team. We've got a lot of stars. They are all leaders. As far as Reggie goes, he's a good player. He'll help the club. Has a lot of power."

"How about jealousy over his salary?"

"No," Munson says, "I don't care about that. He signed as a free agent. I hope he makes $10,000,000. Is that all?"

Munson turns away and begins to talk to a businessman about a shopping center they hope to build in Florida.

It's late in the afternoon and Reggie Jackson is taking extra batting practice. The only people left on the field are Thurman Munson and Chris Chambliss. And a young pitcher, a rookie who is new to me.

Jackson fouls off a couple of pitches, and Chambliss looks at Munson and says, "Show time!" There is a real bite in his kidding.

"Hey," says Munson, "are we out here to see this?"

Jackson digs in and fouls off a few more.

"Some show!" says Munson. "Real power!"

Jackson tries to laugh it off, and finally connects on a pitch. It falls short of the fence, and Munson and Chambliss smile at one another. Munson steps into the cage, but Jackson hurries into the locker room.

I am about ready to leave, and I thank Reggie for his cooperation, but he seems disturbed by my going. "Listen," he says, "I'd like to know what the guys thought of me. You talked to them. How about telling me?"

"Okay," I say, "I'll meet you back at the Banana Boat."

An hour later, at the Banana Boat, I tell Jackson that Lyle had said the team didn't need him, that Lyle said it was nothing personal, but the Yankees needed a righthanded hitter more. Then I tell him that Munson had denied there was any problem, and I mention that Chambliss had said, "I haven't had a chance to talk to him yet."

"Yeah," says Jackson. "You see it's a pattern. The guys who are giants like Catfish, the guys who are really secure . . . they don't worry about me. But guys like Munson. . . . It's really a comedy, isn't it. I mean, it's hilarious. . . . Did you see him in the batting cage? He is really acting childish. Like the first day of practice he comes up to me and says, 'Hey, you have to run now . . . before you hit.' You know he's playing the team captain trying to tell me what to do. But I play it very low key. I say, 'Yeah, but if I run now I'll be too tired to hit later,' and Munson says, 'Yeah, but if you don't run now, it'll make a bad impression on the other guys.' So I say, 'Let me ask the coach,' and I yelled over to Dick Howser, 'Should I run now or hit,' and Howser yelled, 'Aw the hell with running. Get in there and hit.' So that's what I did. It really made Munson furious. But I did it so he couldn't complain. Listen, I always treat him right. I talk to him all the time, but he is so jealous and nervous and resentful that he can't stand it. If I wanted to I could snap him. Just wait until I get hot and hit a few out, and the reporters start coming around and I have New York eating out of the palm of my hand . . . he won't be able to stand it."

Jackson delivers all this with a kind of healthy, competitive and slightly maniacal glee. It's as if he has said to himself, "Okay, they aren't going to love me. So I'll break 'em down. I'll show them who's boss." And he might. I can't help but think that the situation would be a lot healthier if the other Yankees had come to him.

"How has Chambliss been treating you?" I ask.

"Standoffish. They all have. You saw Piniella in there yesterday. He said that stuff about me being the horse and him being the cart. That's how they feel. But at least he talked to me. That was a kind of breakthrough. That and the thing with Whitey, with the sweater. That was good, too."

"Maybe you are overreacting," I say. "It is a new year, and everyone has heard about your legend, and maybe they feel like they can't be the ones to come up to you and try to break the ice because then it will look like they are trying to kiss your ass, and they'll feel embarrassed and self-conscious."

Jackson nods hopefully.

"Yeah, it could be that. I know it could be. Say, did you talk to Billy Martin about me?"

"Yeah," I say. "He told me that the Yankees had a team leader."

"Yeah? Who?"

"Munson."

Reggie laughs ruefully.

"But maybe he's gotta say that," I say. "It wouldn't look good to say you are the team leader this early. It would hurt Munson's pride."

"That's right," Jackson says. "I just want you to know that [coach] Elston Howard came up to me today and said, 'No matter what anybody says, you are the team leader.' So I think there is some real heavy stuff going on. But it is weird. You know, up until yesterday Martin had hardly said two words to me. But he has made me feel I'm all right. Still, I don't understand it."

"It could go back to your verbal ability," I suggest. "I mean, a lot of athletes are suspicious of people who can talk well. It makes them feel dull and stupid so they resent the other guy and get hostile toward him."

"Right," says Jackson. "That's true. I've been through that one before. But you know . . . the rest of the guys should know that I don't feel that far above them. . . . I mean, nobody can turn people on like I can, or do for a club the things I can do, but we are all still athletes, we're all still ballplayers. We should be able to get along. We've got a strong common ground, common wants. . . . I'm not going to allow the team to get divided. I'll do my job, give it all I got, talk to anybody. I think Billy will appreciate that. . . . I'm not going to let the small stuff get in the way. . . . But if that's not enough . . . then I'll be gone. A friend of mine has already told me: 'You or Munson will be gone in two years.' I really don't want that to be the case . . . because, after all is said and done, Munson is a winner, he's a fighter, a hell of a ballplayer . . . but don't you see. . . ."

Reggie pauses, and opens his hands in a gesture that seems to imply, "It's so apparent, why can't Munson and Chambliss and all the rest of them understand the sheer simplicity . . . the cold logic?"

"Don't you see, that there is just no way I can play second fiddle to *anybody*. Hah! That's just not in the cards. . . . There ain't no way!"

This is the story that started it all. Freelance writer Robert Ward spent a few days at training camp interviewing newly acquired free agent Jackson and other Yankees and then filed his story. He knew he'd gotten something special, but no one could have predicted just how much of an impact the story would have.

Advance copies reached the Yankee clubhouse on May 23 and everything hit the fan. Jackson was immediately ostracized from most of the team and less than a month later would be pulled off the field at Fenway Park and publicly humiliated by Martin, precipitating one of the most bizarre periods in team history as Steinbrenner, manager Billy Martin, and Jackson lived a public soap opera. The era that Graig Nettles dubbed "The Bronx Zoo" was in full swing.

HENRY HECHT

GOODBY, AND GOOD RIDDANCE

from *The New York Post*, July 24, 1978

KANSAS CITY: It's four in the morning and I'm thinking how much I hate covering the Yankees and how I should be happy now. Billy Martin has to be fired for calling his boss a "convicted" liar. Billy is a brutal man to deal with. Forked tongue and all that. The constant crisis atmosphere. The crude attempts to manipulate everyone around him. He lies to players and you know about it but you back off because the little unprintable is still the manager and you have to deal with him.

But he's also a pathetic figure, self destructive, childish, a man who will go to pieces if he can't get another job managing. Does anyone doubt what will happen if there are no more owners willing to take a chance. If there are, finally, no more owners crazy enough to think they can change Billy and handle him? Billy is 50 but he still doesn't know how to handle himself. Drinking too much is almost a real death wish.

The thought of Martin without a team to manage is almost sickening. He would shrivel up and die. I cover sports because dealing with the real world outside of work is quite enough, thank you. This Yankee team is hateful to me, as it is to all the beat guys. We like the individuals but not the collective madness George Steinbrenner has gathered. Give me the Mets and last place, anytime.

We all read and heard about the printed rules Billy came up with after the Reggie Jackson incident. There is no discipline on the Yankees because Billy doesn't know how to discipline himself. Thursday night in Minnesota he didn't appear in the clubhouse until 6:10, when almost all the Yankees had gotten dressed and gone out to wait for the start of batting practice. He said, later, he was in the ballpark visiting, but his players certainly didn't know that. They just figured he was late again. Well, late is not quite the right term because the manager can show up when he wants.

But I know of no manager who keeps the hours Billy does. Managers get to the park early. Maybe they sit in their office and pick their noses, but they're there. If you're a Yankee and you hear all this bull about rules, what do you think when the next day the manager isn't there on time?

Billy was wild when I brought this up to Cedric Tallis, his general manager. I make the rules, I don't have to abide by them, I just enforce them, Billy said. That attitude is infantile. It's like he's trying to defy authority, just to prove something, maybe that he can get fired less than a year after winning a World Series.

And with this childish urge to defy comes a certain child-like arrogance. Billy thinks he's the cleverest SOB to come down the pike. He tries to manipulate people and thinks he can get away with it all the time.

Yesterday was the pluperfect example. He tried to set up Reggie Jackson as a liar. He knew Jackson was not being literal when he said Martin had not talked to him in a year and a half. But that was Martin's plan: call Jackson a liar and think the bluff will work. That you'll buy it, that you'll somehow not know Jackson was dealing on a different level.

The same arrogance is evident in his dealings with his players.

"He lies and he does it so much he forgets what he told to different guys," one Yankee said. "How can he get away with it when he lies to so many guys? He can't remember what he said and he keeps getting himself into deeper trouble because he can't shut up and he ends up getting no respect at all."

Other Yankees besides Reggie hate Billy Martin; Reggie is just the most significant. The more I probe and think about last Monday, the more I realize that what Billy has done and tried to do to Reggie was the reason Reggie's mind went south. Reggie was wrong for doing what he did, but I think bunting against orders was the act of an irrational man, a man who did not comprehend the magnitude — that's Reggie's word — of his act. Defiance? In the strict sense, yes.

But he might not have consciously realized what he was doing. Reggie is like that, as tortured in some ways as his manager.

And in a way I'm glad Martin precipitated this explosion. Get yourself fired. End this madness. There was no way he was coming back next year anyway.

And when he does get fired he will blame the usual people. Lying sports writers. Jealous people. Dissatisfied players. A boss who doesn't know bleep about baseball. Everyone but himself.

He wanted to manage the Yankees so much, just like Casey Stengel, and he got his wish. He even won a World Series. Friday night, waiting out some rain, he talked about the Old Man for 30 minutes. Oh, Billy can be a charmer and you forget what he's really like. But not for long.

For a time, the poisoned relationship between Billy Martin, George Steinbrenner, and Reggie Jackson made watching the 1978 Yankees not only painful but uncomfortable, as though one were sitting in the middle of an argument between strangers.

The fatigue this situation engendered among the press covering the Yankees was palpable. Hecht perfectly captured the collective emotions of everyone when Martin was finally let go. No one could have predicted that less than three months later the Yankees would be world champions; that Jackson, after hitting three home runs in the Series finale against the Dodgers, would be lionized; and that Martin would eventually return as manager not once but four more times.

PAUL SOLOTAROFF

THE LAST YANKEE

Don Mattingly is the end of the line, the
point after which one of sport's great
traditions shrivels and dies

from *The National Sports Daily*, July 6, 1990

It begins, of course, with Babe Ruth, the god of thunder, who invented the home run and the 12–hot dog breakfast. It runs through Lou Gehrig, the first baseman built like a center field monument, and through Joe DiMaggio, the center fielder straight from central casting. It culminates in Mickey Mantle, that beautiful wreck who played hard, lived hard, and once remarked in his forties that if he'd known he was going to live so long, he'd've taken better care of himself. "It," of course, is the lineage of the One Great Yankee, the player who taught his generation about class and success, and set boys everywhere dreaming about pinstripes.

It wasn't, God knows, anything like virtue that made Ruth an icon. What signified him to his age was his invincibility — he won everything in sight, and devastated teams doing it. His 500-foot shots were like bombs over Nagasaki; whenever he hit one, the other side just collapsed.

But the mythos of the Great Yankee has as much to do with heart as muscle. DiMaggio played on crippled heels; Gehrig, the last couple of years, could hardly bend to take grounders, so ravaged was he by ALS; Mantle hobbled through much of his career, his knee done in by a sprinkler head. Nonetheless, they endured like soldiers, Gehrig for 17 years, Joe D. for 13, the Mick for 18. Gehrig lasted through '39, by which time DiMaggio was securely established; DiMaggio until '51, when Mantle broke in. No one, alas, stepped up for Mantle, but his legacy of courage and pride survived, in trust, for his eventual heir.

Beyond the monster home runs and memorable catches in center, though, what the One Great Yankee did was set absolute standards — Yankee standards. DiMaggio must have uttered all of 10 words his entire career, but his mute ferocity put the fear of God into his teammates. He once cornered Vic Raschi, who was 21–8 that year but had a nasty habit of squandering big leads, and told him that if he ever blew another one, he'd beat the hell out of him then and there. Nor was there any malingering permitted. If DiMaggio was going to go out there every day on splintered shins, then, believe it, everybody was going to play. One shudders to think what would have happened if Joe D. had ever played with Rickey Henderson.

Mantle may have been the culmination of the line — no one has ever had his combination of lefty-righty power and speed — but he was not the last of the Great Yankees. Reggie, with his drink-stirring swagger, was as true a son of Ruth as any of them. Forget the fact that he was only there for seven years. They were titanic years, full of glorious theater; no one since the Babe has so enlivened the franchise.

And then, of course, there is Don Mattingly. All line drives and silence, he is the very incarnation of Gehrig: solemn and single-minded and as untaintable by George Steinbrenner as Gehrig was by Ruth. But this is where the lineage ends. When Mattingly goes, there will be no more like him. Rome is burning, the royal family disgraced. Soon, nothing will remain but the mad fiddler and his running slaves.

"My place in Yankee history?" sniggers Donald Arthur Mattingly. "I'll tell you what my place in Yankee history is. It's hitting .260 on a struggling ballclub, and letting everyone down in here. At the moment, I don't exactly feel too much a part of Ruth or Gehrig or DiMaggio."

It is three hours before game time, and Mattingly, sheathed in sweat and silver bike shorts, is sitting in his corner cubicle, the *place d'honneur* in the Yankee clubhouse. The other players loll about, most of them still in street clothes, grazing on fruit or playing three-handed rummy, but Mattingly has already put in a fierce hour in the batting cage. His black bat propped beside him, he looks like he wants nothing so much as to go back there now, to the temple of his solemn devotions.

In the batting cage, there is the pure release of hard work, and the pleasure of attacking one baseball after another. But mostly, there is the relief of being away from this team, a collection of can't-win, don't-care, no-account strangers, the most faceless bunch to ever set foot in here. Two years ago, this room was electric, acrackle with the likes of Henderson, Willie Randolph, Jack Clark, and Dave Winfield. Now, peopled by Velardes and Leyritzes, it's got all the flavor of a bus station. Surveying the scene, Mattingly's eyes say, "Can these guys really be Yankees?"

"Man, oh man, this is just so tough," he says. "It hasn't been like this since I was 13 playing for a Babe Ruth team. We were horrible. Awful. Plus, we had bad uniforms. Ugly green things. It was terrible."

Mantle-Maris-Berra-Howard. Munson-Nettles-Jackson-Gossage. Those teams won because they were star-laden, yes, but also because they were blood-and-knuckles competitive. Year in, year out, they played as tough as pirates, tromping on good teams of lesser wills. Not so these Yankees. They give up before the first shot rings out.

"By the seventh inning we're getting pounded again, or we're down a run and we don't expect to win, and you think, 'This is another night we're not going to get over the hill,'" he laments. "We're not even making tough outs. . . . It's really pretty ugly, to tell you the truth. What they need to do is get rid of anyone who doesn't care. I take it home every night, and some guys just leave it. That ticks me off, to see a guy laughing and joking around when we lose. . . . You don't want any of those kind of guys on your team."

It is hard to say which is sadder, the dismantling of all this glorious tradition, or the desolation of Don Mattingly. Once the centerpiece of the gaudiest lineup in baseball, he is, for all intent and purposes, alone out there now. In '88, he hit behind Henderson and Randolph, who, regardless of their averages, drew 100 walks apiece, and were constantly dancing off of first and third for him. Now, he hits behind Roberto Kelly, who walks about as often as Mario Andretti, and Steve Sax, an opposite-field hitter whom American League pitchers seem to have figured out.

"It was such a different situation with Rickey and Willie," he says wistfully. "They put pressure on the pitcher. When there's nobody out there, the pitcher doesn't feel any tension. The only thing that'll hurt him is a home run."

The loss of Henderson and Randolph, both of whom Steinbrenner essentially gave away, is only the half of it, though. The other half is the subtraction of Clark and Winfield, who combined for 200 RBI behind Mattingly in '88. In baseball, this is called protection, and without it you stand about as much chance as a stray blonde in a biker joint. In Mattingly's first five full seasons, only four players hit more homers than he did (137); near the halfway point of this one, he has exactly five. And nobody in baseball had more RBI over that stretch (574); to date, he has 33. Thanks entirely to George's machinations, the Yankees are dead last in the league in hitting, slugging, runs scored, total bases, and on-base percentage. And so the team that won more games than anyone else in the '80s stands every chance of losing 105 this year. If this were any other kind of business, federal investigators would have been called in long ago and a conservator appointed.

None of which is to exempt Mattingly from blame, or to suggest for a moment that he exempts himself. His recent castigation of the team was the first of its kind, an outburst after a disastrous sweep in Boston during which manager Bucky Dent got canned and the wheels came off this abysmal club. By nature, Mattingly is unceasingly upbeat (read, deluded) about his teammates, and brutally hard on himself. Never mind that all the talent has gone elsewhere — to his mind, the losing this season is somehow his fault, his particular responsibility. On a team batting .240, it is not enough anymore to hit the ball hard and field his position flawlessly. He has to drive in every runner, though he hasn't had a pitch to hit in weeks; he has to turn this team around, though no one has a clue what direction it's headed in the first place; he has to take outfield practice, extra batting practice, more extra batting practice . . .

"I have no excuses for this year," he says, despite the built-in excuse of a chronic back problem, which flared again this week. "You look at yourself in the mirror and say, 'You haven't been getting it done, have you?' I've swung at bad pitches, I haven't been patient — there's a whole lot of things I haven't done. Naturally, you try to do too much, but I'm not even doing what I'm supposed to be doing."

He bites the sentence off, chewing on his self-acrimony. He is generally about as expressive as prairie grass, disclosing as little about himself as is humanly possible. But this year he's been even quieter than usual, stewing in a broth of exasperation. "If you're around him every day, you can tell," says first base coach Mike Ferraro. "He has a lot of anxiety to succeed. He's a very intense person, a perfectionist. Mantle was exactly the same. A quiet guy, but boy, you didn't want to be anywhere near him when we lost."

"I can tell you exactly where the season went south on him," says Tony Kubek, the Yankees' color man extraordinaire. "It was about a month ago in a game here against K.C. The Yankees are getting one-hit, 3–0, it's the bottom of the ninth, they've got men on first and second and Mattingly up. [K.C. Manager John] Wathan runs out and tells his reliever, 'Do what we did to [Wade] Boggs last year — walk him. I don't care if there's no base open and he's the tying run — put him on.' He goes back to the dugout, [Steve] Farr throws Donnie a curve that just does break over the plate, and he hits it back into the right field seats. The next day, the word goes out around the league: 'There's nobody else on this team that can beat you — do not pitch to Mattingly.' I don't think he's had a ball to drive since."

For the last six years Don Mattingly has simply been the best player in baseball. Over that stretch, he is first in the majors in total RBIs, third in hits, fourth in BA, fifth in HRs. He's won a batting title, an MVP, five Gold Gloves, set a consecutive-game home run streak, has been the AP Player of the Year three times running and an All-Star every season. He didn't get there on talent — not, at any rate, the sort of head-turning talent with which superstars are usually favored: the blinding bat speed, for instance, of Canseco, or the magic eyes of Ted Williams. No, Mattingly is the first self-made Great Yankee, a 19th-round draft pick from Evansville, Ind., who, through the alchemy of smarts and desire, turned modest gifts into exquisite skills.

"Don Mattingly's the best first baseman I've ever seen," Kubek says, "because he practices harder than most guys play. Intensity pays in the game, and Donnie's focused from the minute he gets to the ballpark. Offensively, defensively, he's just so tuned in. It's his mental sharpness more than anything that makes him so special."

Mattingly's hitting coach, Darrell Evans, agrees. "A lot of guys work hard. The great ones work smart, know themselves backwards and forwards. I saw that in Atlanta, with [Hank] Aaron, and in Detroit, with [Alan] Trammel. Other guys may realize their potential, but the Mattinglys exceed theirs."

Baseball people extol the work habits of Dave Stewart and such, but no one in the sport puts in the hours Mattingly does. He grew up in the mirror, emulating his hero, Rod Carew — hands back, knees bent in that old man's crouch — and has been perfecting and refining the stroke practically every day since. Like a guy with a vintage car, he always has it up on the blocks, sweating the little things like the set of his shoulders, the tilt of his hips.

But something has gone wrong with his swing this year that no amount of tinkering has fixed. Jumping at the bait of that enormous contract he signed in April (five year, $19.3 million), he has tried to be the savior of this team. Instead of taking what the league is giving him and lining the away pitch to left, he is contorting himself, trying to jerk it into the short porch in right. That is breaking faith with his one commandment to himself, to hit the ball hard, and never mind where it goes.

"Donnie had fallen into some pretty bad habits before I got here," says Evans, who came over as hitting instructor when Champ Summers was fired with Dent. "Normally, he's the most patient hitter in baseball, but this year he's just lunging at balls. I guess it's easy enough to see why."

That it is, though not without a little history. In '88 when Mattingly signed his last contract (three years, $6.7 million), he got off to his habitual slow start and was roundly savaged by Steinbrenner for "lacking leadership," George's code word for wimpishness. The belittlement stunned and ate away at Mattingly, and at the All-Star break he exploded, telling the national press that he'd never "gotten it [respect] around here." A hideous snit between the two ensued; for days, the back pages were bloody with George's threats to trade him.

The whole business deeply embarrassed Mattingly, who is, as Kubek describes him, "Yankee class from head to toe — and I mean the kind you don't see around here anymore." Whether Mattingly knows it or not, he is surely trying to pre-empt another strike by George, flexing muscles he doesn't have, breaking his back to be The

Man. It is an old, old story — Steinbrenner signing someone to a fat contract, then promptly and publicly impugning his manhood — but it is the last time we shall see it play out here. None but the lame (Pascual Perez) and desperate (Dave LaPoint) will take his money anymore, though the Mark Langstons will of course be happy to use him shamelessly to drive their price up elsewhere. Money is money, and every owner in baseball has it. What George has frittered away is the only capital that mattered: the cachet of being a Yankee.

It spoke to Mattingly this spring — "It would kill me if I left and two or three years later the Yankees won" — just as it had spoken to Reggie Jackson 15 years before him, and 50 years before Reggie, to a strapping architecture student named Lou Gehrig. "Just putting on a Yankee uniform gave you confidence," Gehrig once said. "It made you better than you actually were." The pride of the Yankees was no insubstantial thing; it was the team's precious equity, built up over time by a succession of the greatest men ever to play this game. Now it is gone, squandered by the little man from Tampa, and New Yorkers are immeasurably poorer for it. They cling to Don Mattingly, cheering even his pop flies and groundouts, because he is the last Yankee, and he is all they have left.

After a decade of drama and controversy for the franchise, Don Mattingly emerged as the one Yankee everyone loved. Against the backdrop of organizational disarray, Mattingly harkened back to an earlier era, providing a standard of excellence and professionalism that stood out in stark contrast to a franchise that rarely seemed to exhibit either during his tenure.

Solotaroff, whose chilling 1991 profile of body builder Steve Michalik, "The Power and the Gory," was included in David Halberstam's Best American Sports Writing of the Century, *wrote this story for Frank Deford's short-lived* National Sports Daily, *perhaps the most ambitious sports publication in history.*

PART VII

NEW YORK, NEW YORK

The Yankees careened out of control through the 1980s as Steinbrenner's exorbitant spending failed to deliver either a championship or serenity. The story of the team became one of opportunities squandered and missed until the franchise finally collapsed under its own weight. The Mets, in the wake of their stunning world championship in 1986, seemed poised to take over as New York's team.

But in the 1990s this team would somehow emerge at the top of the heap again. Sinatra's voice would ring out across the Bronx, championship banners would fly again, and the dynasty would be renewed.

Where did it begin? With George Steinbrenner's petty battles with Dave Winfield and his resulting suspension? With Don Mattingly's stoic example of excellence? The trade for Paul O'Neill? The hiring of Joe Torre? A TV contract that gave the club a license to print money? Or was it just the birth of one Derek Sanderson Jeter, born to be a Yankee and destined to follow in the tradition of every Yankee star to date?

Writers exhausted themselves tracking the details, for the reasons why the Yankees won seemed as endless as the ways in which they did. The game became the subject again. All these factors and a thousand more combined to create a dynasty equal to that of any team in the history of baseball. And in 2001, it all seemed not only justified but well earned. At a time when the city and the nation needed something, anything, to distract itself from the horror of September 11, the Yankees rose to the occasion and gave New York three weeks of the most dramatic baseball it has ever seen, turning the city that couldn't sleep into the city that couldn't stop cheering. Although they fell at the end to Arizona on a broken bat single by Luis Gonzalez on a pitch from Mariano Rivera, the loss was tempered by the knowledge that even in defeat, the city had risen again, and together, had stood as one.

DREAM COME TRUE; KALAMAZOO'S JETER TAKES DRAFT SPOTLIGHT

from *The Detroit Free Press,* May 27, 1992

KALAMAZOO — Children and their dreams go through stages.

Initially, a youngster might want to become a policeman or fireman. Then a sweeper-truck driver or cowboy. Perhaps later, an astronaut or Michael Jordan. Eventually, those dreams relent to reality.

Derek Jeter's dreams never changed. Whenever an adult asked what he wanted to be when he grew up, the answer was always the same — a major league baseball player.

"At first, people would laugh," Jeter said. "Then they'd tell my parents: 'You shouldn't put those ideas in your son's head.'"

Dot and Charles Jeter didn't plant the seed of professional baseball in Derek's mind, but they did nothing to alter his thinking. In fact, they nourished the notion.

"We've always told our kids they could be better than anybody else," Dot said.

Derek will find out Monday just how much better he has become. That day, major league baseball conducts its annual amateur draft. And Jeter, a senior shortstop at Kalamazoo Central, appears to be a surefire first-round pick. *Baseball America* rates him the top high school player in the country.

Cincinnati has the fifth pick in the first round, and word is the Reds are high on Jeter.

"The fifth pick, huh?" said Michigan baseball coach Bill Freehan. "Have you talked to Houston lately?"

Houston has the No. 1 pick.

This spring, the Jeters have met with representatives from Milwaukee, Kansas City, Cleveland, Cincinnati, Houston, Detroit, Los Angeles and Minnesota. Scouts and cross-checkers have flocked to Kalamazoo.

Freehan's interest in Jeter might be academic in a few days. Last fall, Jeter signed with U-M, but he might be lured away by a pro contract.

"He's the best player I've seen, but we've only been allowed to recruit for a year-and-a-half," said Freehan, whose recruiting was limited by NCAA restrictions stemming from violations by his predecessor, Bud Middaugh. "Derek's an outstanding young man on top of it, too. You can tell that by the way he conducts himself around the house and the times he's been here. He's the type of young man you want in your program."

Despite a severely sprained ankle early this spring, Jeter has a .508 average.

"He has good foot speed, he hits well and he hits with power," Kalamazoo Central coach Don Zomer said. "He's got a gun for an arm. He was timed at 91 miles per hour from shortstop to first. One of the problems was getting a first baseman who could handle his throws.

"He's got it all, and I still say he's a better person than a baseball player."

Jeter's father played baseball at Fisk University, so Derek's excellence at the sport is no accident. Neither is his prominence in academics.

Jeter has a 3.82 grade-point average (on a 4.0 scale) and scored 23 on the American College Test. His parents are college graduates, and his father has master's and doctorate degrees from Western Michigan.

"He's a serious student," his father said, "and we're serious about his education."

That is why a pro contract won't be the first contract he has signed. Each fall, Jeter and his sister, Sharlee, 12, sign contracts with their parents detailing what is expected of each of them during the school year.

"First of all, we want them to do well academically," Charles Jeter said. "And we want them to be involved in things. The contract outlines study hours, curfews and participation in school activities."

Derek also started on the basketball team and is a member of the National Honor Society and president of the Latin Club.

But right now, baseball takes precedence.

Jeter began the season in grand style. He was 6-for-9 and hit three home runs in his first seven at-bats before the sprained ankle. He missed three games and was the designated hitter in others while trying to recover, which hampered his performance.

But he still had 30 hits in 59 at-bats, scored 28 runs, and knocked in 25, with five doubles and four homers. A year ago he batted .557 with 34 RBIs and stole 22 bases. He struck out once in each of the last two seasons.

"Let me tell you," Zomer said, "the one this year was a bad call."

The call now for Jeter is whether to attend Michigan this fall or sign a pro contract. A new draft rule allows major league teams to retain rights to a draftee for five years or until a year after the draftee withdraws from college. This is seen as a way to help lower the huge bonuses some high school players were commanding.

"If they want to sign you they'll pay you," Jeter said. "I don't think they want to risk injury in college. But I don't think guys will be getting the $1.55 million Brien Taylor got last year." (With the No. 1 pick, the Yankees selected Taylor, a left-handed pitcher from Beaufort, N.C.)

Jeter does not expect to become a millionaire, but he should get enough dough so the 1981 Datsun with 127,000 miles and all of those rust spots no longer will be his mode of transportation.

Yet, when Jeter is alone at night he doesn't dream of a new Porsche. He dreams of simply playing ball.

"I want to play in the major leagues; I don't want to make $7 million," he said. "I mean, the money crosses your mind, but I just want to play."

Jeter began playing baseball when he was four and his grandmother put a ball on a tee for him.

"My husband always told Derek to compare himself with kids who really wanted to play ball," his mother said. "It's his dream to play ball. It's right around the corner, and he just has to make the right turn. We told him if he worked hard he'd have options. Right now, he has options."

And Jeter appreciates his parents' support.

"I always wanted to be one of the best," he said. "My mom said I could be if I kept working.

"I guess she was right."

Derek Jeter grew up in Kalamazoo, Michigan, with one goal: to play shortstop for the New York Yankees. This portrait of Jeter on the precipice of his professional baseball career reveals a player already mature beyond his years — he had yet to be contacted by the Yankees and tells the reporter his dream is simply to play shortstop in the major leagues. For the Yankees were the only team in baseball that had yet to express interest in Jeter. They did so two days later. When he indicated that he would sign, they made him their first-round pick on June 1, 1992.

THE BIG PAYBACK

from *Sport*, March 1993

Elba is a couple of acres of prime real estate, hugging the shoreline of Tampa Bay, Fla. On any given afternoon, the place is populated with tanned Adonises and bikini-clad women, but on this December day, it is a bit too chilly for sun worshipers, and George Steinbrenner has chosen to entertain in the dining room of his Bay Harbor Hotel.

"It's a beautiful setting," Steinbrenner says, while munching on a tuna-salad sandwich. "Napoleon had his Elba. I guess you could say this is mine."

For the past two years, Steinbrenner has spent the better part of his time serving as vice president of the U.S. Olympic Committee and tending to his hotel and his shipbuilding business, a short fly ball from the Bay Harbor. During that time, his visits to New York have been few and far between. He has not set foot in Yankee Stadium since Aug. 21, 1990, when he tossed an emotional farewell luncheon for his employees and then, fighting back tears, exited the building through the left-field loading dock to a waiting limo.

At the time, there had been a genuine finality to it all. Steinbrenner had, after all, signed away ownership of the New York Yankees by agreeing to be placed on baseball's permanently ineligible list. The alternative was to take a two-year suspension for the crime of giving $40,000 to an admitted gambler named Howie Spira in exchange for damaging information on then-Yankees superstar Dave Winfield. Certainly, no one could have foreseen the dramatic turn of events ahead, which saw baseball commissioner Fay Vincent, himself, be run out of the sport a few months after he announced that

Steinbrenner could resume his role as Yankees owner this coming March.

"I'm bitter at what Fay Vincent did to me and my family," says Steinbrenner. "I wasn't given due process, and I was deprived of my rights as a United States citizen, and that's one of the reasons why he's gone and I'm coming back. He hurt the [Yankees] partnership by forbidding me to participate in the 'extraordinary financial considerations' that were specified in the agreement I signed."

So on March 1, he comes back — the only owner in the history of baseball to be both suspended and reinstated by two different commissioners. But if there is one constant that we have come to know about the Steinbrenner persona in his 20 years as Yankees owner, it's that he is a man who gets mad and even.

Winfield can certainly attest to that. Before he ever donned Yankees pinstripes, he found himself at war with Steinbrenner. In the center of the controversy was the Winfield Foundation to which Steinbrenner had agreed to donate $300,000 per year as part of the new Yankee slugger's deal. In nearly 10 years in New York, Winfield learned just what extremes the boss would go to get even. There were the charges and countercharges regarding the foundation and the unfortunate comparisons of Winfield to Reggie Jackson ("Reggie is a winner . . .") that were punctuated by the infamous "Mr. May" tag Steinbrenner pinned on Winfield during a fit of anger in September of 1985, when the Yankees were in the process of dropping three in a row to the Toronto Blue Jays.

"It was a mistake to have made that 'Mr. May' statement," Steinbrenner says. "He and [Don] Baylor weren't delivering. It was made as a frustrated fan."

Nevertheless, Steinbrenner shows no regret over trading Winfield and does not appear inclined to ever patch things up as he did with Jackson, Lou Piniella and Graig Nettles. Instead, Steinbrenner points with pride to the court victory he won in September of 1989 in which Winfield was forced to reimburse the foundation for $30,000 in misappropriated expenses and another $229,667 in delinquent payments.

"I did not agree with what went on in the foundation," Steinbrenner says. "That caused our real problem. [Former San Diego Padres team president] Ballard Smith told me, 'You'll live to regret ever signing Winfield because of the foundation.' The foundation was always baggage.

"If Winfield brought all that he was said to have brought to Toronto and their world championship, then why did they let him go?"

So it would seem that his two years in Napoleonic exile have not made him a kinder, gentler Steinbrenner. Should we be surprised by that?

"Did he really ever go away?" asks Dallas Green, who managed the Yankees in 1989 before being fired a few months later after one too many clashes with Steinbrenner. "George has shown time and again he's not going to change. I know that better than anyone. I got fooled too. If we're all looking for changes in George, that's not gonna happen. He's gonna come back with some kind of 'I'll get back' at his enemies. In George's defense, he had legitimate gripes about what they did to him."

Steinbrenner shrugs and gazes out at the sea gulls skydiving into Tampa Bay when asked if it's true that he really hasn't been mellowed by his exile. "I honestly don't know what I'll be like or if I'll be any different," he says. "I do know I've missed the players — the relationships with them — and I've missed some of the owners. Above all, I've missed the challenge of building a winner."

Though he never fails to recite his accomplishments — two championships, four American League pennants, owner of the winningest team in baseball during the 1980s — Steinbrenner is careful to downplay the Yankees' steady decline leading up to his departure in 1990.

Once the most visionary of owners when it came to free agency, Steinbrenner lost his touch in the late '80s. A steady stream of disastrous free-agent signings — Ed Whitson and Pascual Perez, to name a couple — all came at the expense of first-round picks.

"You have to look at the whole 20-year record," he insists. "It's the nature of the beast to have down years in sports. . . . Did it pass the Dallas Cowboys by in football? Did [Dodgers owner] Peter O'Malley suddenly learn to lose? Did the Mets?"

Yet, in Steinbrenner's absence, the Yankees' farm system has managed to produce, and even flourish, despite not having No. 1 draft picks. If there's been any beacon of optimism around Yankee Stadium these past couple of years, it has been the development of something that hasn't been witnessed in the Bronx in more than a quarter-century: a bevy of homegrown talent, which includes the likes of pitcher Sam Militello and outfielder Bernie Williams.

Tempering that optimism, however, is the fear that Steinbrenner will not have the patience to allow these kids to reach their potential as Yankees, that he will resort to his old ways of signing or trading for more established, marquee players, only to discover they have had their best years with their former teams.

Those fears were no less alleviated last summer when the Yankees announced that they were cutting out their instructional-league program and reducing their scouting staff because of "budgetary reasons" — strange, indeed, considering that they've been making a mint from CBS and the Madison Square Garden Network.

"We cut the instructional league because we felt we could serve the same purpose by working with just a few players prior to spring training," Steinbrenner says. "By cutting back on our minor-league teams, we feel we'll cull out all the players who were never going to make the major leagues anyway. . . . As for the scouts, it's great to have a lot of 'em, but they gotta be productive."

Ironically, as he talks about his budget cuts, Steinbrenner's son-in-law, Joe Molloy (serving as the Yankees' managing general partner until Steinbrenner officially re-assumes control of the team on March 1), is over on the other side of the dining room, negotiating a contract with the agent of five-time batting champion Wade Boggs. The signing of Boggs, coming off his worst season, blocks out third base for another homegrown Yankees product, Hensley Meulens. But Steinbrenner scoffs at the suggestion that he's again trying to buy a pennant.

"I like getting guys coming off a bad year," he says. "They have something to prove. Besides, Wade Boggs is a guy people might come out to see. We haven't had any guys like that lately.

"You know, I keep hearing so much about how the Blue Jays did it the 'right' way. Now, [Blue Jays vice president of baseball operations] Pat Gillick is a sound baseball man. We trained him. But when I keep hearing and reading how he did it the 'right' way, I have to laugh. What was Winfield? A free agent! What was Jack Morris? A free agent! And old free agents, at that! Out of the Blue Jays' starting lineup, they had two players — Pat Borders and John Olerud — who came up through their system. And they had the highest payroll in baseball! So how come when I was doing it and I had the highest payroll in baseball, they said I wasn't doing it the right way?"

Perhaps because Steinbrenner was doing it amid constant turmoil and turnover in both his front office and manager's chair. Eventually, all the firings and re-hirings of Billy Martin, interspersed with the firings of equally popular and successful managers such as Piniella, Dick Howser and Yogi Berra, took their toll on the Yankees organization. Stability, the primary ingredient of success for any organization, had no place with Steinbrenner's Yankees. And there are ominous signs that this will be the case in years to come.

Case in point: While Molloy was negotiating the Boggs contract, Gene Michael, the team's general manager, was totally removed from the process. Ever since the departures of his first two general managers, Gabe Paul and Al Rosen, Steinbrenner has been bent on setting up a kind of two-headed front office in which one side frequently operates without the other's knowledge. It is the old divide-and-conquer theory, but as evidenced by the Yankees' free-fall to the Cleveland Indians' depths of the American League East, Steinbrenner's methods have been self-destructive.

"I honestly think George wants to win," says Green. "He just doesn't know how to go about it. He should stick to the business end of the organization and let his baseball people do their jobs. George's problem is he thinks the agents are his friends. The fact is, nobody wants to help George Steinbrenner — the owners, the general managers, nobody."

Says Michael, who thought he was going to be Steinbrenner's baseball man: "He tried to get rid of me, but I think down deep he respects my opinion on players. He knows I'll tell him the truth. . . . I'll argue with him, and that's when we'll have trouble, but I've found that he's not so stubborn if you keep going back at him."

When it comes to Steinbrenner's managers, though, there's no going back at him. Seventeen managerial changes in 20 years is sufficient proof that the man simply can't help himself.

"At times, I was a little too anxious to make changes," he confesses. "I think the time away has taught me to be more patient, but that's not to say anything is forever."

Hardly reassuring words for the present Yankees manager, Buck Showalter, who's beginning his 17th year in the organization.

"I have reasons for everything I do," says Showalter, "and I look

forward to working with him. If I'm afraid of my ideas being questioned, then maybe they're not that good. I've learned that anything
that comes easy isn't worth having. Mr. Steinbrenner is not one of
our problems. In a lot of ways, he's our biggest asset."

The anticipation of spring training in Fort Lauderdale and his
triumphant return to a Vincent-less baseball clearly excites Steinbrenner.

"It's going to be a happening," he says unabashedly. And then, as
he gets up from the table to return to his shipbuilding office down
the road, he turns to his visitor and adds, "You know, there are times
when I would rather be owner of the New York Yankees than president of the United States."

The Daily News' *Bill Madden, co-author with Moss Klein of* Damned
Yankees, *is one of the more cogent observers of the Steinbrenner regime. Here, he captures Steinbrenner at his nadir, the end of his two-
year suspension. In retrospect, both the suspension and Steinbrenner's
return were the best things that could ever have happened to the team.*

BOY OH BOY OH BOY

from *The Washington Post*, October 13, 1996

Enough with this kid. I am referring, of course, to The Kid who leaned over the right field railing at Yankee Stadium, stuck out his glove and gave the Yankees a gift home run.

Jeffrey Maier, 12, has gotten so much attention that he's retained a publicist.

A publicist! He's 12! At that age, the only thing he should be retaining is his front teeth. How much publicity is The Kid gonna get? What is he, Tommy Hilfiger?

It's a sad commentary on my profession that the debate between two of the most dynamic political figures in America, Vice President Al Gore and that other guy, was hardly noticed because my colleagues were infatuated by a 12-year-old boy with a baseball glove.

As a journalist, I'm embarrassed by this. The Kid's been on the front page of the *Washington Post,* the *New York Times,* the *New York Daily News,* the *New York Post,* the *Far Eastern Economic Review, Hustler* and *Sri Lanka Today.* He has been on *Letterman, Good Morning America, Rosie O'Donnell* and *Live with Regis and Kathie Lee.* I hear he's been booked on Ted Koppel's show to discuss his views on a Middle East summit.

Enough, already.

OK, here's my take on The Kid.

He's a punk, I sez.

I was at the game in New York, I seen the play, so listen up:

First, The Kid cuts school to go to the game. So he's a truant, and I think he should be suspended from school for five whole days. But not during the playoffs. Starting next season. (Inside baseball joke.)

Second, what was he doing out at night in just a T-shirt? He could catch cold. What kind of parents does he have? A child welfare agency should take him away and put him in an orphanage and feed him gruel.

And third, he DROPS THE BALL!

Kid has it in his glove, and it pops out like a poultry timer. What a doof.

Envy for The Kid's Effort

Tony, this is the lowest you've ever sunk. He's a 12-year-old boy, and he's as cute as a button. So what if he hurt the Orioles? Stop pandering to the Washington audience. All he did was try to catch a fly ball. You'd have done the same thing yourself.

Actually, I wouldn't have.

I was in Jeff Maier's shoes once. This is a true story. I was just a year or so older. I, too, had gone to a baseball game in New York, in the old Polo Grounds. I, too, had brought my baseball glove. And I, too, had a ball hit near me. It was a foul ball, coming right at me, at about the same speed as that flying cow in *Twister*. Any kid worth his spikes would have lifted his glove hand and easily caught the ball.

Instead, I panicked and ducked. The ball sailed over me and clobbered the old man sitting behind me. It hit him in the forehead, knocking him out. It hit him so flush I could see the stitch marks from the ball on his face. I thought he was dead. I felt like a murderer.

That moment of cowardice has stayed with me for almost 35 years. It haunts me now when I take my kids to sporting events. I fear having good seats because I know those seats expose us to sharply hit foul balls. My kids will be depending on their famous sportswriter dad to keep them safe from any missiles, and I know I won't catch them if they come my way. I'll duck like the coward I am. And my kids will take the shot in the labonza.

What ever happened to . . .

So, in truth, I envy The Kid for trying, for getting a glove on the ball. By the same token, I fear for him. He is already past the high point in his life and coming down the other side.

By next week, he'll be nostalgia. He's 12 years old, and it's over for him. Where does he go from here, *Hollywood Squares*?

See, in our minds, Jeff Maier will always be this 12-year-old kid who reached over the rail and gave the Yankees a home run they shouldn't have had. But you can't stay 12 forever. Think about it: The kid who played Eddie Haskell is almost 50 now.

I'm looking 30 years down the road and seeing this kid in an Atlantic City lounge wearing a bad hairpiece and nursing a martini. By then, he'll have been divorced three times, and he'll have gone bankrupt after sinking all his money into a roasted-chicken franchise. He'll be reduced to autographing glossy pictures of himself from that magic night at Yankee Stadium at card shows.

His siblings will hate him; they'll go on TV shows and criticize him for being the favored child in the family and being the cause of their own identity crises. His parents will go on those same shows and express chagrin at his alienation from them. Everyone will agree that it started with the night he reached out and tried to catch that ball at Yankee Stadium.

And they'll blame the media.

The Yankees' recent dynasty has many fathers. But if not for twelve-year-old Jeffrey Maier, the dynasty might never have gotten off the ground. He reached over the right-field fence at Yankee Stadium and snatched victory from defeat in the 1996 playoffs against Baltimore, giving Derek Jeter a home run and turning the tide in the Series. The team would go on to win its first world championship since 1978.

Maier, whom bleacher fans immediately serenaded with chants of "MVP, MVP," was alternately lionized and ripped over the next few days, as in this hilarious column by the Washington Post's *Tony Kornheiser.*

IT'S SIMPLY GREAT DAY FOR DONNIE

from *The New York Post*, September 1, 1997

The man who stood behind home plate, the main attraction on a special day named after him at the Stadium, was no different, really, than the no-name who broke into the big leagues as a prospect a couple of tools shy of can't-miss.

He was all baseball then, all baseball yesterday. Therein lies the secret of Don Mattingly's stranglehold on the hearts of Yankee fans.

A common man with uncommon reflexes ideally suited for baseball, he suffered from no delusions of grandeur. He did not believe because he could hit a baseball and catch one with such grit and grace it made him an authority on the stock market, fine wines, rock and roll.

It should come as no surprise then that Mattingly, when asked what he wants to do with his life, said nothing about being appointed to presidential commissions or any other such ego outlets for self-important retired stars.

Rather, he said he intends to report to Yankees spring training to help young players learn the finer points of first base play and hitting mechanics. He wants to give to the kids what Catfish Hunter and other retired Yankee greats gave to him all those hot afternoons under the palm trees.

Mattingly was a ballplayer, that's all, a great one for half a decade, a Yankee great forever; a ballplayer whose No. 23 was painted in huge digits along the first and third base lines yesterday.

"I always wanted to keep it strictly baseball," Mattingly said. "When the fans thought about me, they thought about baseball, not about a commercial or about a celebrity or anything like that."

Mattingly succeeded in that mission and 55,707 came out to the Stadium on the first NFL Sunday to thank him for that.

The highlights from the 45-minute ceremony: Tino Martinez, No. 24, presenting No. 23 with a ring as they shared a rocking joint ovation; Wade Boggs and Paul O'Neill flanking him in Monument Park for the unveiling of his plaque; Jordan, the third and youngest of Don and Kim's sons, darting about like a mosquito in search of blood; the film clip of Mattingly chasing a foul ball headed for the stands and coming away with a mouth-full of popcorn.

It was Mattingly, forced out of the game prematurely by a dead back that stole life from his bat, who knew when it was time to go. But it was Tino's hot bat that made Mattingly's fans accept Donnie Baseball made the right call.

When Mattingly walked out to throw out the ceremonial first pitch, from first base, Tino deferred to him.

"Go ahead," he told Mattingly. "This is your spot. Do whatever you want."

The moment was nearly as crowd-pleasing as the replay of Mattingly stealing the young boy's popcorn, a memory that brought a smile back to Donnie Baseball's face.

"The ball was only about 12 rows back and everyone turned around to look," Mattingly said, "except for that one kid who was looking right at me, like this [eyes wide, mouth open]. So I said, "Can I have some of that?" And I grabbed some and ate it. It was in one of those 70–90 years. I learned to appreciate the fans more and have a little more fun with them during those down years."

The down years made Mattingly the major league player with the most service time without playoff experience, until the Yankees sprinted through September of 1995 to qualify for the wild card. What a finish.

Mattingly batted .417, doubled four times, homered and drove in six runs in the five-game, overtime loss to the Mariners. Such a finish would have convinced most players they had too much talent left to go home. Not Mattingly.

"It feels great, knowing I went out that way, instead of going out struggling," Mattingly said. "I always felt I would rise to the big moment and it was important for me to prove to myself I could. I felt like I did."

Mattingly called the final days of his career the highlights. How many athletes can say the same?

"The first game of the playoffs, that was special," Mattingly said when reminded of the "Don-nie Base-ball" chants of that night, chants that resurfaced yesterday. "That, more than anything, I'll never forget. When I first stepped out of the dugout to run before the game, I felt like I was floating across the outfield."

His back even cooperated, granting him one more series played at superstar level, after a half-dozen years of diminished production.

He looked the part of superstar only when in Pinstripes. Joe Torre and Tino perfectly captured him with identical words yesterday when they said Mattingly was a superstar who never acted like one.

He has forgotten neither his roots nor where they took him. Mattingly, 36, resides in native Evansville, Ind., but means it when he says he has two hometowns.

"I never thought I would say this coming from a small town in Indiana, not that small, but when we come to New York, we feel like it's home," Mattingly told the crowd before the 3–2 win over the Expos. "I tried to keep it pure. I tried to keep it simple. I tried to play great baseball for you over the years. I hoped you appreciated it."

He didn't hope they appreciated it. He knew it. But to say so would not fit his humble nature. Just like he couldn't say what he later revealed he considered saying: "Michael is No. 23 everywhere else in the world, but not in this stadium."

Should have said it. Some 55,707 would have roared agreement.

No Yankees player has ever played so many games for the club without winning a world championship. Yet many later Yankees, like Paul O'Neill and Derek Jeter, credit Mattingly with setting the tone that later resulted in the championships under Joe Torre. Oddly, Mattingly's failure to collect a World Series ring has made him even more popular with and respected by Yankees fans. Tom Keegan now hosts a radio show on ESPN Radio.

DAVID HALBERSTAM

....

TORRE MAKES A GOOD BOSS

From ESPN.com, November 12, 2001

This is in praise of Joe Torre. What a pleasure it has been to watch the Yankees during the years he has managed in New York. May I also suggest that this year he had what was probably his best year of managing, this being a Yankee team that was aging and somewhat vulnerable, and seemed, especially in the beginning of the season, better on paper than it was on the field.

Joe Torre and his staff have changed the atmosphere in the Yankees clubhouse. It is in praise of him not merely as a baseball man, but in the more complete sense as a man, for the two are not always the same. To understand the difference, all you have to do is think back to the appalling turmoil that surrounded the cartoon-like Billy Martin era in the Bronx years before Torre arrived.

Torre is as complete a person as high-level professional sports can produce, especially in this hyped-up era with its higher visibility, where the rewards are greater than ever, and where therefore the shelf life of a coach or manager tends to be briefer — you go up higher and faster than in the past, and you can descend even more quickly. The role of the media, after all, is greater than ever, which imposes an immense temptation to take care of yourself at the expense of your players, to indulge in me-first leadership.

Torre has been successful in New York for any number of reasons: He has had very good players, by dint of George Steinbrenner's passion to win, and his players are by and large, mature, unusually self-reliant men (especially when calibrated on the Richter Scale of contemporary athletic maturity, where sheer ability and the willingness to accept responsibility for your actions are not necessarily on the same team).

But I think it is important not to underestimate how well Torre's own exceptional human qualities have served him, his honesty and sense of humor, and his instinct, despite all the media pressures on him, to be exceptionally straight in his dealings. This has helped shape the clubhouse and made these Yankees a team that sportswriters coming from venues that are nominally violently anti-Yankee have come to respect, if not actually like.

Torre is the type of manager that most major-league players want to play for. So, in one of the three or four most heavily scrutinized institutions in the country (perhaps less scrutinized than the Pentagon, but more scrutinized than the Department of the Interior) and with an exceptionally demanding and highly volatile owner, he has managed to be true to himself, and his players know it. If they are straight with him, he will play it straight and protect them — if need be, even from the owner.

Somehow, when I think of Torre, I conjure up the opposite vision of Steve Spurrier, the immensely successful coach of Florida who (a) always seems to be running up the score, but more importantly (b) seems to give out the impression by body language and facial expression that when things go wrong, it is not that he coached poorly, but because his players did not execute his game plan as well as they should.

I do not know Torre very well personally, but even my limited dealings with him gave me added respect for him. We met about eight years ago, when I was working on a book about the 1964 World Series between the Yankees and Cardinals. Torre had not played in that Series — he joined the Cardinals a few years later — but he was a great friend and admirer of Bob Gibson, who was the star of the Series and a central figure in my book. He was obviously intrigued that someone who is not nominally a sportswriter was going to write about one of the greatest athletes and fiercest competitors he knew.

Therefore, he went out of his way to be helpful. There was nothing in it for him, which for most readers probably does not mean much. But for anyone writing about sports it means a great deal — by and large, when you deal with an athlete or an ex-athlete, one of the things that hangs quite heavily in the air is one of the oldest questions of all time — what's in it for me?

It struck me that Torre went out of his way to be generous, not because he cared that much who I was, or wanted to ingratiate himself with me, for there was no way I could help his career or get him back into baseball at that time, but because he thought I was serious, and — most of all — because he loved Bob Gibson and he wanted to be sure I got him right. Torre's generosity was about something very old-fashioned, loyalty to a magnificent teammate, years after they had played their last game together.

I remember leaving the interview that day, impressed not merely by the wonderful quality of Torre's stories about Gibson, but about the nature of the man I had just finished interviewing. He had an old-fashioned sense of honor and loyalty to a teammate. It told me a good deal about two men, Gibson, the man who inspired that loyalty, and Torre, the man who, in such an egocentric line of work, still possessed it.

I was impressed at the time, and had made it a point in the years after to pay attention to Torre, and he has not disappointed me. He always seems to be in character, very much the man I dealt with then, albeit in ever-more explosive and pressurized circumstances.

I am always a little wary of journalistic psychological assumptions, but I have come to believe that Torre behaves this way because it is who he is, and the way he was raised, his home, his religion, the nurturing of an admired older brother, and that he was taught to deal with people in a certain way, the way he would like to be treated by them. He seems to be a man secure in his knowledge of who he is, and secure in his faith. Equally important, though he would obviously prefer to win rather than to lose, how he behaves as a man and how he sees himself is not based on his career winning percentage.

It is a rare quality these days, and it extends far beyond sports. My wife, who is not a devoted baseball fan, has watched him over the years, in all kinds of difficult situations, especially in this year when the Yankees made their great postseason run, with the shadow of the New York tragedy hanging over them, and she was stunned by Torre's constant grace under pressure, the test Hemingway set up for men years ago — he is, she says, the most elegant of men; he always seems to get the situation he is in right and to say the right thing.

George Steinbrenner might respect Torre's results, but he still showed who was boss when it came time to talk about a contract extension.

She is right. The key to Torre is that he is a good baseball man, but he also knows there is much more to life than baseball, and that, finally, it is how you behave, most obviously when things are not going on well, that defines you.

If Torre is a man who has come to peace with himself, George Steinbrenner has seemed, at many times in his career (less so now than in the past), a man far from comfortable with himself, often given to bullying those around him and denigrating his players during losing streaks. Some of his pettier qualities have been reined in recently, and I suspect part of the change is simply a factor of age. He was 71 this year, and most of us become less volatile as we get older.

But one of Torre's great successes has been to serve as an insulator to protect his players from the owner and, whenever possible, to take the heat himself. Another has been to be able to change the ambiance at the Stadium from the time, just a decade ago, when the Yankees could not get the free agents they wanted, and were being used by shrewd agents to bid the price up for other teams. Does anyone think Mike Mussina would have come to the Yankees in the Billy Martin era?

The Steinbrenner-Torre relationship is a fascinating, constantly shifting one of balances and counterbalances. Torre serves, as all managers do, at the owner's whim, and Steinbrenner has more whims than most people, and they come to him more quickly. If he knows he needs this manager, there is also no doubt that he has no small amount of envy for Torre's larger public and media popularity and, as such, we get the occasional reminders of his irritation, the long delay in re-signing Torre, and the occasional throwaway lines that Torre never won until he came to the Yankees, and thus managed the players Steinbrenner signed. There is a good deal of truth to that, but it is also true that the clubhouse ambiance has changed dramatically in the Torre years, making the Yankees more attractive to the free agents Steinbrenner wants to sign.

Torre's popularity with the fans and the media certainly isn't lost on Steinbrenner. One of the things that has always fascinated me when looking at men who are engaged in fierce pursuits, in the military or sports, for example, is the difference between being strong and being tough. Steinbrenner, for whatever insecurities, has always struck me as someone who wants to be tough (there was an unusually stupid Howard Cosell piece about him years ago which called him the George Patton of the Yankees — though, of course, Steinbrenner had never heard a shot fired in anger), but does not know the difference between being tough and strong. From his own background, and from his own self-doubt, I suspect, come a certain amount of swaggering, bullying and tough guy talk, as if that is the way real tough guys talk.

Torre is, very quietly, something quite different. He is quietly strong — a strength that comes from a healthy sense of accurately appraised self-value, and a willingness, if need be, to walk away from any situation which might be unacceptably difficult or abusive. As such, there has been an invisible line drawn in the sand at the Stadium without him ever having to draw it. Because of that, he has not only done an exceptional job managing the Yankees, but has also helped do something that a number of us thought once could not have been done — he has helped turn George Steinbrenner, though still a work in progress, into a good owner.

When Joe Torre was first hired as Yankee manager in 1996, the press called him "Clueless Joe," for as a manager in Atlanta, St. Louis, and with the Mets, he had done little to indicate that he was capable of leading a team to the World Series. How wrong they were.

Award-winning journalist David Halberstam is one of many who have been impressed by Torre's understated yet unquestionably effective approach. The team seems to take its emotional cue from Torre, never appearing flustered and always focusing on the task at hand — winning the World Series.

PROBING MR. CLEMENS

from ESPN.com, October 25, 2000

NEW YORK — After a thorough review of the videotapes followed by probing interviews with the principal participants and long, thoughtful analysis, baseball's Minister of Justice Frank Robinson announced before Game 3 of the World Series that Roger Clemens did not intend to hit Mike Piazza with the barrel of the broken bat he threw during the first inning of Game 2.

He was really aiming for Keith Olbermann's mother.

What a thing. A five-time Cy Young winner snaps during a World Series game, firing the jagged edge of a broken bat near the All-Star player he beaned in the head earlier in the season, and days later people everywhere still are trying to figure out what happened. Fans are pretty evenly split on this issue. Half think Clemens threw the bat at Piazza intentionally and should have been ejected. Half think he didn't know Piazza was there and deserved no punishment. And Todd MacFarlane isn't sure what Clemens' intent was, but he's bidding $3 million for the broken bat anyway.

What was Clemens thinking when he threw that bat? Thanks to the wonders of modern phrenology, magnetic resonance imaging and *Gray's Anatomy,* we can help answer that question by taking you on a guided tour of that most mysterious of nature's objects: Roger Clemens' brain.

(Sorry, due to the graphic nature of this tour, no children are allowed without parental supervision. If you are under 17, please click off this web site and return to www.lustynakedcheerleaders.com. As for the rest of you, keep your hands inside the vehicle at all times.)

Cerebral cortex: Controls hand-to-eye coordination, allowing Clemens to throw a small, leather-covered spheroid at speeds approaching 95 miles per hour with pinpoint accuracy. Note: Neurons occasionally misfire in this section, causing the ball to "get away" and hit batters square in the head.

Optic nerve: Controls visual acuity, allowing Clemens to take in visual images and determine their color, size, shape and other characteristics. Warning: Occasional synapse misconnections may cause temporary problems differentiating between objects of similar size and shape, such as an eight-ounce white baseball and a broken 32-ounce wood bat.

Cerebellum: Contains the melody and the lyrics to *The Dukes of Hazzard.*

Cerebrum: Stores every word ever written by every reporter who ever worked in Boston, New York or Toronto the past 15 years, especially those bastards who wrote that I asked out of Game 6 of the 1986 World Series, which I didn't and anyone who says differently is A DAMN LIAR!

Frontal lobe: Controls impulses of rage and violence. Sorry, Wally World is closed for repairs. Moose out front should have told you.

Medulla oblagata: "There are 108 stitches on a baseball. Two minutes to Wapner. K-Mart sucks. I'm an excellent driver. . . ."

Left hemisphere: Entire Charles Bronson film catalogue.

Right hemisphere: Dan Duquette's address. Heh, heh, heh.

Middle cerebral artery: HTML for Victoria Secret's web site.

Frontal cortex: Fear of fire.

Basal ganglia: "Purity of essence. Essence of purity. Our precious bodily fluids . . ."

Foramen of Monro: Pi calculated to one hundred thousand digits.

Temporal lobe: "All work and no play makes Jack a dull boy. All work and no play makes Jack a dull boy. All work and no play makes Jack a dull boy. All work and no play makes Jack a dull boy. All work and no play makes Jack a dull boy. All work and no play makes Jack a dull boy. All work and no play makes Jack a dull boy. All work and no play makes Jack a dull boy. . . ."

■ *When Yankee pitcher Roger Clemens threw Mike Piazza's bat off the field and dangerously close to Piazza during the 2000 subway series between the Yankees and the Mets, he provided a rare tabloid moment in recent Yankee history. ESPN's Jim Caple found the question of exactly what was going on in Clemens's head irresistible.*

....

THE HAMMER OF GOD

from *Esquire,* June 2001

Not enough has been written about the art of the autograph. Oh, we have had earnest disquisitions concerning the science of the auto-graph, an unfortunately integral element of which has become a twelve-year-old boy standing forlornly in the lobby of a hotel at two in the morning while his greasy pimp daddy lurks nearby behind a potted plant. And, alas, the economics of the autograph have taken an even more staggering turn for the worse: After the arrest of Jeffrey Dahmer, two officers at a Milwaukee jail were busted for hav-ing solicited the late cannibal's signature. There has been more than ample examination of the laissez-faire elements of the autograph industry. But the art of the thing, the aesthetic of the signature itself, has gone sadly unremarked upon.

Look at them, you suckers. Look at all the autographs on all the baseballs in all your sweaty little collections. What might be capital letters — and what might just as well be dancing caribou — followed by indistinct horizons of bumps, loops, and jagged peaks. Look at this one here. It's Orel Hershiser's. Of course, by all the observable evidence, it could also be John Philip Sousa's, Warren Harding's, Orville Wright's, Muddy Waters's, Charles the Simple's, or Rin Tin Tin's. A .240-hitting journeyman outfielder could sign himself as Charlemagne and it would be years before anyone noticed.

Part of it is the medium. It is hard to write legibly on something round, which is why important legal documents are never written on baseballs. More of it, though, is that autographs have become a volume industry. They are signed in bulk and in haste. Players can sign using only the far fringes of their peripheral vision, and the best players are the best ones at it, because they have the most practice.

Which makes this all the more curious a scene. It is opening day — oh, pardon me, Opening Day — for the Tampa Bay Little League. The teams have had their parade, and they have scuffled around on the infield, raising clouds of dust into the bright morning air. They have pledged allegiance to the flag and to the Little League, which itself has an oath, just the way the Army does. Now, though, most of the league is lined up in front of a card table in the shade of a live oak tree where Mariano Rivera is signing whatever comes by.

He is old enough to be a parent coaching here. His eyes are set wide and dark, and his face is broad and open. In shorts and a sport shirt, in the cool shade of a tree, he looks more substantial than he does in a baseball uniform on the mound at Yankee Stadium, clinging to a one-run lead in the ninth inning of a World Series game, two men on and one man out, the forgotten starting pitcher back in the dugout icing his arm while he watches Rivera — who has ice in his heart. There he looks modest, slight, even mild, until he throws the ball and the game ends like a great iron door slamming shut.

We are in the fourth Yankee era, as dynasties are now reckoned. Given that the team has been the central pivot around which baseball has revolved over the past five years, and given Rivera's importance to the way the Yankees construct and win their games, a very compelling case can be made that Rivera is the single most valuable player in the sport. He doesn't throw a ball off the plate unless he wants to. There is very little about what he does that is accidental. In the last three years — which is to say, during the Yankees' three consecutive championships — Rivera has walked a total of sixty batters. Last season, he saved thirty-six of forty-one games, and he struck out fifty-eight batters in seventy-six innings pitched, and this in a year in which his ERA rose from 1.83 to 2.85. In fact, there was some talk that he was slipping, and even more talk that the four-year, $40 million contract he signed in February might well have been more of a reward for services rendered than anything else. It's a substantial commitment for a team to make to a thirty-one-year-old closer, but Rivera's value lies far beyond the mathematics dear to statisticians or accountants.

The rest of the case — the best part, the dramatic soul of it — comes from the fact that Rivera's presence changes every game long before he enters it. Consider: From July 8, 1999, until June 24, 2000,

nearly a flat year, including the 1999 World Series, Rivera did not allow a single inherited runner to score. Not one. This means that
teams must play the Yankees in accelerated time. They have to win
in seven innings, or maybe in eight, and the pressure cracks many of
them long before Rivera even begins to warm up. That thing that
baseball's tiresome aesthetes profess to love — that each game, theo-
retically, could last forever, that it is timeless (Five minutes, Mr.
Costner!) — is demolished when a team decides to place a mental
curfew on itself to win the game before the end of the game, before New York goes to its bullpen and brings out the Hammer of
God.

"I had [Anaheim Angel] Darin Erstad in the All-Star game last
year," says Yankees manager Joe Torre. "You'd have trouble getting
two words out of the guy. Anyway, I was saying, 'Come on, let's get a
couple more runs, guys.' And he comes up to me and says, 'Is Rivera
pitching the last inning?' I said, 'Yeah.' He says, 'You don't need any
more runs.' I found that pretty amusing."

He does not walk the ragged edge that many closers do. He is not
the fearsome, wild-eyed, intimidating presence the position once
appeared to demand. His power seems almost illusory, given his demeanor. He pitches briskly and efficiently, relying on a delicately
manipulated fastball that he either throws straight past the hitter or
cuts so it sails in on the hands and dives away. In the fourth game of
last year's World Series, for example, facing Matt Franco of the Mets,
Rivera threw a clutch of cut fastballs that danced like swallows and
flummoxed Franco so completely that he looked wonderingly at the
perfectly straight fastball that ultimately struck him out.

Knowing all that, then, watch him under the tree, signing baseballs, a breeze stirring the dust on the little infield behind him.
Watch his fingers work. They are long and pianistic, unscarred and
almost pristine in their movements. Watch as he brings the baseball
up close to his eyes. See the rounded M and the R with the jaunty little downswept tail. Then watch every single tiny letter, shaped and
sharpened, as though the letters were being sewn into the cover of
the baseball like stitches. It's like watching a monk illuminate a
manuscript, and it happens with every baseball, every time. Then
think of those dozens of tiny, jeweled movements, a choreography
of bone and muscle and tendon, making a baseball move at ninety-

eight miles per hour, and see how the art of the autograph works to make the economics of the autograph possible.

"I like to be precise," Mariano Rivera says later. "I like to be neat."

Their place in Tampa is as quiet as a law firm these days, loud only with the swish and swirl of two fountains and raucous only with the call of large swamp birds. This is where the Yankees train now, but more important, this is the place where the Yankees are, and they are in a good place, and it's not just because they've won three world championships in a row.

After all, they've had these dynastic exercises before, except that the previous ones all were attended by garish petulance, sybaritic barbarism, and the general charm and elegance apropos of the annual gathering of the Ostrogoths. The first bunch had Babe Ruth, all seven deadly sins rolled into a single beer gut. The teams from the forties through the sixties tore up New York at night as thoroughly as they did the American League during the day. And the seventies crew managed to win a lot of games despite giving the impression that the whole enterprise might one day dissolve into gun-play. That latter character persisted well into the eighties, long after the Yankees again had stopped winning pennants.

I can vividly recall being around the Yankees during the days of the extended fandango between George Steinbrenner and Billy Martin. I would see the Yankee beat writers at the beginning of the season, all bright-eyed and full of hope. By the All-Star break, they'd look as if they'd been with Napoleon on the retreat from Moscow.

Now, though, either because Joe Torre has set a tone and stuck to it, or because there are conspicuously fewer outright lunatics in the clubhouse, or because the principal owner finally has found being a cartoon plutocrat more exhausting than being an actual one, the Yankees hum along like a great, efficient machine. This latest dynasty is the Rockefellers, not the Medicis.

"You feel it all through the minors," Rivera explains. "The Yankees are a dynasty. That's what it is all along, and being a Yankee, you're part of that. The Yankees are the Yankees."

He is of a piece with his team and with its times, bounding through the clubhouse, quiet and merry at the same time. Everybody is bro, the way everybody is dude to some other players. His

English is good, laden with thoughtful pauses indicating that he doesn't think it's as good as it actually is. His team is relaxed, and he is relaxed, and there is no little correlation between the two. His presence puts the team at ease, as if it knows it has to hold a lead through only seven or eight innings. "In the seventh and eighth innings, we relax," says Jorge Posada, the catcher whose career in New York closely parallels Rivera's. "It's a nice way to play." If this Yankee team has a collective personality, Derek Jeter may be its public face and Bernie Williams its heart and soul, but Rivera is its definition.

He's been part of it almost from its inception, signing a minor league contract in 1990 after no major league team drafted him. Rivera grew up in Puerto Caimito, a fishing village on the southern coast of Panama, where his father was captain of another man's boat. Mariano worked the boat himself as a teenager. He was an athlete before he was a baseball player, and he was a baseball player before he was a pitcher. He played soccer first, then moved on to baseball, where he began as a kind of all-purpose player. When he was nineteen, his team needed a pitcher, so he pitched, beginning his real baseball career relatively late. "It didn't matter if I was a position player or a pitcher, I just loved to play," he recalls. "One day, we didn't have no pitcher, so I pitched. Or, I guess, I threw the ball. That was it."

Within a year, he was tearing up the Gulf Coast League as a twenty-year-old starting pitcher, his ERA a ridiculous 0.17. Over the next six years, he moved slowly through the Yankee chain, where he saw the central pieces of this team begin to fit together. Williams came through, then Jeter. By 1996, Rivera was in his second major league season, and his obvious talents placed the Yankee bullpen in something of a delightful bind.

Torre arrived that same year, and he quickly saw that he had been blessed with what amounted to a two-headed closer out of his bullpen. Rivera would succeed the starter, pitch the seventh and eighth innings as a "bridge" man, then hand the ninth over to John Wetteland, a talented veteran. This arrangement helped narrow an opposing team's window of opportunity to six innings.

However, Rivera was so dominant in this strange, hybrid role that he gradually made Wetteland expendable. In 1996, his year as a bridge man, Rivera was 8–3, struck out 130 batters in 108 innings, and walked only 34. He even got some votes for the league's Most Valuable Player award. When Wetteland's free-agent number came up that winter, the Yankees gambled and let the veteran move on to Texas. Then they handed Rivera the ninth inning.

Rivera's success was not instant. He grew into the role throughout the 1997 season, finally having his defining closer's moment when Sandy Alomar beat him with a home run in the fourth game of that fall's divisional playoff series.

"It was a turning point for him, not just because he became more determined, but because he dismissed it," Torre says. "He was able to put it behind him and get that little incentive to go out and see how good he can be. Being a closer is more like being a regular player than any other pitcher is. Going 0-for-4 as a regular player, you can go out there the next day and atone for it. On the other side of the coin, though, if you have a good day, you don't get a chance to enjoy it. You have to go lace them up again."

After 1997, and up until a brief slide last season, Rivera was nearly untouchable. Refining his fastball by "cutting" it — slipping his fingers sideways across the ball so that it sails — he has become a one-pitch pitcher with more than one pitch. Rivera's cut fastball behaves like a conventional slider except that it loses no velocity. His cut fastball remains a fastball — which, in Rivera's case, means ninety-five plus. He also warmed to the role of being a closer, a job for which, upon first glance, he would seem physically and emotionally ill suited.

"How you are doesn't have nothing to do with it," Rivera says. "You still have to throw the ball. It doesn't matter if you're cool or nasty out there, or if you're mean. You have to throw the ball over the plate.

"The game's unpredictable. Sometimes you feel good, and that's one of your bad days. Sometimes you feel worse, and that's one of your good days. But if you try to be someone you're not, it's never going to work."

He is modest and mild. He is neat and quiet. Closers are not. They snarl and spit. They rage and howl. They are wild and unkempt, hooligan cowboys, living and dying with every pitch. One of them still hangs around the Yankees, helping the relief pitchers. The hair's thin now, and gray. The mustache still droops, and it's gray, too. He's the old rancher with a rifle above the door that nobody asks about. Be they as precise as Mariano Rivera or as fierce as this old gentleman, closers make their own special marks, always, as long as they sign in blood.

I saw him throw a fastball once, a high riser in a still moment, toward Carl Yastrzemski as the long shadows lengthened throughout Fenway Park. The pitch caught Yastrzemski tight on the hands — "sawing him off," as the old-timers say — and the Red Sox outfielder popped the ball high into the purpling autumn evening toward Graig Nettles at third base. It was the end of the prolonged and baroque 1978 season, Rich Gossage was on the mound, and suddenly we were all standing in the O.K. Corral, our ears ringing and cordite thick in the air.

Gossage has watched Rivera evolve into a different kind of closer. There is no talismanic moment — Gossage's glare, say, or Dennis Eckersley's slingshot delivery, with his hair flying like a cavalier's in a duel. Rivera is precise and careful, whereas they seemed more reckless. Rivera looks like a movie star, a tango dancer, whereas the old guys looked like the front row at a Metallica concert. But the sharp edges of the job are the same.

"The one thing you don't want to do is get beat on your fourth-best pitch," Gossage explains. "If I got beat in a ball game on my fastball, well, you just go out and do it again the next day. But if I got beat trying to throw a slider, it was a sleepless night. That's the biggest lesson Mo had to learn. That home run that Alomar hit in '97, I think Mo was trying something there instead of just throwing his fastball. He learned from that game. It made him a closer."

He is throwing batting practice now, serving them up on a back diamond to some Yankee farmhands with (at best) triple-A Columbus already in their eyes. It is as far from the chill of a playoff game as you can get, and even more distant from the great throb of those moments. There are perhaps fifteen people watching Rivera throw on a lazy February afternoon to batters of no consequence, one of whom catches a D-level fastball late, shattering his bat. There's a great cackle then from the homuncular presence of Don Zimmer, who looks more than anyone else like a human designed by committee.

"I heard that, Mo," Zimmer cries. "I heard what you did."

On the mound, Rivera laughs as he flows into another pitch. His power seems like some sort of physical trompe l'oeil, its source a mystery locked inside the elegant movement of his pitching motion. The power is in there somewhere, coiled and mysterious and re-morselessly reliable. Otherwise, he looks as if he's tossing a tennis ball against the side of his garage. If he has an identity as a closer, it is that he throws the same pitch at the same speed with the same fluid motion every time, impeccable and contained and neat, like his handwriting, like his career.

"You don't know about things," he says later. "Once you get to the mound, you still don't know how your pitch is going to feel. So that's the things you don't know."

They are waiting for him after he's done, lined up behind a metal barricade along the cinder path that leads back to the clubhouse. It is a place for scrawls and scribbles, tossed off with a major leaguer's disdainful aplomb. Sign this hat, this ball, these cards. Sign your name. Sign Charlemagne. Who'll know?

He stands in front of them, one at a time. He takes every object and brings it up in front of his face. His fingers move in a tiny dance. The big M, then all the sharp, clear letters. Then the R, with the down-swooping tail. You can read his name clearly over his shoulder. One of them gets restless, impatient.

His eyes alight, he never looks away. He is finishing up that last a, and as much work goes into it as went into any of the other letters. The impatient girl waves a ball. He brings it toward his eyes. He starts to sign. You can read the M from across the path. "Ma-ree-ahnn-ohh!" bleats the impatient young fan.

"Yes, mami," sighs the Hammer of God.

Is the key to the Yankees' recent success simply the right arm of Mariano Rivera? Leave it to the inimitable Charles P. Pierce to find the answer in the curving script of Rivera's autograph. The author of Sports Guy *and* Hard to Forget, *he has since left* Esquire *for the* Boston Globe Sunday Magazine.

JETER RUNS TO BALL, PICKS IT UP & FLIPS TO PLACE IN HISTORY

from *The New York Daily News,* October 14, 2001

There was no good reason for Derek Jeter to be floating like this from short toward the mound, then toward the first base line, backup for the backup on a relay throw from Shane Spencer in right.

Jeter ran there anyway in the bottom of the seventh, the way that Larry Bird would sniff out an errant pass or Jerry Rice would find the perfect spot in any end zone. The Yankee shortstop aligned himself behind Tino Martinez and Alfonso Soriano, a third of the way up the line from home plate, waiting. Surely, this was a redundant, token gesture of diligence, lifted from some overeager spring training playbook.

Yet with this one instinctive and uncanny play, Jeter would wrap all of the Yankees' greatness into a 10-second package of opportunism. He would embody four Yankee championships and a relentless talent to make something grand out of a minuscule detail.

Incredibly, Spencer overthrew both cutoff men from the deep corner, and the baseball started bouncing, dying, kicking outside the foul line, heading nowhere, slowly.

Except that Jeter was there. With Terrence Long running toward second, with Jeremy Giambi rumbling around third, the shortstop's positioning suddenly looked so logical now.

"That's my job on a ball in the corner," Jeter said, shrugging. "You've got to react to the play. I don't have time to turn around and set up and throw. You've got to make the quickest play possible."

Jeter grabbed the ball, then flipped a backhanded shovel pass right on target to Posada, who tagged out Giambi rumbling toward the plate.

Giambi didn't slide, even though his teammate, Ramon Hernandez, was waving him down into the red, clay dirt. "I got him on the leg on the way down," Posada said of the tag. The play was close, and now so is the series. The Yankees held on for dear life behind Mike Mussina and Mariano Rivera, 1–0, in Game 3, the only way they know how.

"He was there and made a sensational play," Joe Torre said of his shortstop. "We'd like a more conventional throw [from Jeter], but he was in a position where he had no choice. The kid has great instincts, and he holds it together. That was obviously the play of the game."

If the Yanks pull this thing out — and there are more reasons today to believe in them than there were yesterday — then people can remember the play in the seventh inning, when Jeter was a genius and Giambi was a standing duck.

It had been a vintage Yankee victory, culled from a minimal number of offensive opportunities, fashioned in such a way to make the beaten opponent say, once again, "Those are some lucky guys."

Jeter's play was not luck, of course. It was his baseball DNA.

"There are players in this league, in baseball, when you play with them every day, you get to see what they come up with," said Mussina, who pitched a gem last night. "It can be as simple as running the bases or the play he made today."

For those who would still dare insist that Jeter is no Alex Rodriguez, there is now a single play at the plate that will argue the point forever. Jeter quieted the largest baseball crowd in the history of Oakland, 55,861 strong. The longer the Yankees stay in this postseason, the bigger that play will grow.

From the start, this figured to be a one- or two-play ballgame, a duel between Mussina and Barry Zito, absent the tiniest margin of error for the defending champions. One mental glitch might have doomed the Yankees to season's end.

Pitches darted and cut to their designated targets, give or take a hundredth of an inch. Zito threw way inside, keeping the visitors off the plate. Twilight shadows crept through the Coliseum, disguising changeups and making two deceptive starters even more difficult.

And then, in the fifth, Zito blinked. Whether it was inexperience or fallibility, the young Oakland lefty threw a high, outside fastball on a 1–0 count to Jorge Posada, one of the few Yankees who remembers how to power the ball. Posada accepted the invitation, depositing a solo homer into the left-field stands.

After 22 innings, for the first time in this series, the Yankees held a lead, a real, honest-to-goodness advantage. It wasn't much breathing space, but it was enough because of Mussina and Jeter.

For those who have trouble fitting this great Yankee team into a single, neat memory, there is now the team's I-formation on Long's double. Spencer in right. Martinez, Soriano and Jeter lined up toward home. Posada at the plate. Even Mussina dashing behind the plate, one final insurance mitt.

The Yankees covered each other's backs last night and won on a piece of inspiration, of instinctive brilliance.

It happens in sports. Gretzky made the pass. Jordan made the jumper. Jeter was in the right spot again, at the right time.

This is the signature account of one of the most remarkable plays in baseball history, one that will be talked about one hundred years from now. Bondy, a columnist for the Daily News, *is also the author, with Harvey Araton, of* The Selling of the Green, *a portrait of the Boston Celtics.*

MARTINEZ AND JETER RESCUE YANKS

from *The New York Times*, November 1, 2001

The dynasty Tino Martinez and Paul O'Neill and Derek Jeter helped build over thousands of innings, in hundreds of games, was almost out of time. The Yankees were two runs down with two outs in the bottom of the ninth in Game 4 of the World Series last night, about to be pushed to the brink of elimination.

But the charter members made a last stand, forming perhaps the most improbable and incredible comeback in the history of this dynasty. Arizona was within one out of taking a three-games-to-one lead in the four-of-seven-game series, some of the Arizona Diamondbacks standing anxiously at the railing, waiting to celebrate. But with O'Neill leading off first base, Martinez slammed a two-run homer off Byung Hyun Kim to center field, tying the game, 3–3.

Then, in the bottom of the 10th, Jeter hit a game-winning homer with two outs off Kim, and Jeter sprinted around the bases before jumping on home plate at 12:04 A.M., in the first moments of a November World Series, with the decisive run in a 4–3 victory. The Yankees and the Diamondbacks are tied, 2–2, and Mike Mussina will pitch against Arizona's Miguel Batista tonight at Yankee Stadium.

It was the first time in World Series history that a team generated a ninth-inning home run to tie the game and followed it with a game-winning home run in extra innings, according to the Elias Sports Bureau.

"You win a game like this, when you are on the threshold of going down, 3–1 — it's huge," Yankees Manager Joe Torre said. "It's huge. It's huge for our confidence."

The Yankees survived the Curt Schilling gambit of Diamond-backs Manager Bob Brenly. Schilling, working on three days' rest, pitched exceptionally for seven innings, allowing only three hits and one run and striking out nine. But the Yankees and Diamondbacks were tied after seven innings, 1–1, in part because of Arizona's inability to capitalize on chances against Orlando Hernández.

El Duque struggled early and threw a series of meaty, hittable pitches in the first innings, and the Diamondbacks kept missing, kept fouling pitches off. Shane Spencer slugged a home run in the third to give the Yankees a 1–0 lead, but Arizona tied the score in the top of the fourth on Mark Grace's home run and nearly assumed a 2–1 lead in the fifth. Spencer, however, threw a runner out at the plate from left field.

Brenly hoped to use Schilling into the late innings and get him out of the game with the lead, and perhaps with few enough pitches to keep him strong in case he must pitch a Game 7. Schilling blew through the Yankees in the bottom of the seventh, and in the top of the eighth, Erubiel Durazo hammered a run-scoring double off Mike Stanton to take a 2–1 lead. Arizona added another run, moving ahead, 3–1, and Brenly decided to go to his bullpen, despite the fact Schilling had thrown 88 pitches.

"It was a very easy decision to take him out, considering he was starting on three days' rest," Brenly said. "We had a lead, six outs left in the ballgame, that's the way we hoped it would work out."

Kim took over for the bottom of the eighth, throwing sidearm, confusing the Yankees, striking out all three batters he faced. The Yankees were down to three outs, and in effect, the dynasty was down to three outs. If the Yankees lost this game, they would have to come back and win three games — two in Arizona, two of the three against Randy Johnson and Schilling, who have allowed nine hits in 23 innings in this Series.

Three outs to go, and they were desperate. Jeter tried bunting leading off the bottom of the ninth and was thrown out. O'Neill looped a single to left field, but Bernie Williams struck out. One out left.

Martinez walked to the plate, 0 for 9 in the World Series, playing perhaps his next-to-last game in a Yankees uniform. He had gone into the Yankees' video room during the bottom of the eighth inning and tried to familiarize himself with Kim, a pitcher he had never seen before. As Martinez walked to the plate, the Yankees were batting .143, 17 hits in 119 at-bats. Martinez made up his mind to look for a high fastball, something to drive. The air was much warmer last night than during Game 3, when balls died in right-center field, knocked down by the cooler air. Martinez was looking to hit something a long way.

Kim threw a fastball, high in the strike zone. Martinez attacked.

The sound of contact was unmistakable, the click of something well struck. Arizona center fielder Steve Finley ran back, back looking up; on Tuesday night, Martinez's drive would have died, but this drive kept going and going, and when it landed in the stands, Jeter leapt from the dugout with both arms outstretched. Tie score, unbelievably, incredibly. Kim's face sagged.

Martinez stepped on home plate and thrust his fists, pumped his arms, adrenaline overpowering him and those who cheered for him. The old warriors of the Yankees' dynasty had dug in, one more time. Martinez kept trading hard high-fives with teammates in the dugout, and he came out for a curtain call, pirouetting and waving.

"Tino has been there for us for six years," Torre said. "He's hit a lot of home runs. If you asked him, this would probably be at the top."

Martinez said, "To get a hit like that was a boost for the team."

The Yankees almost won in the bottom of the ninth. Jorge Posada reached on a walk and David Justice on an infield single, but Shane Spencer struck out, and the game moved into extra innings, Mariano Rivera taking over for the top of the 10th and getting three quick outs.

Jeter fouled off a handful of pitches in the bottom of the 10th, and he seemed to be locking in a little more with each pitch, his swings getting stronger. Jeter typically hits the ball to the opposite field, but in the first 36 innings of this Series, he had kept pulling grounders to the left side, uncomfortably. That was why he bunted in the ninth, out of desperation.

Kim came at him again, the ninth pitch of the at-bat, and Jeter swung and hit a drive toward right field. Instantly, his teammates rushed forward from the bench, peering out toward the right-field corner, and when the ball disappeared, they all rushed the field, Martinez leading them.

Jeter jumped at home plate, Mr. November in the World Series, the fans at Yankee Stadium erupting. The dynasty that was running out of time was alive and well again, in an immortal moment.

Day by day, moment by moment, the 2001 postseason became ever more dramatic and improbable as the Yankees inched ever closer to defeat only to continue to win in ever more improbable fashion.

It all peaked just after midnight on November 1, and New York Times beat reporter Buster Olney somehow managed to capture the moment for the morning paper.

RUNNING STORY, GAME SEVEN, 2002 WORLD SERIES

(Unpublished), November 4, 2001

PHOENIX — If this is the final monument to a dynasty that couldn't be broken by its opponents but will be by finances and free agency, it is also the one that stands the tallest of them all, ultimately fulfilled by an aging legend, a postseason phenomenon and a kid who was never supposed to be on the roster in the first place.

The Yankees are World Champions again. They outlasted a terrific Arizona team 2–1 to win their fourth straight World Series title and fifth in the last six years. They won another championship Sunday night when Alfonso Soriano became a playoff name for the ages by hitting a game-breaking solo home run off of Curt Schilling in the eighth inning. It was the margin that ended one of the finest World Series of an era. Roger Clemens, who despite all his accolades had never carried a team from start to finish as he did this year, won the clincher, outdueling his old pupil Curt Schilling. He struck out 10 in 6 $\frac{1}{3}$ innings and once and for all has erased any talk of his inability to lead a champion. In a shaky ninth, it was Mariano Rivera, the unstoppable one, who gave up a hit, made an error, but settled to close out his fourth straight World Series championship.

When the Yankees and Diamondbacks were finished squeezing every drop from this joyous World Series, the Yankees were champions again. They won the World Series by hitting .183, by cheating death nightly, but always having enough strength for yet another moment. The 39-year-old legend Clemens beat the boastful and gallant 20-game-winning Schilling. The Yankees didn't hit, but enough to win another title. With Soriano halfway home to glory, Joe Torre

made the call to Mariano Rivera, the most dependable weapon in
World Series history, who closed the door on this season by striking
out the side in the eighth and escaping to glory in the ninth. When
the Diamondbacks broke through in the sixth with a run, the Yankees immediately tied it in the top of the seventh. As usual, the catalyst was Derek Jeter. When Danny Bautista doubled home the first
Arizona run in the sixth, it was Jeter who made a spectacular catch-
and-throw to nail him trying to stretch the double into a triple.

Jeter then led off the seventh with a single off of Schilling. He
then was running on the next pitch, which Paul O'Neill singled up
the middle. After Bernie Williams' force play, Tino Martinez ripped
a hard single off Schilling to tie the score. But the run was created by
Jeter, first defensively by throwing out Bautista and then at the plate.
In big games, there is nobody like him . . .

*Of course, it didn't happen that way. But Yankee fans can dream, can't
they?*

*During every game, beat writers create a running story so that at
its conclusion they can quickly file on time for the morning edition.
Howard Bryant shows the difficulties such deadlines pose. His Game
Seven story of the Yankees' anticipated twenty-seventh world championship and fourth in a row stops abruptly. As every Yankee fan knows,
the Diamondbacks surged back against reliever Mariano Rivera in the
ninth inning to win the most dramatic World Series in recent memory.*

*Get me rewrite. Bryant and every other writer in the press box had
to stop on a dime, turn around, and then write* that *story. Seventeen
minutes after Luis Gonzalez singled to center field, Bryant, who is also
the author of* Shut Out: A Story of Race and Baseball in Boston —
and who is now a staff writer for the Boston Herald — *filed his account of what really happened. His report, which follows, was the only
game story from the Series to win an award from the Associated Press
Sports Editors.*

FOUR-GET IT

Yanks Denied When Rivera Fails in 9th

from *The Bergen Record*, November 5, 2001

It happened a way it had never happened before. The Yankees and a dynasty fell on top of the very man who had made it so indomitable.

Mariano Rivera, so untouchable for the last three years and especially in this playoff season, took a 2–1 lead into the bottom of the ninth inning with another monument to a dynasty on the line. But he gave up two hits, made an error, hit a batter, and finally yielded a flare single to Luis Gonzalez to give the Arizona Diamondbacks a stunning 3–2 win and their first World Series title.

"I was just trying to choke up," said Gonzalez, whose hit to center field was blooped over the Yankees' drawn-in infield. "I knew [Rivera] would come in.

"They have a great ballclub over there, but this team was relentless," Gonzalez said.

A Yankee team that had built a championship by being perfect in the toughest and most difficult of moments, lost a championship by being dealt a fatal blow in the same method they had inflicted in all of their conquests.

And with the noise deafening, Roger Clemens, magnificent in the biggest game of his career, would be left with nothing. Alfonso Soriano had been the hero until an unforeseen rally ended one of the greatest runs any baseball team has ever had.

If this is the end of the dynasty, then let it be known that these Yankees did not crumble or decay as all great teams do, but used every resource to keep its light shining bright. But in the end, even the greatest of teams ultimately fall.

"We're obviously disappointed with the results, but not the effort," Yankees manager Joe Torre said. "We did our best. . . . You don't always win."

When the Yankees and Diamondbacks were finished squeezing every drop from this joyous World Series, the Diamondbacks were unlikely, giddy champions.

"What a fitting end to the season," co-MVP Curt Schilling said. "Every time we had our backs to the wall, we came back. This is a dream come true. I hope it was fun to watch because it was intense."

The Diamondbacks won the World Series not only by being the better team, but by defeating the team that has never known how to lose.

Randy Johnson, who won Games 2, 6 and 7, was named the co-MVP and became the first pitcher with three Series wins since Detroit's Mickey Lolich in 1968.

"For a lot of people who felt he was not a big-game pitcher, at least I hope this has erased that from his resume," Diamondbacks manager Bob Brenly said.

When the Diamondbacks broke through in the sixth with a run, the Yankees immediately tied it in the top of the seventh. As usual, the catalyst was Derek Jeter. When Danny Bautista doubled home the first Arizona run in the sixth, it was Jeter who made a spectacular catch-and-throw to nail him trying to stretch the double into a triple.

Jeter then led off the seventh with a single off Schilling. He then was running on the next pitch, which Paul O'Neill singled up the middle. After Bernie Williams' force play, Tino Martinez ripped a hard single off Schilling to tie the score. But the run was created by Jeter, first defensively by throwing out Bautista and then at the plate. In big games, there is nobody like him.

Game 7 started out as nothing but the classic it was advertised as. There were so many side plots that would all carry weight before the first pitch was thrown. Afterward, it was nothing but two pitchers — who were once in the same farm system — fighting each other for the last word of a classic World Series.

That Roger Clemens hadn't always come up huge in big games is rapidly becoming — if it is not already — a distant memory. Clemens struck out Matt Williams to end the first with a man on. He put two men on with one out in the second, but struck out catcher Damian Miller and Schilling. In the third, he gave up two singles, but struck out the side. And in the fourth, he gave up a one-out single to Mark Grace but struck out Miller and Schilling in succession to end the inning.

That was eight strikeouts in four innings. In this battle between the student and the master, Clemens was brilliant. Schilling reminded everyone of the conversation the two had back more than a decade ago, when both were in the Red Sox organization and Clemens, already established as a major league pitcher, told Schilling he wasn't applying himself and was wasting his talent.

Schilling took the talk to heart and here they were facing one another. Schilling accepted Clemens' challenge and froze Derek Jeter to start the game, Tino Martinez to lead off the second, and Clemens to end the third. After Jeter flied out to right in the fourth, Schilling struck out Paul O'Neill and Bernie Williams to end the inning.

The two had at each other all night, providing a fitting end to what had been a tantalizing World Series.

After the fifth, there was no score. In the sixth, Schilling struck out two more, and retired Clemens on a fly for the third out.

But in the sixth, Arizona broke the ice on Clemens. Steve Finley singled and Danny Bautista — 6 for 10 to that point in the World Series — hit a double to center to score Finley. Bautista, foolishly, was thrown out trying to stretch a double into a triple.

Schilling had yielded but one hit — a one-out double to O'Neill in the first that he escaped when O'Neill was gunned down trying to stretch it into a triple — and struck out eight.

This is what the season came down to: two 20-game winners, both needing a crown only one could wear. The game itself was not seamless for the Yankees, as O'Neill committed the baserunning blunder in the first. Clemens also committed an error in the first, dropping a Martinez feed on a Craig Counsell fly ball. The Yankees committed another error in the fifth, when Soriano booted a Matt Williams grounder. All of that would take a back seat to the two men on the mound.

O'NEILL LEAVES GAME WITH HITS AND CLASS

from *The New York Daily News,* November 5, 2001

The Yankee clubhouse opened after the game last night and you almost couldn't recognize the place without the champagne spraying in your face. George Steinbrenner was yelling at a public relations official from the league. Rudy Giuliani was making his way toward Steinbrenner — toward a final, lame-duck mayoral hug.

And there was Paul O'Neill, away from these sideshows, leaning steadfastly against a cubicle with his left arm, done with baseball. It was the saddest sight of all, more the end of an era than a 3–2 loss in Game 7, than Luis Gonzalez's bloop single to left-center in the ninth.

The pillar was leaving the building.

"I'm finished," O'Neill said, finally acknowledging his retirement. "But that has nothing to do with it. There are some people in this room I need to sit down and talk to on the plane tonight.

"We made a mark on this game in the huge history of baseball, I'm proud to say. The way baseball goes, people will leave this week and I may never see them again."

It's strange. All those years of banging water coolers, of throwing helmets around over the slightest bad call or run of luck, and now O'Neill was staring straight ahead without a trace of that famous temper.

He was fighting back something, but it wasn't a tantrum. Maybe tears. Maybe the flood of recollections. At age 38, with aching body parts and wounded heart, he searched for calm in this proud defeat.

All nine years spun through his head as he talked about his remarkable career in New York. He came to the Bronx in 1992 in a swap for Roberto Kelly, not knowing what to expect from the big city. He produced four straight 100-RBI seasons and earned four championship rings in five years.

He didn't bring any of them to the game last night. He wore his dad's wedding ring instead, for good luck. On the eve of Game 7, he'd prayed that he would be relaxed enough to play well.

He was good. He was bad. O'Neill doubled in the first inning off Curt Schilling, only to be nailed trying to stretch the hit into a triple. O'Neill had to laugh at himself on that one.

"The way I was running around today, stumbling toward third, I'm glad I won't have to relive that feeling again," he said.

He singled in the top of the seventh, helped to build a run-scoring rally. O'Neill stood in right for the bottom of the seventh, the last time out there before he would be pulled for pinch-hitter Chuck Knoblauch against Randy Johnson.

All his rituals were on display in the field, one last time, for all his fans. He threw his shoulders back, whirling his arms backwards over his head. He tipped his bill. He walked around impatiently and flexed his left knee. He pounded his mitt.

O'Neill left the game with a one-run lead. It was only a matter of time, he thought.

"We were World Champions with three outs to go and the best pitcher in the world on the mound," O'Neill said. "Without Mariano, we don't have even one ring. I wanted to finish this run. But you can't fight hits like that — no way around it."

O'Neill, symbol of this dynasty, was ready to move on, he said. He won't be a coach, won't be a manager, for the foreseeable future. He will leave the crowded stadiums and clubhouses to those who revel in them.

O'Neill never enjoyed the waves of reporters, the adoration, though he fully understood them. He cooperated, reluctantly, with a sense of honest responsibility to his profession. He tipped his glove to the Bleacher Creatures. He talked to the writers, and then again to the broadcast reporters, after he'd whined about how they were stealing his time.

He worked in New York. He loved the Italian food, the Stadium. He lived in Cincinnati, though. Still does.

"I'm looking forward to my first July 4th at home, to Memorial Day, to Labor Day," he said. "I have three kids. I want to help coach them. I had my fun. I had a riot. I can't be more blessed than I was."

All around O'Neill last night, the reporters rushed about to grab Tino Martinez, to get Steinbrenner and some of the others. O'Neill was still answering questions. You knew he wasn't enjoying this, but this was the last time and he was going to do it right.

Somebody asked him again about his teammates, and whether he drew consolation in their accomplishments.

"A lot of people would say they'd want to be in the other locker room right now," O'Neill said. "I don't want to be in the other locker room. I want to be right here."

He leaned harder against his locker. Maybe it wasn't the perfect ending. But it was a very good way to leave, for sure.

It was an open secret that Paul O'Neill would retire following the 2001 World Series. Moments after the Yankees' loss, Bondy captured O'Neill's first few moments as a private citizen, as the Yankee right fielder looked back on the bittersweet end to both his career and an unforgettable postseason. Over three weeks of some of the most exciting baseball the city has ever seen, O'Neill and his teammates gave New York a brief respite from the pain of September 11. So did the writers, who by their work covering the team allowed those moments to continue a bit longer.

CREDITS AND PERMISSIONS
INDEX

CREDITS AND PERMISSIONS

INDEX

Albone, Frankie, 250

Alexander, Grover Cleveland, 73, 80, 81

Alexander, Pete, 77

Allen, Mel, 124, 125, 184, 197–98, 217

Alomar, Sandy, Jr., 240, 313

American League Championship 1976, 255–58

American League Park, 17

Amoros, Sandy, 164, 165

Anson, Pop, 19

Arizona Diamondbacks, 319–22, 323–24, 325–27

Babich, Johnny, 95

Bagby, Jim, Jr., 136

Baker, Frank "Homerun," 31, 41

Baltimore Orioles, 223, 259, 296

Barnett, Barney, 151

Barrow, Ed, 69, 101, 102, 213

Barsocchini, Reno, 140–42

Barstow, Rogers L., Jr., 10–11, 12

Bartell, Dick, 86, 87

Baseball, 27, 100

Baseball America, 285

Batista, Miguel, 319

Bauer, Hank, 157, 159, 164, 165, 170, 183

Bautista, Danny, 324, 326, 327

Baylor, Don, 229, 290

Beacher, Bob, 105

Bell Syndicate, The, 44, 64

Belmont, August, 5, 10, 12

Bengough, Benny, 71, 80, 84

Benson, Vern, 147

Bentley, Jack, 45, 48, 49, 50, 51

Bergen Record, 325

Berra, Yogi, 111, 114, 159, 161, 162, 171, 183, 204, 205, 208, 293

Bevens, Bill, 113, 114, 115

Bird, Doug, 231

Bodie, Ping, 41, 42

Boggs, Wade, 279, 292, 299

Bonham, 121

Borders, Pat, 292

Boston Pilgrims, 17, 24

Boston Post, 18

Boston Red Sox, 31, 34, 38, 181, 220, 229

Bottarini, Frank, 98